NIHILISM AND TECHNOLOGY

NIHILISM AND TECHNOLOGY

Nolen Gertz

ROWMAN &
LITTLEFIELD
INTERNATIONAL
London • New York

Published by Rowman & Littlefield International, Ltd.
Unit A, Whitacre Mews, 26-34 Stannary Street, London SE11 4AB
www.rowmaninternational.com

Rowman & Littlefield International, Ltd. is an affiliate of
Rowman & Littlefield
4501 Forbes Boulevard, Suite 200, Lanham, Maryland 20706, USA
With additional offices in Boulder, New York, Toronto (Canada), and London
(UK)
www.rowman.com

British Library Cataloguing in Publication Information
A catalogue record for this book is available from the British Library

ISBN: HB 978-1-78660-702-7
ISBN: PB 978-1-78660-703-4

Library of Congress Cataloging-in-Publication Data

Names: Gertz, Nolen, author.
Title: Nihilism and technology / Nolen Gertz.
Description: Lanham : Rowman & Littlefield International, 2018. | Includes bibliographical refer-
    ences and index.
Identifiers: LCCN 2018022468 (print) | LCCN 2018024763 (ebook) | ISBN 9781786607041 (Elec-
    tronic) | ISBN 9781786607027 (cloth : alk. paper) | ISBN 9781786607034 (pbk. : alk. paper)
Subjects: LCSH: Technology--Philosophy. | Technology--Social aspects. | Nihilism.
Classification: LCC T14 (ebook) | LCC T14 .G38 2018 (print) | DDC 601--dc23
LC record available at https://lccn.loc.gov/2018022468

Printed in the United States of America

TABLE OF CONTENTS

PREFACE

This book is the result of my work at the University of Twente, and the result of my nihilism. With regard to the former, this book grew out of the vast variety of perspectives on technology that I have been able to engage with at UT. Teaching in modules in departments as varied as Industrial Design, European Public Administration, Communication Science, and Philosophy of Science, Technology, and Society has allowed me to discuss and develop my ideas with students and faculty who have a wide range of backgrounds and expertise. It was particularly illuminating to see firsthand how UT students and faculty were able to so thoroughly diagnose the dangers created by technologies in the past and in the present, and yet so optimistically, and so consistently, prescribe the development of new technologies and of new technology policies to avoid such dangerous situations in the future.

That we are technological beings living in a technological world was rarely if ever questioned, as instead the primary question students and faculty both sought to answer was how to make our technological world better. It was in response to the optimism required to have such a single-minded focus on technological solutions—a focus that, again, I found to be consistent even though the people holding this view came from such different backgrounds and areas of expertise—that I began questioning my own relationship to technology. For while I taught the techno-pessimism of thinkers like Martin Heidegger, Jacques Ellul, and Lewis Mumford, I nevertheless chose to teach these thinkers by using PowerPoint, using Word, using Google, using Blackboard—by using technology. Consequently I was made more and more sympathetic to the view that technologies are fundamental to what it means to be human, that technologies mediate our relationships to ourselves and to the world, and that we should investigate technological mediations in order to shape them rather than merely be shaped by them.

However, thanks perhaps to my training at the New School for Social Research, I could not avoid my nagging suspicion that there was something wrong with this techno-optimism. While I came increasingly to rely on technologies in my personal and professional life, I yet did not feel optimistic about my relationship to technologies. I did not enjoy relying on FaceTime to connect with my brother and sister. It is often like a chore to use Twitter to try to keep up with current events. I was never confident in my decision to use PowerPoint slides, slides filled with pop culture references found on Google Images, as a way to engage with students. Such technologies were a ubiquitous part of my daily life, but that felt less like a welcome development than simply a fact of life that could not be avoided. I did not love technologies. I did not hate technologies. I merely acquiesced to a life lived with technologies and through technologies.

At the same time I found myself more and more invested in trying to keep my son away from technologies, in trying to get my son outside as much as possible, in trying to get my son to prefer forests over *Frozen* and playgrounds over *PAW Patrol*. I knew my son liked technologies and that I could not prevent him from using technologies. I also knew that familiarity with technologies could only help him to advance in our technological world. But he wanted to use technologies a little too much. He got a little too upset when I took them away. He could be a little too absorbed in the technologies he was using. And it often felt a little too easy for me to turn to technologies as a way to solve parenting problems. In other words, I did not want my son to become as dependent on technologies as I had.

Thanks to these conflicting experiences I came to realize that my concern over techno-optimism was less about whether we are wrong to seek technological solutions to our problems and more about whether we are wrong to see so much of life *as problems*. For to view an experience as a problem is to be led to seek a solution, a solution to that experience, a solution that would help us to avoid again having such an experience. Further, to view a technology as such a solution is to view a technology as a way to avoid certain experiences, to avoid experiences viewed as problematic. But once we discover that technologies can help us to avoid problematic experiences, it is hard not to make the further discovery that technologies can also help us to avoid undesirable experiences. Consequently, we are led to the final discovery, that technologies can even help us to tailor experiences to our desires. In this way trying to solve a problem, a problem like not wanting to take the bus to get to work, becomes trying to raise money for a start-up devoted to *disrupting commuting*, devoted to the vision of a world where no one ever has to take a bus again.

It may seem at first like there is nothing wrong with such a vision, with such disruption, with such a problem-solving mindset. But the issue is how this mindset can lead us toward techno-utopianism rather than toward self-discovery, rather than toward asking ourselves why we would find an experience like riding a bus to be a *problem* in the first place. To seek solutions to problems is to be able to avoid not only the recurrence of the problem but to be able to avoid reflection, as we are not led to ask questions about experiences if we are no longer having the experiences. Using technologies to try to create a problem-free world, a world where we can avoid problematic and undesirable experiences, can also be seen therefore as using technologies to try to create a reflection-free world, a world where we can avoid problematic and undesirable questions.

In other words, my concerns were not focused on technology but on humanity, on investigating why we are so drawn to the problem-solving mindset, and why the problem-solving mindset is so drawn to technology. These concerns were motivated by the realization that the problem-solving mindset can lead us not only toward techno-utopianism but also toward *techno-nihilism*. Philosophically, as well as etymologically, this should come as no surprise, as utopianism and nihilism—or no-where-ness and no-thing-ness—are two sides of the same coin. To want a perfect world is to both want a world different from the world in which we live, and to see the world in which we live as so imperfect as to need to be replaced.

It is for this reason that I wrote this book, this book which is a turn to Nietzsche in order to analyze human-technology relations, as Nietzsche's analyses revealed that nihilism could result in either pessimism and dystopianism or in optimism and utopianism. Thanks to Nietzsche we can see that someone who is morbid and someone who is cheerful could have the same reality-denying attitude but merely express that attitude in opposing ways. Though Nietzsche analyzed the relationship of such nihilistic attitudes to morality and to religion rather than to technology, I believed that Nietzsche's analyses could nevertheless be applied to technology. A Nietzschean philosophy of technology is possible not only because we pursue moral goals through technologies and because technologies cultivate a religious faith and devotion from users but more generally because Nietzsche diagnosed the life-denying nihilism at the heart of the problem-solving mindset, a mindset that existed in the Christian moral world as much as it exists in our technomoral world.

This book is not meant to be a work of Nietzsche exegesis but rather is a work inspired by Nietzsche, a work intended to develop a critical, Nietzschean perspective on our relationships with technologies. I provide an interpretation of Nietzsche's views on nihilism in order to develop my own views on nihilism, not in order to provide a definitive "explanation" of Nietzsche. Similarly, it should be noted that I use the word "we" throughout this book, not in order to suggest that I am describing tendencies and experiences universal to *we humans*, or universal to *we Westerners*, or *we English-speakers*, but in order to avoid the confusion that the use of "I" and the use of "they" can create. I would prefer readers think I am describing tendencies and experiences that I believe they share with me and share with countless others ("we"), rather than think I am describing tendencies and experiences that I believe only apply to me ("I"), or that I believe apply to everyone but me ("they"). There is of course still a danger of confusion with the use of "we," but I believe that the benefits outweigh the costs (and of course you are welcome to exclude yourself from the "we" should you be so lucky to have lived a nihilism-free life). To paraphrase Nietzsche, this book was written for everyone and for no one (that is, for no specific academic or cultural group in particular).

ACKNOWLEDGMENTS

This book would not have been possible without the generous support of my colleagues and students in the Department of Philosophy at the University of Twente. In particular I have greatly benefited from being a member of Peter-Paul Verbeek's research group, a group that has kindly invited me to present chapters from this book during various colloquia held over the past two years. The critical feedback I have received from Peter-Paul Verbeek, Ciano Aydin, Michael Nagenborg, Melis Bas, Jonne Hoek, Olya Kudina, Bas de Boer, Philip Brey, Marianne Boenink, Michael Kühler, Steven Dorrestijn, and many others has been immensely helpful throughout. My research assistants Ana Fernandez Inguanzo and Anna-Carolina Zuiderduin worked with me early in the writing process, identifying possible technologies for me to analyze, and my research assistant Emīls Birkavs aided me with the completion of this project. I must give special thanks to David Douglas, Melis Bas, Babette Babich, Jon Greenaway, and Miranda Nell for having been so generous as to read each chapter and provide me with such valuable feedback.

Portions of this book have been presented at various conferences and colloquia, not only at the University of Twente but also at TEDx-Frankfurt; the Philiminality Society at Cambridge University; the ADAPT Centre at Trinity College Dublin; the Machine Learning Symposium at the University of Liverpool; the Forum on Philosophy, Engineering, and Technology (fPET); the joint conference of the Society for Social Studies of Science (4S) and the European Association for the

Study of Science and Technology (EASST); the Culture, Technology, Communication (CaTaC) conference; and the Thomas More Summer School at Utrecht University. I thank Mark Coeckelbergh, Joseph Savirimuthu, Wessel Reijers, James Dickinson, Kevin McMillan, Srdjan Vucetic, and Stephanie Igunbor for their invitations to present my work at their institutions. I also benefited from presenting my work to two companies (which asked me to sign nondisclosure agreements). Serving as the Coordinator of the 4TU.Centre for Ethics and Technology's Task Force on Risk, Safety, and Security further enabled me to present work relevant to this book in various workshops and panel discussions.

It is often thought that teaching and research are two distinct and perhaps even opposed aspects of academia, but for me teaching and research feed off of each other and thus my teaching was vital to my research for this book. Many arguments from this work made their way into my lectures over the past two years, for which reason I am grateful to the many students at UT who engaged in debates with me about these arguments both in class and in their assignments. I am especially grateful to the students who asked me to work with them on their Master's theses as either their supervisor or as a member of their examination committee. Working so closely with Ana Fernandez Inguanzo, Christian Pauli, Peter Segers, Gerald Munters, Gijs de Boer, Duuk Baten, Anna Melnyk, Selen Eren, Samantha Hernandez, and Denise op den Kamp has not only been delightful but has been very helpful in developing my own philosophical arguments about technologies while working with them on developing theirs. I also benefited from having three groups of students (Simone Casiraghi and Roos de Jong; Anna Melnyk and Chris Fries; Selen Eren, Alan Houot, and Joonas Lindeman) in the PSTS course PhiloLab write papers based on chapters of this book.

Many people have provided me invaluable guidance and inspiration over the years, such as my former professors Jay Bernstein, James Dodd, Simon Critchley, Nicolas de Warren, Agnes Heller, Yirmiyahu Yovel, James Miller, and James Willson-Quayle. I am also grateful (in no particular order) to Miles MacLeod, Dominique Behnke, Mayli Mertens, Johnny Søraker, Aimee van Wynsberghe, Saskia Nagel, Lantz Fleming Miller, Brandt van der Gaast, Margoth Gonzalez Woge, Stéphanie Gauttier, Luisa Marin, Stefan Koller, Robert-Jan Geerts, Per-Erik Milam, Petra Bruulsema, Ada Krooshoop, Jan Nelissen, Sabine Roeser,

Sven Nyholm, Gemma Calderon, Iris Huis in 't Veld, Noel Sharkey, Robin James, Patrick Lin, Chelsea Harry, Michael Neu, Bob Brecher, Irna van der Molen, Christina Kousiounelou, Marlene Nowotny, Matthew Beard, Jan Mieszkowski, Nastaran Tavakoli-Far, Ephraim Rosenbaum, Sara Murphy, Britta Schnoor Loftus, Christina Nabholz McLeod, Scott Stephens, Robert Rosenberger, Krista Thomason, Philip Laughlin, Albrecht Fritzsche, Charles Ess, Thom Brooks, Shannon French, Stephanie Carvin, John Adams, and Marina Adams. I also wish to thank Isobel Cowper-Coles, Natalie Linh Bolderston, Sven Ove Hansson, and everyone else who provided me support and assistance from Rowman & Littlefield.

I am grateful to my family, especially to my grandmother Sylvia, who was perhaps the first to motivate me to turn off the TV and go outside. I am thankful that my brother Bennett (and Katie, Dylan, and Ethan) and my sister Lynne (and Mike and Tyler) have always been there for me. My partner Miranda has provided not only invaluable feedback throughout the writing of this book but has been a great motivator, interlocutor, and, well, partner. My son Zachary has been a constant source of inspiration for me, both because of his terrifying ability to quickly master any technology put in front of him and because of his awe-inspiring ability to make even the darkest moments seem comical. If this book was written for anyone, it was written for him.

I

NIETZSCHE AND CHILL

1.1 LEISURE-AS-LIBERATION

A family is playing together in their living room. Mom and daughter are inside a couch cushion fort, a fort that dad is moments away from invading. The daughter is happily watching the family dog, who is too busy with a chew toy to guard the perimeter. Alongside this happy family in their happy home happily playing on their happy carpet is a large hockey-puck-like machine sitting on the floor. The black machine appears in stark contrast to the bright sunny situation surrounding it. The machine's function is not made obvious, but its purpose is clear as we can see that this machine is what enables this family to be so happy, and thus we can further conclude that without this machine, the happiness would be gone.

What I am describing is not only an ad for a Roomba[1] but an ad for a trend in the design of technologies, a trend that has become so pervasive, so dominant, so ubiquitous, that advertisers need only hint at it for us to immediately understand that what is being sold to us is not the technology but a way of life, a way of life that only the advertised technology can make possible. The Roomba ad needs no text as the image tells us everything we need to know. The large black hockey puck in the corner works so we do not have to, so we can instead play, so we can instead be happy, so we can instead be human.

I call this the *leisure-as-liberation* trend in technological design. The idea behind this trend is very simple: the role of technologies is to liberate us from the chores that prevent us from having the leisure time we need to be human. This is the idea we see at work not only in the Roomba but also in online shopping, in voice-activated assistants, in predictive algorithms, and in the development of autonomous cars, autonomous robots, and autonomous drones. Technologies can clean for us, they can buy and sell for us, they can check the weather for us, they can write texts for us, they can drive for us, they can do manual labor for us, and they can even kill for us.

Technologies can do so much for us that we are beginning to wonder which of life's tasks, if any, will be left for us to do. In other words, while it is clear that technologies are advancing at an incredible rate, that technologies are becoming more and more capable of performing tasks previously assigned to humans, it is not as clear that humans are necessarily advancing, that humans are becoming more capable rather than merely more dependent on the capabilities of technologies. Yet as technologies become more capable, they also become more entrenched in our everyday lives, for which reason it is increasingly difficult to even determine where technologies end and we begin. Hence it is perhaps a mistake to think that technologies could advance independently of humans, or that humans could become dependent on technologies, as it could instead be argued that the human/technology distinction is merely a leftover from our more traditional dualistic ways of thinking.

Contemporary thinking about technology—both in design and in philosophy—suggests that rather than distinguish humans and technologies we should instead recognize that technologies have always played a formative role in human life. Rather than worry that technologies are turning us into the helpless blobs depicted in *Wall-E*, we should realize that we would not be who we are without technologies, that, as was shown in *2001: A Space Odyssey*, we can draw a straight line from our prehuman ancestors' discovery of tools to our present-day exploration of outer space. As technologies have always been part of human development, we should not fear what they are doing to us but strive to learn more about them and to take a more active role in their design, as technologies have been and will continue to be part of human development whether we like it or not.

Such contemporary thinking about technology is not meant to champion technophilia but instead to move us away from what is seen as the counterproductive concerns of technophobia. These contemporary thinkers—thinkers such as Peter-Paul Verbeek, Shannon Vallor, Luciano Floridi, and Bruno Latour—would likely argue that they are simply technorealists, that either loving or hating technologies is less useful than studying technologies, than engaging with developers and actively participating in the design process. Yet such study, engagement, and participation would necessarily require that we invest a lot of time and energy into thinking about technology. In other words, it appears that we must develop technologies that can liberate us, in order to have leisure, in order to think about technologies, in order to develop technologies that can liberate us, in order to have leisure, etc., etc., etc.

However, for the technophobic thinkers of the past—thinkers such as Jacques Ellul, Martin Heidegger, Herbert Marcuse, and Lewis Mumford—what was at issue was not the question of whether technologies had a role in human development but rather the question of whether the *in-order-to* mindset of modern technological thinking was perverting human development. Modern technologies appear to function not by helping us achieve our ends but instead by determining ends for us, by providing us with ends that we must help technologies achieve. Thus the Roomba owner must organize their home in accordance with the maneuvering needs of the Roomba, just as the smartphone owner must organize their activities in accordance with the power and data consumption needs of the smartphone. Surely we buy such devices to serve our needs but, once bought, we become so fascinated with the devices that we develop new needs, such as the need to keep the device working so that the device can keep us fascinated.

Technologies go beyond providing us with goals and shaping our activities, they can also influence our values and shape our judgments. The values of efficiency and of objectivity lead us to necessarily judge technologies to be superior to humans, for which reason we not only prefer technological solutions to our problems but we increasingly see humans as inefficient, as biased, as *problems*—problems to be replaced by more trustworthy and dependable technologies. Likewise our use of social media leads us to constantly redefine the values of privacy and of friendship so that we see Facebook as just another form of communication, with pluses and minuses like any other, rather than seeing it as intrusive and alienating in ways that were unimaginable before its presence.

Just as contemporary thinkers would not see themselves as techno-philiacs but as technorealists, so too these thinkers of the past would not have seen themselves as technophobes but as technorealists. Indeed these earlier thinkers would have probably suggested that the label of *technophobia* is itself symptomatic of the effect modern technologies have on us, as to challenge the perceived positive benefits of technologies is to be seen as either a Luddite, an ingrate, or a paranoid conspiracy theorist. In other words, contemporary thinkers accuse thinkers of the past of not understanding what it means to be technological whereas thinkers of the past would accuse contemporary thinkers of not understanding what it means to be human.

It is important to realize that the opposition between these two perspectives is not merely an esoteric theoretical argument. If we can indeed take an active role in determining how technologies influence us, then to treat tech companies as our enemy is to risk letting tech companies determine these influences *for us* rather than *with us*. Alternatively, if technologies are warping our goals, our values, and our judgments in ways that we do not realize, then the more we try to work with tech companies, the more we will be at risk of becoming entrenched in a technological mindset, consequently making us less and less able to take a critical stance toward technologies. Working out which of these perspectives is correct is thus vital for ensuring that technologies are providing us leisure as a form of liberation rather than providing us leisure as a form of dehumanization.

1.2 FROM TECHNOLOGY TO GENEALOGY

The question of whether our practices are leading us to become liberated or dehumanized, to become freer or more deluded, is a question that has arisen not only due to practices concerning technology. In the nineteenth century, Karl Marx attempted to answer this question with regard to Capitalism, and Friedrich Nietzsche attempted to answer this question with regard to Christianity. For Marx, Capitalist ideology convinces workers that anyone could become wealthy if they only work hard enough when, in reality, workers are exploited by the wealthy and alienated from themselves, from other workers, and from their humanity.[2] Yet because the wealthy not only seek to keep profits from their workers but also from each other, Marx argued that the wealthy would inevitably fight each other, train the workers to fight their battles against their rivals, and consequently destroy themselves by having inadvertently revolutionized the working class.[3] In other words, the more that brands advertise that their competitors are lying to us, the more we should learn to distrust advertising, to distrust brands, and to distrust Capitalist ideology.

For Nietzsche, it would come as no surprise that Marx's predicted revolution has not taken place, that we have not become distrusting of Capitalism, nor even of brands, but have instead developed brand loyalty, identifying with brands, taking sides in brand wars, choosing to destroy ourselves rather than Capitalism. Whereas Marx thought that we are distracted and deluded by ideology, by external influences preventing us from learning the truth of our situation, a truth that, once learned, would immediately lead us to unite and revolt, Nietzsche thought that we are distracted and deluded because *we want to be*. According to Nietzsche, we should be concerned less with dangerous external influences than with dangerous internal influences, internal influences such as our tendency to view life as a source of suffering rather than as a source of challenges that force us to adapt and grow. This tendency leads us to turn against life, to embrace both opportunities to be distracted from life and ideologies—no matter how delusional—that promise us a way to a better life, even if such a life is to be found only through death.

From a Nietzschean perspective, what we need to learn to recognize and fight against is not exploitation but *nihilism*. For we will never revolt against our exploitation so long as our nihilism—our tendency to turn against life—leads us to prefer being exploited to being free, to being responsible, to being human. In other words, Marx took for granted that we want to be our own boss instead of being bossed around, and he did not appreciate the degree to which we might like having a boss, having a boss whom we could blame for our suffering, a boss who could tell us what to do, a boss who could prevent us from having to face the burden of making decisions for ourselves.

In his philosophical writings, Nietzsche diagnoses various ways that we turn against life, various ways that we distract and delude ourselves, various ways that we seek leisure, not as a way to become more human but as a way to avoid being human. What is important for Nietzsche is that we live a life of contradictions since we do not recognize our every-day practices as being contrary to life but have instead developed a moral framework that valorizes our anti-life practices, defining such practices as means to the sole end that life should have: *being good*. It is for this reason that Nietzsche focuses on Christianity as he traces the genealogy of our paradoxical value system—a value system that defines someone who is bad at being human as good at being moral—back to the victory of Christianity over paganism. Using his philological exper-tise, Nietzsche reveals that our moral values are not based on universal human experience or on pure concepts discovered by reason but are the product of a struggle between competing value systems, a struggle that took place so long ago, and that ended so decisively, that we no longer realize that alternative value systems are even possible.

If "good" could have multiple competing meanings, then so too could "progress," for which reason Nietzsche does not ask whether humans have achieved progress since the dawn of Christianity; he asks how we define "progress" and whether this definition accords with what it means to be human. It is for this reason that I believe Nietzsche—though he did not write much specifically about technology—can still help us to address the question of whether technological progress ac-cords with human progress. Nietzsche in particular can help us to avoid the simple reduction of this inquiry to a question of whether technolo-gies are making us more moral as we can see, thanks to Nietzsche, that the relationship between moral progress and human progress must be interrogated rather than taken for granted. By turning to Nietzsche, we can, for example, investigate not just whether technologies that monitor and report shifts in moods might help save lives[4] but also what sort of "life" is being saved by using such surveillance technologies, technolo-gies which could motivate the very mood shifts that they are designed to monitor and report.

1.3 OUTLINE OF THE BOOK

The aim of this book is to investigate how our nihilism became techno-logical and how technologies become nihilistic. The goal of this investi-gation is to move us away from the endless debates between techno-optimists and techno-pessimists about whether technological progress is making us better or making us worse, to move us instead toward interrogating how we define concepts like "progress," "better," and "worse," toward interrogating how technologies both shape and are the result of such ideological definitions.

In chapter 2 I begin this project by clarifying what nihilism is, what nihilism means, and why we should not underestimate nihilism by thinking of it as merely an affliction of overprivileged teenagers. For existential philosophers like Sartre, nihilism has become so normalized in everyday life that we take for granted that nihilism is only experienced by those who claim not to care about life, and thus we do not recognize how even what we think of as "caring about life" can be nihilistic. By recognizing the pervasiveness of nihilism in everyday life, we can better understand Nietzsche's arguments about the role of nihilism in the history of Europe, and in particular in the history of Christian morality. For Nietzsche, nihilism and morality are intertwined historically, for which reason Nietzsche challenges us to question the value of our values so that we can see that our values of self-sacrifice and self-denial are nihilistic and self-destructive. Though we might think that Nietzsche's arguments no longer apply to the technological world we live in today, by investigating transhumanism we can see how vital an understanding of nihilism is for appreciating the nihilistic underpinnings of the "posthuman" that this movement is championing.

In chapter 3 I turn from developing a philosophy of nihilism to developing a philosophy of technology. As Heidegger's "The Question Concerning Technology" has become a rite of passage for contemporary philosophers of technology—a text that one must criticize in order to establish trust that one is not a technophobic determinist—I begin with this text as well. My aim is not to attack Heidegger in order to assuage fears about my own views but instead to show how Heidegger's philosophy of technology both points toward and breaks from Nietzsche's philosophy of nihilism. Heidegger's concerns about modern technology ushering in a conformist society can be read as an argument about the relationship between nihilism and technology. Yet, like Marx and unlike Nietzsche, Heidegger ends up blaming the external influence of technology for humanity not achieving its destiny. For this reason I move from Heidegger to Don Ihde, as Ihde's philosophy of technology is based on trying to separate Heidegger's helpful insights into the use of technologies from his philosophically problematic and politically dangerous views about human destiny. Ihde's analyses of what he calls human-technology relations show how we can combine Nietzsche's philosophy of nihilism and Ihde's philosophy of technology and investigate what I call *nihilism-technology relations*.

Having developed the theoretical underpinning of this project in chapters 2 and 3, chapter 4 begins the application of this theoretical framework by investigating the nihilism-technology relation that I call *techno-hypnosis*. After discussing Nietzsche's analysis of "self-hypnosis," of the practices we engage in to try to put ourselves to sleep, of practices like meditating or drinking, I show how this analysis can be applied to technology. What Nietzsche saw as our attempts to avoid the burdens of consciousness can help us to recognize the hypnotic appeal of such technologies as television, streaming entertainment services, and augmented reality and virtual reality devices. I conclude by discussing the danger of techno-hypnosis as can be seen, for example, in such technologies not only helping us to relax but helping us to become complacent with the status quo, to become complacent with lives lived staring at screens.

Chapter 5 is focused on the nihilism-technology relation that I call *data-driven activity*. Nietzsche's analysis of "mechanical activity," of the practices we engage in to try to avoid the burden of decision-making, practices like obeying orders and routines, can help us to recognize how we use technologies to keep ourselves busy and to keep ourselves organized. By investigating our use of Fitbit, Pokémon GO, and our increasing reliance on algorithms, we can see how these technologies not only help us to avoid making decisions but how they make decisions for us. The danger of such data-driven activity can be seen, for example, in the increasing inequality between how much algorithms know about us and how little we know about algorithms, an inequality that requires that we not only put our faith in machine learning but that our faith be blind.

Chapter 6 is an investigation into the nihilism-technology relation that I call *pleasure economics*. According to Nietzsche, we use "petty pleasures" as a form of compensation for our powerlessness as we enjoy helping others because, in giving to others, we experience power in both reducing others to their neediness and in elevating ourselves through our ability to be givers. This analysis can be applied to the technologies of the sharing economy to help us to understand why so many people make online donations, rent out their homes, and get into cars with strangers. By comparing such technologies as Kickstarter, Airbnb, and Uber to technologies like Tinder, we can see how they all have in common this dynamic of other-reduction and self-elevation. The danger of pleasure economics can be seen, for example, in the swiping activity essential to all of these technologies, as they allow us to not only enjoy the power of generosity but also the power of cruelty, in particular the power of judging others as worthy or not worthy of our generosity.

Chapter 7 is concerned with the nihilism-technology relation that I call *herd networking*. For Nietzsche our "herd instinct" leads us to join with others, partly because there is strength in numbers but also because of the opportunity to lose ourselves in a crowd and thus avoid the burden of having to continue to be who we are. Applying these insights to social media technologies, from CB radios to emojis to Facebook, can help us to see why social networking has become so popular and so pervasive, as these technologies have expanded from serving as an outlet for our desire to engage with others to fundamentally reshaping what we think engagement means. The danger of herd networking can be seen in how social networking platforms not only lead brands to act like people but lead people to act like brands, crafting identities and producing content in accordance with the platform-induced need to attain and retain followers, followers whom we cannot be sure are interested in us beyond our content as we ourselves are no longer sure who we are beyond our content.

Chapter 8 delves into the world created by the nihilism-technology relation that I call *orgies of clicking*. Nietzsche separates the fifth and final of his human-nihilism relations—"orgies of feeling"—from the first four by describing these orgiastic nihilistic practices as "guilty," for they involve outbursts, releases of pent-up urges, emotional explosions, all of which are attempts to experience the ecstasy of evading the burden of accountability, evasions that incur a cost that we must later pay. Yet when technologies provide new ways to indulge our ecstatic urges, such as when technologies allow us to post anonymous comments, form flash mobs, and become cybervigilantes, our explosive tendencies can move beyond the self-destruction of guilt to the other-destruction of shame. The danger of orgies of clicking can be seen, for example, in the escalation that takes place when trolling and flash mobbing merge to create shame campaigns—as those who rally to a hashtag to pillory the latest social media outlaw can themselves be pilloried, as trolling incurs counter-trolling, which leads to doxing and counter-doxing—creating a world so toxic that shame campaigns and political campaigns become more and more indistinguishable.

Having seen in the previous chapters how technologies both enable and expand our nihilistic tendencies, allowing us to evade the burdens of consciousness, of decision-making, of powerlessness, of individuality, and of accountability, the final chapter is an attempt to answer the question of how we should respond to the relationship between our nihilism and our technologies. To develop such a response I begin by turning to Nietzsche's "madman," the madman who, in *The Gay Science*, declared that "God is dead." For after our journey through the nihilistic underbelly of the technological world we have created, it is hard not to experience what the madman experienced, a loss of orientation, of direction, of certainty. Just as God once functioned as the star by which we could always guide ourselves, a guide without which we felt lost and the world felt uncanny, so today Google similarly functions as such a guide, as we look to Google Search for answers, to Google Maps for directions, and to Google DeepMind for the cure to our suffering. We even look to Google for morality, as "Don't be evil" is certainly easier to remember than the Ten Commandments.

Google, however, is not proof that we have killed and buried God or that we have taken up the responsibility of giving our lives meaning, the responsibility that we had formerly outsourced to God. Google is instead proof that we have not yet escaped our nihilistic reliance on external sources of meaning. Hence even the death of Google would only lead to a search for the next Google to take its place. It is for this reason that we must not blame technologies or try to evade technologies—as if turning off technologies would turn off the influence of technologies on us—but instead endeavor to find ways to stop trying to evade ourselves and what it means to be human. One way to do this is by turning from passive nihilism to active nihilism, by turning from destruction for the sake of destruction to destruction for the sake of creation. Whereas passive nihilism is leading us to equate human progress with technological progress and to pursue becoming technological posthumans as the goal of human progress, active nihilism can lead us to take a more critical stance toward such goals, to recognize and criticize the ascetic values underlying this techno-human view of progress. Though passive nihilism may not lead to active nihilism, just as the death of Google may only lead to a search for new Googles, by continuing to investigate nihilism-technology relations we can nevertheless seek to motivate the move toward active nihilism, to motivate a search for new values, new goals, and new views of what "progress" should mean.

NOTES

1. Steve Dent, "The Roomba 960 Is iRobot's Cheaper App-Driven Robot Vacuum," *engadget*, August 4, 2016, https://www.engadget.com/2016/08/04/irobots-roomba-960-is-its-cheaper-app-driven-robot-vacuum/.

2. Karl Marx, "Alienated Labor," in *Karl Marx: Selected Writings*, ed. Lawrence H. Simon (Indianapolis: Hackett, 1994), 61–64.

3. Karl Marx, "The Communist Manifesto," in *Karl Marx: Selected Writings*, ed. Lawrence H. Simon (Indianapolis: Hackett, 1994), 166–167.

4. Paul Biegler, "Tech Support: How Our Phones Could Save Our Lives by Detecting Mood Shifts," *Sunday Morning Herald*, November 12, 2017, http://www.smh.com.au/technology/innovation/tech-support-how-our-phones-could-save-our-lives-by-detecting-mood-shifts-20171106-gzfrg5.html.

2

THE WILL TO ¯_(ツ)_/¯

2.1 WHAT IS NIHILISM?

Though "nihilism" is a philosophical concept with a long and complicated history,[1] in everyday usage it is taken to mean something roughly equivalent to the expression: "Who cares?" In other words, when we say that someone is a "nihilist" we mean that this person is both someone who does not care and someone who believes that, in general, no one else cares either.

Not caring, however, seems impossible. Though we might often say we do not care in response to a question like "What do you want to do?" or "What do you want to eat?" we tend to feel that even in these mundane instances the expression of not caring is insincere. Surely we cannot *not care* about how we spend our time. Surely we cannot *not care* about what we put in our bodies. In such instances it seems that "I don't care" is less an expression of detachment from the world and more an expression of simply trying to avoid making a decision.

Yet these two expressions are importantly interconnected. To avoid making a decision, even a seemingly trivial decision, is to be detached from the world. Preferring to let others make decisions for us—whether because we want to avoid being wrong or being held accountable or because we want to avoid having to think or to expend energy—is how we cut ourselves off from what makes our lives meaningful. That we justify our lack of interest in making decisions by asserting the meaninglessness of the decisions signifies precisely how easy it is for this way of thinking and acting to mutate from the mundane to the nihilistic. Or, to put it another way, we have grown so comfortable with our nihilism that we do not even recognize that it has become mundane, ordinary, *normal*.

2.2 SARTRE AND THE NORMALCY OF NIHILISM

The nihilism of everyday life was precisely what Jean-Paul Sartre was trying to capture in both his philosophical and his dramatic works. In *Being and Nothingness*, Sartre uses various mundane examples in order to analyze what he calls "bad faith"[2] and in particular the "patterns" that it takes. "Bad faith" for Sartre is the consequence of the fact of having "to deal with human reality as a being which is what it is not and which is not what it is."[3] For example, Sartre analyzes the situation of a man suddenly taking hold of his date's hand, leading the woman to distance herself from having to confront the *fact* of the situation by *transcending* it, by reducing the situation's significance by elevating herself above such petty concerns. As Babette Babich points out, although Sartre gives the man a "free pass," bad faith is so pervasive that both the man and the woman on the date are "dancing the same mind-above-body dance."[4]

It is hard to see why situations such as hand-holding are deserving of philosophical analysis rather than simply seeing the woman's reaction as nothing more than the innocent rationalizations of which we are all occasionally guilty. Yet the fact that we see nothing terrible about such rationalizing, that it seems silly to even spend so much time analyzing these situations, is the very problem that Sartre wants us to finally see as a problem, as perhaps *the* problem. To distance ourselves from our situation is to lose sight of the very freedom that defines us. In any given situation, at any moment, we have within ourselves the capacity to make decisions and, in making those decisions, to make ourselves.

But this freedom is a burden, one that we tend to not want to bear. To recognize the actions of another during a date as possibly laden with meaning, as intending more than they appear to be, is to have to face the choice of either accepting or rejecting such intentions. To recognize that the other may want more than just dinner is to be forced to reckon with the possibility that, in agreeing to dinner, the other may believe that the "more" has been implicitly agreed to as well. When we wish to avoid such realizations, we pursue—knowingly or unknowingly—various strategies, such as not thinking about the present moment by instead thinking about the future, as for example when we think of ourselves in the future looking back and laughing at the present moment. The danger of such thinking is that life is lived in the present, not in the future, so to focus on the future in order to avoid the present is to essentially avoid having to live one's life. To see in the future the past of the present is to let the future become the past without ever having been present.

This is what is meant by the existentialist motto: "Existence precedes essence."[5] *That* you are always comes before *what* you are. But the fact of existence, the bare fact, leaves us with the pressure of defining it, of clothing it in the choices we make. When this pressure becomes too much we are tempted to use "duplicity,"[6] as Sartre puts it, to avoid the truth of our situation. This is not to say however that this is deception. To deceive one must be conscious of the truth so as to best hide it from view. If this were the case then we could simply stop deceiving ourselves or others about who we are and just *be*. Yet, like Nietzsche's insight that forgiveness requires not just forgetting the offense but forgetting that one forgot,[7] here we find ourselves confronted by a deceiver who has been deceived, with the deception being that one sees oneself as actually *being sincere*.

But what would it mean to *be* sincere? As Sartre points out, "sincerity presents itself as a demand and consequently is not a *state*."[8] We can no more *be* who we are than a waiter can *be* a waiter. Just as someone impersonates you by acting *like you*, so too does a waiter act *like a waiter*, or, as Sartre writes, "he is playing *at being* a waiter in a café."[9] But who am I if not *myself*? The problem here is that we make something of a category mistake when we try to understand what such a question is asking. We try to answer the question in the same way that we would answer, "What is a table?" We provide a description, we offer details, we list facts, and in so doing we make ourselves into a thing that can be so described. We feel that just as a table is a flat surface supported by legs that is used as a place to keep objects, we too have an *essence*, something that defines me as *me* and not *you*. And yet the harder we try to offer up this definition, the more tempted we are to simply point at ourselves, as though that should tell you everything you need to know, much as how a child would probably tell you what a table is by simply pointing at one. This is how we come to fear that we, so to speak, are everyday impersonating ourselves, that I present myself as *me* while I believe, within my heart of hearts, that this is not who I *am*. Furthermore, this is how others can tell you that you are "not being yourself" and you both have a shared understanding of this to mean that you are not *acting like yourself*.[10]

What Sartre illustrates is how willing we are to focus on the "bigger picture" in order to not have to focus on the "small stuff," consequently losing sight of the fact that the bigger picture is nothing but the accumulated small stuffs. Life is a series of nows, each now is significant, each now is integral to the unfolding of every other now. One cannot therefore remove the meaning from any one now without removing meaning from all other nows. And yet we do this all the time. This is why Sartre focuses on mundane incidents in mundane events. "What are you doing right now?" someone asks you, and you respond, reflexively, "Nothing." And this response is not seen as alarming, as depressing, as indicative of a nihilistic reduction of the meaningfulness of existence, but as perfectly normal. Or, again, such a nihilistic reduction *is normal*.

It is the normalcy of nihilism that the nihilist points to when uttering "Who cares?" to express that *nobody cares*. This is not a question but a challenge, a dare to whoever is listening to find someone who actually cares. Even those who appear to care, who appear to make decisions and want to be held accountable, are, as this challenge suggests, either insincere or abnormal. What is held to be sincere and normal then is not caring, not wanting to make decisions, not wanting accountability. These are burdens, and no one wants to be burdened. And nihilism, as Sartre has shown, is how we unburden ourselves from the burden of being ourselves.

The danger of the nihilism of everyday life is that if it is human to make decisions, to make oneself accountable, to be responsible, then to avoid decision-making is to avoid being human. But to understand this human, this *all-too-human*, attempt to avoid being human requires that we turn from Sartre to Nietzsche. For now that Sartre has helped to introduce us to nihilism, to what nihilism can look like in everyday life and to how it can even play a role in everyday situations like dating, we are better prepared to look to Nietzsche to help us to understand nihilism's relationship not only with our everyday lives but with life itself, to understand where nihilism came from, what nihilism means, and what nihilism does.

2.3 NIETZSCHE AND THE GENEALOGY OF NIHILISM

In the first note of the first book of *The Will to Power*, Nietzsche writes:

> Nihilism stands at the door: whence comes this uncanniest of all guests? Point of departure: it is an error to consider "social distress" or "physiological degeneration" or, worse, corruption, as the cause of nihilism. Ours is the most decent and compassionate age. Distress, whether of the soul, body, or intellect, cannot of itself give birth to nihilism (i.e., the radical repudiation of value, meaning, and desirability). Such distress always permits a variety of interpretations. Rather: it is in one particular interpretation, the Christian-moral one, that nihilism is rooted. [11]

Nihilism confronts us, arriving not from within but from without. Yet, as a "guest," it is not necessarily uninvited. Such a guest is not a stranger, though it is the strangest, the "uncanniest" of guests, a guest who, upon arrival, can make us feel somehow as though we are no longer at home. But what is such a guest who could be so strange as to make us feel like strangers in our own home, and where did this guest come from?

Nietzsche tells us almost immediately. This guest is "the radical repudiation of value, meaning, and desirability,"[12] a repudiation that comes, not from some cultural or physical decline, nor from some sort of feeling of "distress," but rather from the "Christian-moral" interpretation of distress. Nihilism is "rooted" in this interpretation says Nietzsche, indicating both that in Christian morality we will find the seeds of nihilism, and that nihilism grew, and has continued to grow, from out of Christian morality.

In subsequent notes we find more and more references to nihilism, to Nietzsche's attempts at working out what nihilism is and what it means. However these notes were collected and published not by Nietzsche but by editors after his death. Rather than delve into the decades of arguments by academics trying to determine not only the meaning but even simply the order of these notes, I believe we should instead turn to Nietzsche's *On the Genealogy of Morals*, which he wrote and published in 1887, immediately after the time during which many of these notes were written.

The *Genealogy*, Nietzsche's most systematic work, can be seen as an investigation into the questions raised by these notes, questions concerning the origin and progression of nihilism through European history, in particular the history during which Christian morality was recognized by Europeans not as the *best* morality, but as the *only* morality. The *Genealogy* thus pursues the origin and progression of nihilism by pursuing the origin and progression of morality, asking how competing moral value systems gave rise both to Christianity and to nihilism. It is for this reason that Nietzsche called the work a *genealogy*, as it is a project tracing out the lineage not of a family of people but of a family of concepts—concepts such as "good," "evil," "guilt," and "sin." Nietzsche treats these concepts therefore not as universal truths but as victors in a struggle for survival between competing moral value systems, a struggle that Christianity won so decisively that we no longer realize that any other morality could even be possible, just as, before Darwin, we had no realization that any other human species could have been possible.

Nietzsche begins the *Genealogy* by pointing out the taken-for-granted nature of morality, arguing that we do not know ourselves because we accept rather than question our moral values. As an example, Nietzsche asks us to consider whether we are wrong to assume that someone seen as "good" is necessarily beneficial to society and that someone seen as "evil" is necessarily harmful to society.[13] So long as we identify the "good" as those who do "good" deeds and the "evil" as those who do "evil" deeds—while never questioning if "good" truly is beneficial and if "evil" truly is harmful—we can never be certain whether these value judgments are themselves benefiting or harming society. Yet because of the circular nature of our moral thinking, because we take for granted that the "good" *are good* and that the "evil" *are evil*, to begin to question these value judgments is to reveal that it is *faith* rather than *certainty* that is underlying the morality we live by. Thus, as Nietzsche says at the outset of the *Genealogy*, we do not *know* ourselves. To achieve such knowledge we must question the value of our values,[14] a questioning which, according to Nietzsche, has never before been undertaken.

In the first essay of the *Genealogy*, Nietzsche uses his training as a philologist to trace the etymological evolution of moral values back to their pre-Christian roots, back to a time when there were at least two competing value systems: "master"[15] morality and "slave"[16] morality. The central concern of the essay is trying to figure out how the Judeo-Christian morality of the slaves defeated the warrior morality of the masters, or, in other words, how the meek inherited the Earth. The answer, according to Nietzsche, is that the slaves, because they were born weak, were forced to become clever, and thus they were able to outwit rather than outfight the masters, because the masters were born strong enough to remain stupid.

The slaves defeated the masters by converting them to Judeo-Christian morality. This was achieved by convincing the masters that humans have a true, but invisible inner life (a "soul"[17]) that can end up in a true, but invisible afterlife (a "Heaven" or "Hell"[18]), and that in order to avoid eternal damnation one must avoid "evil"[19] (where "evil" is what the masters defined as "good"[20]). Such avoidance was possible by acting like the slaves, by becoming "good,"[21] by becoming "cultured,"[22] by learning to *abstain* from acting on one's instincts.

The theme of abstinence runs throughout the *Genealogy*, as Nietzsche identifies it as the value that becomes dominant in both the rise of Christian morality and the rise of nihilism. In the first essay, abstinence is what turns the strong into the weak and the weak into the powerful, as the masters—in the hopes of achieving salvation—chose to abstain from their "evil" ways, to abstain from their "vigorous, free, joyful activity,"[23] and thus created a world ruled by the weak. In the second essay, abstinence is seen as what kept the Christian world from falling apart, as the instincts of the masters—the instinct for cruelty especially—never disappeared but was merely suppressed, creating in each person a buildup of instinctual energy that demanded to be released.

Managing this explosive situation was the job of the priests, who successfully redirected the instinct for cruelty by inventing the concept of "guilt,"[24] by inventing a cruelty that we could joyfully experience, though only by being cruel to ourselves. By punishing ourselves for our "sinful"[25] instincts, we could both become "virtuous" through pursuing "good" habits like "self-denial" and "self-sacrifice,"[26] and we could experience the pleasure of cruelly forcing ourselves to deny our instincts and sacrifice our desires. These denials and sacrifices were of course not made in the name of cruelty, nor even in the name of virtue, but were made in the name of "God,"[27] in the name of a being who knew of all of our sinful instincts, and who had made the ultimate sacrifice of dying to save us from our sins, providing us with a debt that could never be repaid, with a guilt that no self-cruelty could ever satisfy.

In the third essay, abstinence appears in the form of "asceticism," or the elevation of self-denial and self-sacrifice from a means for individuals to redirect destructive instincts to the ideal way of life to which we all should aspire. According to Nietzsche, ascetic ideals have become so valued, in so many different areas of European culture, that modern life has become a nihilistic "self-contradiction."[28] Looking at not only religion and morality but at art, philosophy, and even science, Nietzsche argues that life has become "paradoxical,"[29] that we live our lives in accordance with life-denying ideals. The reason for this is that the victory of the weak over the strong did not actually result in the weak becoming strong as the weak, even in victory, were still weak, still frail, still susceptible to disease, still mortal, still *like slaves*.

While the victory of the slaves made life safer, easier, and less dangerous—because there were no more masters to terrify us—it also made life boring, complacent, and less meaningful—because there were no more masters to inspire us. Exchanging freedom for equality resulted in not only a Christian moral world but also in a *sick* world, a world where we are sick of being mortal, sick of being human, and sick of being ourselves. It is for this reason that Nietzsche sees the preachers of asceticism, the "ascetic priests,"[30] as having the vital role of protecting the Christian moral world from the nihilism it produces, protecting society from those made sick by it, as the ascetic priest is the one who *"alters the direction of ressentiment."*[31]

"Ressentiment"[32] is Nietzsche's concept for the essential characteristic of the weak, what in the past drove the slaves to destroy the masters and what in the present drives the sick to destroy themselves. The slaves did not merely *resent* the masters, the slaves did not merely feel bitter about having been born weak and frail while others were born strong and healthy, instead the slaves hated the masters, they blamed the masters for *being masters*, for being who the slaves thought they could and should be if there were no more masters standing in their way. This all-consuming reactive feeling of hatred and blame is what Nietzsche named *ressentiment*, a feeling which did not end with the

death of the masters since their death did not result in the death of the slaves; those who were weak and frail still remained weak and frail.

With the masters gone, the victorious slaves became sicker and sicker as there was no one left to hate for one's weakness and frailty, no one left to blame for one's weakness and frailty, leaving only the Christian moral world itself to hate and to blame. For this reason ascetic priests became increasingly necessary for preventing the destruction of the Christian moral world, giving us ways to manage our *ressentiment*, and less dangerous targets for our *ressentiment*. Importantly for Nietzsche the ascetic priest does not make the sick healthy but rather makes the sick "tame"[33] for, as was the case with the invention of guilt, the ascetic priests turn our sickness inward rather than allowing it to be vented outward. As Nietzsche argues, the ascetic priest is therefore not a "physician"[34] because the ascetic priest only relieves symptoms, never attempting to cure the disease itself.

In other words, the aim of the ascetic priest is not to combat nihilism but to make nihilism palatable, to help sufferers to live with their suffering rather than letting them spread their suffering to others. Nietzsche identifies five different tactics that the ascetic priests employ to achieve this aim: self-hypnosis, mechanical activity, petty pleasures, herd instinct, and orgies of feeling. The ascetic priest preaches that we should meditate, that we should keep busy, that we should help the needy, that we should join with others, and that we should punish the wicked. Relaxation, work, charity, community, and justice are in other words all forms of "priestly medication," the medications prescribed by the ascetic priests that Nietzsche raises a "fundamental objection" against because these activities soothe rather than cure our nihilistic suffering.

Of course these activities do not seem to us to be medications; we perceive them to be healthy, normal, even necessary parts of life. But it is precisely the necessity, normality, and, in particular, the healthiness of these activities that Nietzsche wants us to question. For in each of these activities Nietzsche finds not the will to life but rather the will willing its own destruction. Life is for Nietzsche the "will to power"[35]— not to achieve political success nor to dominate others but, rather, the will *to will*. To will is to strive, to pursue, which requires both something to strive after, an end to pursue, and the ability to do what is necessary to achieve one's goal, the ability to recognize and carry out the means to one's end. Willing is thus more than mere wanting; there are many things we want but, lacking the will to get them, such things remain fantasies rather than realities we are willing to create.

The will to power is to strive after striving itself, to pursue pursuing, to have no other end but to be able to continue to will. "Power" here means overcoming, overcoming obstacles, limits, but also oneself, to overcome what one has already achieved and the gravitational pull that one's achievements can have, dragging the will away from power to instead focus on preservation. But if life is the will to power, the will to overcoming, then the will to preservation, the will to maintaining the status quo, is the will turning against life, the will turning against willing, the will turning toward *asceticism*.

Having defined life as the will to power, Nietzsche sees the activities that have come to be regarded as normal and necessary as *unhealthy* because they are aimed at turning the will against itself. To meditate, to relax, is to not act, to will not to will. To work is to work for someone else, to bring about what someone else wills, to keep oneself too busy to be aware of one's own will. To help is to feel powerful, not by willing but by being recognized for what one has already, for what one has to give to those in need. To form groups is to compromise one's will in the service of the will of the many. To punish is to vent, to use the pretext of justice as a way to exercise one's will against someone else, as a way to compensate for otherwise having ceased to exercise one's will.

But we do not see these activities as unhealthy, or even as having been prescribed to us by others, for which reason we pursue these activities as normal, as necessary, without ever making the connection between how we *live* our lives and how we *feel* about our lives. Each of these activities allows us to feel as though we are living, as though we are willing, and thus our Christian moral world is preserved, even though preserving the world is what continues to make us sicker and sicker. For, as Nietzsche warns, humans cannot live without a goal, even if that means that we would "rather will *nothingness* than *not* will."[36]

Nietzsche finds no ideals competing with the ascetic ideals, as the ideals he finds in art, in philosophy, in science, are still ultimately focused on preserving the world rather than overcoming it, and are thus in the service of asceticism, in the service of soothing rather than curing our nihilism. It is because Nietzsche is able to diagnose asceticism even in the field of science, even in the field that is meant to be most opposed to the Christian moral world, that I believe Nietzsche can help us to explore the field of technology, and even help us to locate updated versions of these priestly medications operating within the technologies we use today. By carrying out a Nietzschean investigation of the technologies that surround us, we can see how technologies impact nihilism and how nihilism impacts technologies, how technologies can soothe our nihilism, and how nihilism can prevent us from realizing the potential of technologies to do more than soothe us.

2.4 TRANSHUMANISM AND THE UPGRADE OF NIHILISM

Before we continue, two important objections to this project need to be addressed. First, it may be asked why Nietzsche was able to be the first to pursue this line of questioning, if no one, not even Kant, had previously been able to see the need for a *"critique* of moral values."[37] We have already seen what Nietzsche's answer to this question is: nihilism. Nihilism is for Nietzsche both the reason why we are *able* to question our values and the reason why we *need* to question our values. Nihilism is the "radical repudiation of value, meaning, and desirability," and thus the more nihilistic the world becomes, the easier it is to see our values as questionable rather than as absolute. Yet the reason we need to question our values is precisely because the world is becoming more and more nihilistic.

As Nietzsche indicates—in another note from *The Will to Power* written at the same time as the *Genealogy*—nihilism can be seen as *"ambiguous,"* as either *"active"* or as *"passive,"* as either "a sign of increased power of the spirit" or as "decline and recession of the power of the spirit."[38] To question our values is to *actively* repudiate the taken-for-granted nature of our values, but our values have become weak enough to be seen as in need of questioning precisely because we have for so long *passively* accepted our values without question. Active nihilism could therefore be seen as both a result of passive nihilism and as a way to prevent the continued growth of passive nihilism.

Passive nihilism could lead us to not only question the value of our traditional values, it could eventually lead us to question the value of having any values whatsoever, to question even the value of questioning. Or as Nietzsche puts it:

the weary nihilism that no longer attacks; its most famous form, Buddhism; a passive nihilism, a sign of weakness. The strength of the spirit may be worn out, exhausted, so that previous goals and values have become incommensurate and no longer are believed; so that the synthesis of values and goals (on which every strong culture rests) dissolves and the individual values war against each other: disintegration—and whatever refreshes, heals, calms, numbs emerges into the foreground in various disguises, religious or moral, or political, or aesthetic, etc.[39]

It is here that we can begin to ask whether technology would be seen by Nietzsche as not only nihilistic but as a manifestation of passive nihilism. For it would appear that technology could belong to this list of the "various disguises" through which passive nihilism "emerges," as technology is what "refreshes, heals, calms, numbs" for so many of us today. Of course it may be objected that technology should instead be seen as active nihilism, as a sign of strength rather than of weakness, of energy rather than of weariness, for surely if there is any domain where we are today questioning traditional values and creating new values it is in the domain of technology.

Before we can begin to make such determinations we should first look at current debates surrounding the relationship between technology and what it means to be human, for a second objection that could be raised is that Nietzsche is simply too outdated to be of any relevance to contemporary issues. Nietzsche could be seen as having taken for granted that to be human is to be embodied, to be vulnerable, to be mortal, and that to be nihilistic is to evade our embodiment, to evade our vulnerability, to evade our mortality. But what if this presupposition is wrong, or at least, obsolete? What if embodiment, vulnerability, mortality are not *necessary* features of being human but are merely *historically contingent* features, features that belong to a phase of humanity, a phase that we may soon be able to leave behind?

This is the question posed by a movement inspired by recent innovations in technology: transhumanism.[40] Transhumanism is the pursuit of technologically modifying the human body in order to improve it (for example, Kevin Warwick turning himself into a "cyborg"[41]). A more extreme version of transhumanism pursues not the modification of the human body but the replacement of the human body with a technological body (for example, Ray Kurzweil's prophesied "Singularity"[42]). In other words, transhumanists want to upgrade *through* technology, or they want to merge *with* technology.

While these might seem like different goals, the underlying perspective of both forms of transhumanism is very much the same: human existence is *imperfect* and it *can* and *should* be fixed. The *imperfection* of human existence identified by transhumanists is that of having a limitless consciousness trapped in a limited body. This idea is of course not new as it is the basis of what has come to be known as *mind/body dualism*. Numerous philosophers and numerous religions have entertained some version of this dualism, some version of the idea that the soul, the mind, the *res cogitans*, rationality, intelligence, consciousness, all of these various names for the thinking part of human life, is pure, infinite, immortal, and caged within a body that is impure, finite, mortal.

This dualistic perspective has been attacked not only by Nietzsche but by phenomenologists, existentialists, feminist philosophers, philosophers of race, critical theorists, structuralists, and poststructuralists, to name a few. On the one hand, this perspective has been shown to be nihilistic, positing the existence of a world beyond ours, a better world, a world that we can achieve through death, whether that death be literal or living (for example, through the ascetic renunciation of life favored by monks both Buddhist and Christian). On the other hand, this perspective has been shown to be ideological, providing metaphysical justification for the political subjugation of those found to be more physical than rational, more emotional than objective, and thus more in need of being controlled than in need of having control (for example, women, persons of color, or more generally anyone who is not a wealthy heterosexual white Christian man).

Transhumanism however simply sidesteps all of these issues by asserting that dualism is not a theory, it is a reality. This is where the *can* part of their perspective comes in. The *can* part of this perspective is the result of technological progress in biomedical technologies with regard to upgrade-focused transhumanism, and in artificially intelligent technologies with regard to merge-focused transhumanism. Implants, modifications, and genetic engineering that allow us to extend human life already exist, giving rise to the dream of not only curing diseases and impairments but of curing death itself. Similarly, machine learning that allows technologies to understand us, converse with us, and compete with us already exists, giving rise to the dream of not only living *with* artificial intelligence but living *through* artificial intelligence.

The *should* part of this theory comes from the shared ideological underpinning of both forms of transhumanism: a rejection of the imperfect, of the natural, of the (traditional) human. As Nick Bostrom writes, in his essay "In Defense of Posthuman Dignity":

> Transhumanists promote the view that human enhancement should be made widely available, and that individuals should have broad discretion over which of these technologies to apply to themselves (morphological freedom), and that parents should normally get to decide which reproductive technologies to use when having children (reproductive freedom). [43]

Transhumanism here appears to be simply an argument for freedom and equality. If there are technologies available that *can* improve human life, then everyone—not just those wealthy enough to afford it—*should* have access to these technologies. This is not an argument that everyone *should be enhanced* but rather that everyone *should decide for themselves* whether or not to make use of enhancement technologies. However, while this argument may apply to "morphological freedom," it quickly unravels when applied to "reproductive freedom," as this freedom can only exist for the parents who make the decisions, not for the children who are the result of the decisions.

Ableism is the belief that there are "normal" human abilities, and that whoever is lacking in those abilities is not only disabled but abnormal, inferior, in need of being fixed, of being made human. To assert "reproductive freedom" is to reveal the ableism of transhumanism. As Melinda Hall writes:

> Transhumanists seek to eliminate or mitigate dependence and vulnerability, while disability rights proponents seek to drain stigmatizing power from those concepts and embrace differences of all kinds. Transhumanists make a universalizing gesture when they categorize all humans as deficient, but this move merely serves to shift, rather than ameliorate, stigma connected to deficiency—thus maintaining and even strengthening ableism. [44]

What is assumed by Bostrom, and by transhumanism, is that any child *would* want to be enhanced, that the unenhanced life is *not worth living*.[45]

It is the assertion of "reproductive freedom" that reveals the true meaning of the normative dimension of transhumanism. As Bostrom continues:

> Transhumanists counter [in response to what Bostrom calls "biocon-servativism"] that nature's gifts are sometimes poisoned and should not always be accepted. Cancer, malaria, dementia, aging, starvation, unnecessary suffering, and cognitive shortcomings are all among the presents that we would wisely refuse. Our own species-specified na-tures are a rich source of much of the thoroughly unrespectable and unacceptable—susceptibility for disease, murder, rape, genocide, cheating, torture, racism. The horrors of nature in general, and of our own nature in particular, are so well documented that it is aston-ishing that somebody as distinguished as Leon Kass should still in this day and age be tempted to rely on the natural as a guide to what is desirable or normatively right. [. . .] Rather than deferring to the natural order, transhumanists maintain that we can legitimately re-form ourselves and our natures in accordance with humane values and personal aspirations.[46]

Or to put it even more bluntly:

> Had Mother Nature been a real parent, she would have been in jail for child abuse and murder.[47]

Among Bostrom's list of the "poisoned" gifts of nature, gifts such as "cancer," "malaria," "dementia," and "starvation," we find "aging," "un-necessary suffering," and "cognitive shortcomings." Cancer, malaria, dementia, and starvation were all, at various points in human history, seen as death sentences but are today seen as problems that either have been or will be solved by technology. The inclusion of aging, unneces-sary suffering, and cognitive shortcomings in this list is clearly meant to imply that these are also merely problems to be solved by technology. The further implication is that it is not the case that these gifts are part of human life because that is what it means to be human, but rather they are part of human life because we have mistaken what is historical-ly contingent for what is existentially necessary.

But is curing cancer really all that similar to curing aging? Cancer is an abnormality, a genetic mutation, which can be caused by inherited or environmental triggers. Aging however is not an abnormality but rather the condition of possibility for normality itself. Nature is change, growth, decay. To see aging as "poisoned" and as a "horror" is to see not what nature *gives* but what nature *is* as poisoned and as a horror. Similarly, to suggest that we can distinguish necessary from unnecessary suffering, cognitive perfection from cognitive shortcomings, is to judge reality against ideality, to condemn bodies and minds for being what they are rather than what—in a techno-utopia—they could be.

This condemnation of bodies and minds becomes even more apparent when Bostrom locates "disease" and "cheating" alongside the "unrespectable and unacceptable" aspects of human nature such as "rape," "genocide," "torture," and "racism." Rape, genocide, torture, and racism are crimes against humanity. If transhumanism sees aging as a poisoned gift, then it should be no surprise that disease is likewise treated as a crime. Cheating, however, is less a crime than a taboo, a break with norms that exist in certain societies at certain times. Moreover, because of its relation to norms, cheating only exists in societies where it is treated as taboo. Indeed, it could be argued that cheating is a product of living in specific societies with specific social structures. Bostrom seems to be suggesting instead that cheating, rape, genocide, torture, and racism are, like disease, products *of nature*, not *of society*, and are thus capable of being "cured" through technology. They are seen by Bostrom therefore not as part of what it means to be human, not as a product of the interaction between individual character and social structure, but as naturally occurring crimes against humanity, as proof that "Mother Nature" belongs "in jail for child abuse and murder."

Transhumanism, as presented by Bostrom, appears to be guilty of precisely the mistaken judgment that he criticizes bioconservatives of making. Bostrom is here using nature as "a guide to what is desirable or normatively right," though not for the purposes of defending nature but for condemning it. What is seen as natural is what is seen as undesirable and wrong. The transhumanist finds all that is wrong with the world in nature rather than in oneself, rather than in society. If the transhumanist suffers, the suffering is seen not as an opportunity for individual growth nor as motivation for social transformation but as evidence that the transhumanist was wrongly made to be susceptible to suffering and as motivation for technological transformation.

And just as transhumanism would accuse bioconservatism of preferring what is natural to what is technological for no other reason than that it is natural, transhumanism is just as guilty of preferring what is technological for no other reason than that it is *not natural*. Transhumanism goes even further than ableism. For transhumanism, the standard against which all are judged is not the "normal" human but the "technological" human, the human who does not yet exist but who is seen as what humanity *can* and *should* strive to become. As Babette Babich writes:

> We want to be anything but human. We want, as Günther Anders already argued in his 1956 *The Obsolescence of Humanity*, to overcome our "promethean shame" and to be like our precisely manufactured objects in all their precision, all their durability, all their replaceability. We wish to be objects with exchangeable parts, infinitely upgradable, as science fiction robot stories have long explored these possibilities. Bad heart? Get a replacement. Bad eyes, replace them with optical sensors, see the way Robocop sees—i.e., in the dark, through walls, complete with grids and autofocus—upgrade to Cyborg vision. Bad spirit, that is to say, afflicted with the "disease" du jour, namely "depression"? There are a bunch of pills to help with that. But what we want, at least we think this, is to live forever.[48]

It is here that we can see the relevance of Nietzsche for helping us to understand what may be motivating and operating beneath the surface of transhumanism. Rather than saying with Nietzsche, "Whatever does not kill me makes me stronger,"[49] Bostrom instead effectively says, "Whatever does not kill me reveals a weakness to be technologically cured."

It may appear that transhumanism is trying to bring about Nietzsche's "overman" (*Übermensch*)[50] for, as Nietzsche writes, "Not 'mankind' but *overman* is the goal!"[51] Yet I believe that Nietzsche would instead view transhumanism as merely continuing the very nihilism that the overman was meant to *overcome*. As Ciano Aydin writes:

> The elaborated view of the Overhuman as an index of transcendence is an attempt to express this paradoxical challenge. Recognizing a dimension in human existence that in no way can be controlled,

appropriated, or domesticated, is a necessary condition for radical self-transformation. By virtue of this transcendent dimension the human can never completely coincide with his current state, which is a conception that is also expressed by Nietzsche's idea that the human being can never be completely determined. Radical self-transformation is only possible if the anticipated ideal in no way can be reduced to the current (and past) self-understanding of the human being. Transhumanists who claim that the human being will be able to completely design his life and fate deny this transcendent dimension and necessarily reduce, in their projections of an ideal human being, the human to a contemporary (humanist) perfect image, to an idol. The human being has from their view no other goal beyond himself.[52]

The overman is a stage in human development for Nietzsche, a stage that could only occur—if at all[53]—after the *valuation* of the masters and the *revaluation* of the slaves.[54] The overman represents the stage of *transvaluation*, the stage of the transcendence of value judgments, of the transcendence of wanting to *reify* values rather than *overcome* them. The masters earn the love of the gods through their actions, the slaves are born beloved of the one true God, but the overman—even if it makes him look like a "madman"[55]—is able to reckon with the realization that "God is dead,"[56] to reckon with the realization that there is no transcendent being or realm upon which we can base any absolute and eternal value judgments.

Again, it may appear that transhumanists are likewise saying "God is dead," but in reality they are saying, "Technology is God." Nietzsche argues that science appears to challenge religion but only perpetuates religion by replacing "faith in God" with "faith in truth,"[57] positing truth as a value without "justification,"[58] taking for granted that it should guide all our actions. In much the same way, transhumanists have replaced "God" with "Technology." In this replacement, the names we give to our values may have changed, but what the values represent, and the functions they serve, has not.

We have long dreamt of shedding our mortal coils in death, allowing our souls to return to where they *truly* belong. Though we may believe that the world is becoming increasingly secular, and that technology in particular is helping to usher in a new atheistic age, this dream still clearly exists. We may have replaced a cloud-filled Heaven with a cloud-computer Heaven—as was depicted for example in the *Black Mirror* episode "San Junipero"—but it is still the same nihilistic dream. It is for this reason that Nietzsche's writings, though over one hundred years old, are still relevant, are still in need of being returned to, so that we can investigate our nihilistic dreams, and try to foresee, if not prevent, our becoming trapped in a nihilistic nightmare.

Bringing together what I call Nietzsche's analyses of *human-nihilism relations* with Don Ihde's analyses of *human-technology relations* (which I will discuss in the next chapter), we can ask whether it is technologies that today best serve to help us live with our nihilism, and also whether it is the designers of these technologies who today serve in the role of ascetic priests, by not combating nihilism but instead only making it more palatable. For if this is indeed the case, if our technologies and the designers who make them are not, as we often assume, *disrupting* the Christian moral world, then they may instead be helping to ensure its survival by providing us *Traditional Moral Values 2.0.* There is a danger then that technologies are not a sign of human progress but of decline, making us more advanced but also sicker, more self-destructive, more nihilistic. The question I will be trying to answer in subsequent chapters is whether our technologies are the product not of innovation but of asceticism, whether technologies are life-denying ideals that we can hold in the palms of our hands.

NOTES

1. Even solely within the realm of Nietzsche exegesis, the attempt to define "nihilism" has a long and complicated history. For a discussion of this history, see Babette Babich, "*Ex aliquo nihil*: Nietzsche on Science, Anarchy, and Democratic Nihilism," *American Catholic Philosophical Quarterly* 84, no. 2 (2010): 231–56. See also the entry on "nihilism" in Douglas Burnham, *The Nietzsche Dictionary* (London and New York: Bloomsbury, 2015), 236–39, and see Andreas Urs Sommer, "Nihilism and Skepticism in Nietzsche," in *A Companion to Nietzsche*, ed. Keith Ansell-Pearson (Oxford: Blackwell, 2006), 250–29.

2. Jean-Paul Sartre, *Being and Nothingness*, trans. Hazel Barnes (New York: Washington Square Press, 1992), 96.

3. Sartre, *Being and Nothingness*, 100.

4. Babette Babich, "On Schrödinger and Nietzsche: Eternal Return and the Moment," in *Antonio T. de Nicolas: Poet of Eternal Return*, ed. Christopher Key Chapple (Ahmedabad, India: Sriyogi Publications & Nalanda International, 2014), 171–72.

5. Sartre, *Being and Nothingness*, 725. See also Jean-Paul Sartre, "The Humanism of Existentialism," in *Essays in Existentialism*, ed. Wade Baskin (New York: Citadel Press, 1965), 34.

6. Sartre, *Being and Nothingness*, 100.

7. Friedrich Nietzsche, *On the Genealogy of Morals and Ecce Homo*, trans. Walter Kaufmann (New York: Vintage Books, 1989), 39.

8. Sartre, *Being and Nothingness*, 100.

9. Sartre, *Being and Nothingness*, 102.

10. Sartre, *Being and Nothingness*, 102: "A grocer who dreams is offensive to the buyer, because such a grocer is not wholly a grocer. Society demands that he limit himself to his function as a grocer, just as the soldier at attention makes himself into a soldier-thing with a direct regard which does not see at all, which is no longer meant to see, since it is the rule and not the interest of the moment which determines the point he must fix his eyes on (the sight 'fixed at ten paces'). There are indeed many precautions to imprison a man in what he is, as if we lived in perpetual fear that he might escape from it, that he might break away and suddenly elude his condition."

11. Friedrich Nietzsche, *The Will to Power*, trans. Walter Kaufmann and R. J. Hollingdale (New York: Vintage Books, 1967), 7.

12. Nietzsche, *Will to Power*, 7.

13. Nietzsche, *Genealogy*, 20.

14. Nietzsche, *Genealogy*, 20.

15. Nietzsche, *Genealogy*, 29.

16. Nietzsche, *Genealogy*, 36.

17. Nietzsche, *Genealogy*, 46.

18. Nietzsche, *Genealogy*, 47–49.

19. Nietzsche, *Genealogy*, 34.

20. Nietzsche, *Genealogy*, 28.

21. Nietzsche, *Genealogy*, 34.

22. Nietzsche, *Genealogy*, 42.

23. Nietzsche, *Genealogy*, 33.

24. Nietzsche, *Genealogy*, 65.

25. Nietzsche, *Genealogy*, 92.

26. Nietzsche, *Genealogy*, 88.

27. Nietzsche, *Genealogy*, 92.

28. Nietzsche, *Genealogy*, 117.

29. Nietzsche, *Genealogy*, 118.

30. Nietzsche, *Genealogy*, 120.
31. Nietzsche, *Genealogy*, 126.
32. Nietzsche, *Genealogy*, 38.
33. Nietzsche, *Genealogy*, 126.
34. Nietzsche, *Genealogy*, 129–30.
35. Nietzsche, *Genealogy*, 78–79.
36. Nietzsche, *Genealogy*, 97.
37. Nietzsche, *Genealogy*, 20.
38. Nietzsche, *Genealogy*, 17.
39. Nietzsche, *Will to Power*, 18.
40. In order to avoid a potential confusion here, a distinction should be made between "transhumanism" and "posthumanism." Transhumanists frequently use the concept of a "posthuman" to describe what technology will allow humans to become. However there are philosophers of technology who instead use the concept of a "posthuman" to describe the ways in which technology reveals ideological presuppositions in the humanistic conception of what it means to be human. Consequently we could distinguish the former as *posthuman-ists* from the latter who are *post-humanists*. In the posthuman-ist camp would belong Kevin Warwick, Ray Kurzweil, and Nick Bostrom. In the post-humanist camp would belong Donna Haraway, N. Katherine Hayles, and Rosi Braidotti. My criticism of transhumanism and of the concept of the "posthuman" should thus be read only as a criticism of the posthuman-ist project. My thanks to the anonymous reviewer who helpfully suggested that I clarify this issue.
41. James Edgar, "'Captain Cyborg': The Man Behind the Controversial Turing Test Claims," *Telegraph*, June 10, 2014, http://www.telegraph.co.uk/news/science/science-news/10888828/Captain-Cyborg-the-man-behind-the-controversial-Turing-Test-claims.html.
42. Lev Grossman, "2045: The Year Man Becomes Immortal," *TIME*, February 10, 2011, http://content.time.com/time/magazine/article/0,9171,2048299,00.html.
43. Nick Bostrom, "In Defense of Posthuman Dignity," *Bioethics* 19, no. 3 (2005): 203.
44. Melinda Hall, *The Bioethics of Enhancement: Transhumanism, Disability, and Biopolitics* (Lanham, MD: Lexington Books, 2017), 133.
45. See for example Steve Fuller, "We May Look Crazy to Them, But They Look Like Zombies to Us: Transhumanism as a Political Challenge," *Institute for Ethics and Emerging Technologies*, September 8, 2015, https://ieet.org/index.php/IEET2/more/fuller20150909.
46. Bostrom, "Posthuman," 205.
47. Bostrom, "Posthuman," 211.

48. Babette Babich, "Nietzsche's Post-Human Imperative: On the 'All-too-Human' Dream of Transhumanism," in *Nietzsche and Transhumanism: Precursor or Enemy?*, ed. Yunus Tuncel (Cambridge: Cambridge Scholars Publishing, 2017), 122.

49. Friedrich Nietzsche, *Twilight of the Idols*, trans. Duncan Large (Oxford: Oxford University Press, 1998), 5.

50. See for example the contributions by Max More and Stefan Sorgner in *Nietzsche and Transhumanism: Precursor or Enemy?*, ed. Yunus Tuncel (Cambridge: Cambridge Scholars Publishing, 2017).

51. Nietzsche, *Will to Power*, 519.

52. Ciano Aydin, "The Posthuman as Hollow Idol: A Nietzschean Critique of Human Enhancement," *Journal of Medicine and Philosophy* 42, iss. 3 (June 1, 2017): 322.

53. Aydin, "Hollow," 312: "The Overhuman, not only has never existed, but will also never exist as something particular. [. . .] By its very nature, the Overhuman cannot be conceptualized nor realized."

54. Nietzsche, *Genealogy*, 33–34.

55. Friedrich Nietzsche, *The Gay Science*, trans. Walter Kaufmann (New York: Random House, 1974), 181.

56. Nietzsche, *Gay Science*, 167.

57. Nietzsche, *Genealogy*, 151.

58. Nietzsche, *Genealogy*, 152.

3

THE HAMMER OF THE GODS

3.1 WHAT IS TECHNOLOGY?

When talking about technology, there are typically three different positions one can take. First, one can take a *pessimistic* position, and describe technology as a dominating force, as a power that is taking over the world, as a power that we must try to stop, if stopping it, or even controlling it, is even possible. Second, one can take an *optimistic* position, and describe technology as a liberating force, as a power that is fixing the world, as a power that we must try to expand, bringing technology to as many people, in as many places, for as many problems, as possible. Third, one can take a *neutral* position, and describe technology as not a force but as a particular set of objects, a set of objects that, like any other objects, are neither positive nor negative, as they are merely means to ends, ends chosen, and made positive or negative, by people.

Technology can be seen as life-destroying, as life-preserving, or as lifelessly instrumental. Yet to claim any one of these positions as defining what technology *is* is to be immediately criticized by those holding either of the two other positions for having overlooked something crucial about the nature of technology. For a pessimist to hold up the iPhone as an example of how technology is turning us all into zombies is to have to face, on the one hand, arguments about how the iPhone has been vital to keeping us informed, entertained, and even politically active and, on the other hand, arguments about how the iPhone is just a device, and a device can have no power other than what we give it. For an optimist to champion the self-driving car as an example of how technology is empowering is to have to face, on the one hand, arguments about how self-driving cars are just another technology that are stealing our jobs and, on the other hand, arguments about how a car being driven by programming is still a car being driven by a human. For a neutralist to point out how even the internet is not a force for good or evil but merely a complicated combination of devices is to face, on the one hand, arguments about how the internet is turning us into trolls and, on the other hand, arguments about how the internet is turning us into gods.

3.2 HEIDEGGER AND TECHNOLOGY

In his 1955 lecture, "The Question Concerning Technology," Martin Heidegger attempted to find a solution to the seemingly intractable problem of defining technology by providing an analysis of the "essence"[1] of technology. According to Heidegger it is only through such an analysis that we can free ourselves from our preconceptions about technology and so "experience the technological within its own bounds." Heidegger continues:

> the essence of technology is by no means anything technological. Thus we shall never experience our relationship to the essence of technology so long as we merely represent and pursue the technological, put up with it, or evade it. Everywhere we remain unfree and chained to technology, whether we passionately affirm or deny it. But we are delivered over to it in the worst possible way when we regard it as something neutral; for this conception of it, to which today we particularly like to pay homage, makes us utterly blind to the essence of technology.[2]

Heidegger here not only makes clear that he is a pessimist when it comes to technology but further suggests that our situation with regard to technology is so dire that it matters little whether we are pessimistic or optimistic. Rather what should concern us according to Heidegger is the neutral position—the position that he assumes most people take—

for it is neutrality that leaves us the most vulnerable, the most "blind," to the essence of technology.

The blindness of neutrality is, ironically, a result of the neutralist being "correct"[3] in defining technology as instrumental, as for Heidegger a definition being *correct* is not the same as it being *true*. While a correct definition is *relevant*, it is not *revelatory* in the way that truth is, and thus it puts forth a part of an answer in place of the whole, like reducing someone's identity to their nationality. For this reason Heidegger moves from asking what the essence of technology is to asking what the essence of instrumentality is, moving, like Socrates, through interrogations of the merely correct in order to reach the ultimate truth. In this way Heidegger discovers that the truth of technology, what is revelatory about technology, is that technology is itself *a way of revealing*. As Heidegger writes, "If we inquire, step by step, into what technology, represented as means, actually is, then we shall arrive at revealing. The possibility of all productive manufacturing lies in revealing."[4]

To produce, to manufacture, is to make something appear, to make visible how physical materials, technical concepts, and cultural practices can be gathered together in order to create a product. This product can be used, can be judged, and can be made significant, such that it can be identified as the product that it was intended to be. In this way, according to Heidegger, technology reveals through the mode of "bringing-forth,"[5] through not only turning what is potential into what is actual but through showing what nature and humanity are capable of, what each means for the other, what each can do for the other. Or at least this was true of ancient technology, for as Heidegger argues, while modern technology is still a way of revealing, it reveals instead in the mode of "challenging-forth."[6]

Ancient windmills and ancient bridges helped people to see the power of wind and the power of water, that wind and water were forces to be reckoned with, to be respected, to be named, honored, and even deified. The windmills and bridges of today still reveal wind and water to us as power, however what is revealed is not power to be respected but power to be "stockpiled,"[7] to be packaged, stored, and made available on demand, like a battery, or what Heidegger calls "standing-reserve."[8] The reduction of nature from a godlike force to a controllable energy source is what Heidegger sees as the defining feature of modern technology, as what has led humanity to take ourselves to be a godlike force, to be the beings for whom not only technology but the natural world that technology mines, harvests, and stockpiles is seen as mere instrumentality, as mere means to our ends, as existing merely to satisfy our demands.

Yet Heidegger points out that this is precisely what is dangerous about the neutralist position, for viewing technology as instrumentality, as instruments *for us*, is to become blind to how we too have come under the rule of instrumentality, how we too have become instruments, instruments *for technology*. That modern technology has reduced nature to an on-demand power source, to a power source that we can control, does not mean that we are ourselves the masters of this process of reduction and subservience, for we have likewise been reduced and made subservient as standing-reserve, as we must be available on demand in order to control and make use of these on-demand power sources as needed. In other words, modern technology not only challenges nature, revealing nature as a power source to be stockpiled, but first and foremost challenges humanity, revealing humanity as the power source to do the stockpiling.

Of course, to refer to something as on *demand*, as available as *needed*, is to be taken to imply that these demands and needs are human, and thus even if humans have been made subservient, they have nevertheless been made subservient to the demands and needs of other humans. In this way we are tempted to argue against Heidegger's pessimism that, even if we are not personally the ones who are in control of instrumentality, humans must still ultimately be in control, and must still be above the level of instrumentality. Modern technology may have reduced nature, but nature has been so reduced *for humanity*. Or at least that is how our situation appears to us. What Heidegger wants us to see however is that while we may work in the service of industries—of industries owned and operated by humans—these industries are operating under a logic that is not a human logic meant to serve human demands and needs but rather the logic of modern technology, a logic meant to serve the demands and needs of modern technology.

Heidegger argues though that what is driving humanity to serve modern technology is not itself anything technological but is, rather, part of the "challenging-forth" that is driving modern technology. What has challenged both humanity and technology to come under the logic of instrumentality is what Heidegger calls "*Gestell*" or "Enframing,"[9] a reappropriation of a German word (*Ge-stell*) meant to make clear how humanity and technology have both been gathered (*Ge-*) and forced to reveal themselves (*-stellen*) in the mode of standing-reserve. Using the example of a lumberjack, Heidegger argues that both a lumberjack and his grandfather could walk through the same forest, but they would not walk through the forest in the same way for the same reasons.[10] The lumberjack in the forest today is there because he is paid to be, paid in order to chop wood, in order to produce paper, in order to make newspapers and magazines, in order to sell products and opinions to the public. The lumberjack may appear to be working for the forestry industry, but the forestry industry is itself working for industries within industries and, therefore, the lumberjack is ultimately working within the logic of the *in-order-to*, the logic of Enframing.

What Heidegger is specifically concerned with here is that while Enframing reveals what we can do with nature—we can use modern technology to turn trees into shapers of public opinion—Enframing at the same time conceals our ability to see nature as anything but what we can do with it, and thus conceals that we can exist as anything other than manipulators of nature. Technology itself does not worry Heidegger—"What is dangerous is not technology"[11]—but rather it is the "destining"[12] of technology to become the challenging-forth found in modern technology that Heidegger sees as the true danger. In particular Heidegger focuses on how the history of technology has culminated in our becoming enraptured by Enframing, by instrumentality, by challenging-forth, and thereby losing sight of the noninstrumental possibilities of bringing-forth that were revealed in ancient technology. Because this outcome was already present as a possibility in ancient technology, as the fate of bringing-forth to become challenging-forth, Heidegger is not simply arguing for a return to ancient technology since today, under the rule of Enframing, we are incapable of seeing ancient technology as anything other than a primitive form of modern technology, as anything other than primitive instrumentality.

Once instrumentality becomes the only mode of revelation and thus becomes simply how everything appears to us, Heidegger argues that we will no longer be aware that revealing is taking place, that a particular way of seeing the world is being revealed to us, resulting in revelation and concealment themselves becoming concealed. It is at this point that humanity would truly have reached the level of mere standing-reserve, seeing the world, God, ourselves only through instrumentality, only through the logic of the in-order-to, relying on the *correct* version of reality to be effectively sufficient such that we no longer inquire into the *truth*, such that inquiry itself would no longer be pursued, except *in order to* satisfy a demand. Yet Heidegger believes that so long as inquiry is possible, so long as we can question the essence of technology, then we can free ourselves from the grip of Enframing. For such questioning to take place however we would need something that could again motivate and inspire our curiosity, and the possible source of such motivation and inspiration Heidegger finds in art. Because art is "akin to the essence of technology" and "fundamentally different from it"[13]—for which reason, according to Heidegger, the Ancient Greeks called both art and technology *technē*—art has a power to reveal, a power to reveal that could rival modern technology's power to conceal.

Much more can be said about Heidegger's lecture but, for our purposes here, this overview should be sufficient to see how Heidegger can help us in trying to make sense of technology. Heidegger is clearly pessimistic about the technological world in which we find ourselves, arguing throughout that we have become enslaved to technology and to the instrumental way of seeing the world that modern technology reveals. However it is important to note that he is not pessimistic about humanity, as he also argues throughout that we are not the ones who have done the enslaving. The history of humanity is not to blame for our predicament, according to Heidegger, but rather something more like the history of Being, the history of revealing, the history of the revealing of Being, in which humans play a vital role, but of which humans are not the prime movers.

As we have already seen, even when Heidegger criticizes those who take a neutralist stance toward technology, he still describes the neutralist as having been "delivered over to" this stance. Similarly, when Heidegger begins to investigate the neutralist stance by questioning what instrumentality means, he moves from instrumentality to causality to Aristotle's "doctrine of the four causes."[14] Heidegger makes this move in order to show how we have today collapsed causality to one cause, to "*causa efficiens*," to the cause where we typically locate the role humans play in causality, a collapse which is indicative of the relationship between instrumentality and causality, of means/ends thinking taking over cause/effect thinking. To challenge this view, Heidegger does not merely argue that we need to return to Aristotle and appreciate the role of the other three causes but rather argues that we need to return to Aristotle in order to see that we are wrong to view humans as *causa efficiens* in the first place. Heidegger writes, "Finally there is a fourth participant in the responsibility for the finished sacrificial vessel's lying before us ready for use, i.e., the silversmith—but not at all because he, in working, brings about the finished sacrificial chalice as if it were the effect of a making; the silversmith is not a *causa efficiens*."[15]

The silversmith does not create the silver chalice but rather participates in the creation, sharing "responsibility" for creation with the three causes, with the *causa materialis* (silver), with the *causa formalis* (chalice-ness), with the *causa finalis* (ritual). The three causes are responsible for the chalice in the sense that the chalice is "indebted" to the causes for its existence. Yet the responsibility of the silversmith seems to be of a different order as, for Heidegger, the silversmith appears to be "responsible" for the chalice in the sense of having the *ability to respond*, in the sense of having *answered the call* of the three causes so as to gather them together to bring forth the chalice. Heidegger's thought here seems to be similar to the description of sculpture by Michelangelo put forth in one of his sonnets, which begins:

> The best of artists hath no thought to show
> Which the rough stone in its superfluous shell
> Doth not include: to break the marble spell
> Is all the hand that serves the brain can do.[16]

The sculptor does not create sculptures from out of nothing but responds to what is present in the stone, revealing what is already there. Heidegger however expands this thought to seemingly apply to any activity we would typically describe as human creativity, even applying it to Plato, as he writes, "The fact that the real has been showing itself in the light of Ideas ever since the time of Plato, Plato did not bring about. The thinker only responded to what addressed itself to him."[17]

The idea that humanity's role is to answer the call of Being, to bear witness to Being, to let the truth of Being reveal itself, can be found throughout Heidegger's philosophy.[18] Yet if the purpose of Heidegger's philosophy of technology is to argue that we need to question Enframing such that we can attain a "free relation" to technology, it is not clear what would be gained by having won our freedom from technology if seemingly we would nevertheless not be free to be much more than passive observers in our relation to Being. As Heidegger writes, "Wherever man opens his eyes and ears, unlocks his heart, and gives himself over to meditating and striving, shaping and working, entreating and thanking, he finds himself everywhere already brought into the unconcealed."[19] Enframing conceals the truth of Being, blocking us from serving our purpose, but if our purpose is merely to serve, to be thankful for having been "brought into the unconcealed," then it appears the "illusion" of freedom presented to us by Enframing might in the end be preferable to the reality Heidegger hopes we can recover. Indeed even when Heidegger explicitly discusses freedom, he still manages to make freedom seem somehow passive and unappealing, as for example when he writes, "Man is only an *administrator* of freedom, i.e., he can only let-be the freedom which is accorded to him, in such a way that, through man, the whole contingency of freedom becomes visible."[20]

Though Heidegger is often described as an *existential* phenomenologist, he is clearly opposed to the idea of freedom that has come to be associated with Existentialism. Heidegger himself states this opposition in his "Letter on 'Humanism'" where he explicitly distances himself from Sartre, and in particular from Sartre's "basic tenet" that "Existence precedes essence,"[21] the tenet that defines humanity as essentially having no essence, as essentially free, free to define our essence for ourselves. Contrary to this idea, Heidegger writes:

> The human being is rather "thrown" by being itself into the truth of being, so that ek-sisting in this fashion he might guard the truth of being, in order that beings might appear in the light of being as the beings they are. Human beings do not decide whether and how beings appear, whether and how God and the gods or history and nature come forward into the clearing of being, come to presence and depart. The advent of beings lies in the destiny of being. But for humans it is ever a question of finding what is fitting in their essence that corresponds to such destiny; for in accord with this destiny the human being as ek-sisting has to guard the truth of being. The human being is the shepherd of being.[22]

To be human is to find oneself in a particular historical period, a historical period determined not by humans but by Being, by the Being that gives us our destiny, a destiny of guarding and shepherding Being. Yet as guards and shepherds of Being we still play no role in shaping Being, no role in deciding how Being or beings or even history appears or disappears. Again, if technology serves to block us from realizing that this is our destiny and presents us instead with the illusion of freedom, it is perhaps no wonder that we have so embraced technology.

Heidegger is not blind to this issue though, as he himself raises in his "Letter" the concern that if we are enslaved by technology, if we are alienated by technology, then surely we need to respond with ethics rather than with ontology, with a focus on humanity rather than with a focus on Being. Heidegger writes:

> The desire for an ethics presses ever more ardently for fulfillment as the obvious no less than the hidden perplexity of human beings soars to immeasurable heights. The greatest care must be fostered upon the ethical bond at a time when technological human beings, delivered over to mass society, can attain reliable constancy only by gathering and ordering all their plans and activities in a way that corresponds to technology.

Yet Heidegger continues:

> Who can disregard our predicament? Should we not safeguard and secure the existing bonds even if they hold human beings together ever so tenuously and merely for the present? Certainly. But does this need ever release thought from the task of thinking what still remains principally to be thought and, as being, prior to all beings, is their guarantor and their truth? Even further, can thinking refuse to think being after the latter has lain hidden so long in oblivion but at the same time has made itself known in the present moment of world history by the uprooting of all beings?[23]

Heidegger here moves from ethics back to ontology, trying to show that even when we are facing an ethical crisis like that presented by technology we should nevertheless remain focused on ontology. An ethical crisis does not automatically "release" us from our "task," the task we cannot "refuse," the task of ontology, of thinking about Being rather than merely thinking about human beings. Heidegger next moves however to merge ethics and ontology, arguing "that thinking which thinks the truth of being as the primordial element of the human being, as one who eksists, is in itself originary ethics."[24] But Heidegger ultimately concludes that this thinking is "neither ethics nor ontology," as this thinking is "neither theoretical nor practical," as it has "no result," has "no effect," but is simply "recollection of being and nothing else."[25] In other words, our task is to be concerned with Being, not for any ethical or even ontological benefit but simply because that is our task, because that is what it means to be human.

We can now see that Heidegger is not particularly interested in technology, nor even in humanity, but only in Being. For this reason Heidegger only thinks about the relationship between technology and humanity from the perspective of Being, and from the perspective of what he perceives as humanity's role in the destiny of Being. Yet, we must ask, does humanity have a destiny? Is there a destiny to which humanity belongs? For Heidegger, such questioning is the *piety of thinking*, such questioning sets us on our way to Being. For Nietzsche, such questioning is the *thinking of piety*, such questioning sets us on our way to nihilism. In *The Will to Power*—in a note which begins with the declaration, "*Against determinism and teleology*"[26]—Nietzsche writes:

> As soon as we imagine someone who is responsible for our being thus and thus, etc. (God, nature), and therefore attribute to him the intention that we should exist and be happy or wretched, we corrupt for ourselves the *innocence of becoming*. We then have someone who wants to achieve something through us and with us.[27]

In other words, to focus as Heidegger does on Being rather than on becoming, on the destiny of humanity rather than on the humanity operating behind the concept of "destiny," is to commit the mistake of not having "ceased to look for the origin of evil *behind* the world,"[28] a mistake that Nietzsche tells us in the *Genealogy* that he "learned early" to avoid. Though Nietzsche is arguing against "theological prejudice," against the thinking that leads us to look *above* or *behind* the world for answers to our questions, we could apply this argument to what we could call Heidegger's "ontological prejudice" by arguing that we should not look *below* or *within* the world either, as we must instead be willing to look at ourselves.

The irony here is that Heidegger questions not only the essence of technology but also "the essence of nihilism,"[29] two questionings that so well parallel each other that one could seemingly replace "Enframing" with "will to power" in order to reveal that the two lectures—lectures that Heidegger gave only six years apart from each other—are two sides of the same argument. Yet it is precisely their similarity that is the problem for, even in his analyses of Nietzsche and nihilism, Heidegger still turns nihilism into a "historical movement," a "fundamental ongoing event that is scarcely recognized in the destining of the Western peoples," and "the world-historical movement of the peoples of the earth who have been drawn into the power realm of the modern age."[30] Heidegger thus turns Nietzsche into a Heideggerian, into a thinker of Being rather than of becoming.

If therefore we disagree with Heidegger and side with Nietzsche, then we can disagree with Heidegger that humanity has a destiny that requires the thinking of Being and instead agree with Nietzsche that humanity has not a destiny but a prejudice toward "destiny" thinking, a prejudice that requires that we investigate *becoming*. We can still retain Heidegger's insights into what technology means for human experience, insights into the ways that technology reveals and conceals the world, but we can do so without having to retain the deterministic conclusions that Heidegger draws from these insights. And such a Nietzschean[31] reappropriation of Heidegger is precisely what we find in the philosophy of technology of Don Ihde, the philosophy that he has named *postphenomenology*.

3.3 IHDE AND TECHNOLOGIES

Postphenomenology is centered on what Ihde calls "human-technology relations."[32] These relations are not meant to be taken as merely how humans and technologies relate to each other, as the latest version of subject/object dualism, but rather as how, through these relations, humans and technologies become what they are. Postphenomenological investigations are therefore investigations into co-constitution,[33] into how technological beings, in a technological world, come to have meaning in, and through, and for each other.

Devices are not inert tools that I can pick up, use, and discard, for in picking up, using, and even in discarding a device I must already have a meaningful relationship with the device such that I can recognize it, manipulate it, and become bored with it. The device must already have a place in my world and must already have the ability to shape, or *mediate*,[34] my experience of the world in order for me to even know that it is a device.

A fork is not merely a metal stick at the end of which are three smaller metal sticks, it is an ability to eat, a way to transform a plate of food into a meal, into a dish of mouth-sized bits of nourishment to be taken up as needed or desired. A fork may start out, perhaps when first seen in one's infancy, as metal to be played with, thrown, stabbed, or drummed, but it quickly becomes so tied to hunger that these once-infantile fork games are only later reverted to as a way of sublimating our frustration for not eating when expected, games we later play with the fork almost as if we see the fork as itself being as frustrated as we are.

To say that a fork is "frustrated" may sound like an appeal to *animism*—suggesting that objects can be alive even if inanimate—or an appeal to *projection*—suggesting that objects are receptacles of whatever desires, feelings, emotions their human users imbue them with. Yet in either case we are returned to the very subject/object dualism that postphenomenology is meant to transcend. In animism a fork can be seen as a subject modeled after human subjectivity, while in projection a fork can be seen as an object that a human subject can manipulate psychologically just as a subject would manipulate an object physically. Rather, what must be seen is that, for the child relating to the fork as a participant in a game or for the adult relating to the fork as a participant in a meal, there is no fork independent of the specific human-technology relation in which it is engaged, just as there is no child or adult independent of that same engaged relation.

As Wittgenstein tried to reveal in his *Philosophical Investigations*, we are easily tricked by language into holding certain philosophical positions, even if we do not realize it. Thus the name "fork" appears to suggest to us an object in the world that is predefined, predetermined, and whose determinate definition is maintained across any and all possible uses we might find for it. In other words, a fork forks, and a fork forks regardless of whatever particular forking we might be trying to engage in at any given moment. From this perspective, to stab someone with a fork is to misuse a fork for which reason we can, and often do, scold others for using forks wrongly, for using a fork in a way that does not correspond to its proper use.

However, from the postphenomenological perspective, to stab someone with a fork is to relate to a fork as a participant in a murder plot. To see a fork as a way to murder someone is to not only constitute the fork as a potential weapon but, vitally, is to constitute myself simultaneously as a potential murderer. The intentional relation of I → Fork → Murder co-constitutes myself as Murderer and the fork as Weapon such that, within the relation, there is no "fork" outside of its weaponness and there is no "me" outside of my murderousness. Unlike the aforementioned deterministic perspective, for the postphenomenologist, here it is not the case that a fork can be seen as a weapon but rather that a weapon can be seen as a "fork," just as it is not the case that a person can be seen as a murderer but rather that a murderer can be seen as a "person." In other words, there is no fork, there is no me, there is only the intentional relation.

Through postphenomenology we have arrived at an ontology based not on subjects and objects but on intentional relations, an ontology that is perhaps the truest realization of Husserl's lifelong attempt to make phenomenology a presuppositionless science of intentionality. Such an ontology is centered not on Descartes's "I think, therefore I am," or even on "I intend, therefore I am," but rather the more radical claim: "Intentional beings intend, therefore intentional beings are." To return to the aforementioned fork example, we can now say that, in the I → Fork → Murder relation, there is the intentional being "I" and the intentional being "Fork," but it is only through the relation "→ Murder" that "I" and "Fork" exist, and exist, more specifically, as "Murderer" and "Weapon" respectively. In other words, to say "I am a murderer" is to say "I, as the being who has an intentional relation with a being intended to be a weapon and a being intended to be a victim, am a murderer."

Contrary to the fears of Heidegger, postphenomenology does not see our relationship with technology as dystopic or deterministic, precisely because of this co-constitutive nature of the human-technology relationship. Postphenomenologists refer to the "multistability"[35] of technologies to point out—as was shown earlier with the fork example—that because technologies have no inherent being outside of intentional relations, there can be nothing inherently fearful or determining about technologies. Like the "duck-rabbit" optical illusion, technologies have no stable essence but only various *stabilities*, or various ways of being related to, none of which can be said to be "true" or "false," "right" or "wrong." This does not guarantee that human-technology relations must be instrumental or beneficial either but instead simply refutes any argument based on making a priori claims about how users *will* relate to technologies or, contra Heidegger, any claim about what technology *is*.

And yet this relational view of technologies does not originate with Ihde; it comes from Heidegger, from the Heidegger of *Being and Time*, from the "positive"[36] Heidegger who Ihde appropriates in order to challenge the "negative" views of the Heidegger of "The Question Concerning Technology." Whereas in the later work Heidegger focuses on the distinction between ancient technology and modern technology in order to illuminate the difference between bringing-forth and challenging-forth, in the earlier work Heidegger focuses on the distinction between functioning technologies and malfunctioning technologies in order to illuminate the difference between "Being-in-the-world"[37] and subject/object dualism. Though in both works Heidegger's primary focus is on Being, and the need for humanity to take up our proper role in relation to Being, nevertheless in *Being and Time* Heidegger explores the uses of *specific* technologies in *specific* contexts without making pronouncements about how the particular historical period we live in must determine our relationship to *any* technology in *any* context.[38]

The most famous example of such an exploration is Heidegger's discussion of using a hammer.[39] When hammering, according to Heidegger, we have a more "primordial" relationship to the world, as we do not pay attention to the hammer but simply use it. In hammering, the hammer is not a hammer but is an "in-order-to," that which we use to do our work, the work that we are paying attention to instead, the work that is the "toward-this" of the hammering. Heidegger's primary insight here—the insight from which Ihde develops his philosophy of technology—is that for the hammer to function as an "in-order-to," in hammering, the hammer must "withdraw"[40] from our attention so that we can do our work, so that the "toward-this" of our work can occupy our attention instead.

This insight helps to explain why we so frequently hit our thumbs when hammering since, in hammering, neither the hammer nor even our own bodies are the focus of our concern. Yet when we do hit our thumbs, when we do use the hammer and something unexpected occurs, our attention is suddenly taken away from our work and put instead solely on the hammer, which we then see no longer as an "in-order-to" but only as a hammer. Or, to be more precise, what we see in such a breakdown situation is not the hammer but the *in-order-to-ness* of the hammer. As Heidegger writes:

> But *when an assignment has been disturbed*—when something is unusable for some purpose—then the assignment becomes explicit. Even now, of course, it has not become explicit as an ontological structure; but it has become explicit ontically for the circumspection which comes up against the damaging of the tool. When an assignment to some particular "towards-this" has been thus circumspectively aroused, we catch sight of the "towards-this" itself, and along with it everything connected with the work—the whole "workshop"—as that wherein concern always dwells. The context of equipment is lit up, not as something never seen before, but as a totality constantly sighted beforehand in circumspection. With this totality, however, the world announces itself.[41]

Not unlike the law of conservation of energy, Heidegger argues that humans have something like a law of conservation of attention, that we can be concerned with work or we can be concerned with the world but not with both simultaneously. The world, as a referential totality, as a totality of every "in-order-to" and "towards-this," only "announces itself" when our work has been "disturbed," when we are taken out of our practical mode of working and are instead led to take up a more theoretical mode, following the suddenly apparent chain of references in order to figure out what went wrong.

Rather than follow Heidegger—moving from the ontic to the ontological, from the everydayness of hammering to the meaning of Being—Ihde remains within the ontic, establishing postphenomenology as a research program into the human-technology relations of everyday life, a research program meant to steer clear of the "negative" conclusions of Heidegger's ontology. Ihde thus turns Heidegger's analysis of hammering into an exemplar of how to carry out analyses of human-technology relations, analyses which lead Ihde to expand the field of human-technology relations beyond Heidegger's examples, resulting in analyses into four types of relations: "embodiment relations,"[42] "hermeneutic relations,"[43] "alterity relations,"[44] and "background relations."[45]

Embodiment relations occur when a technology functions for a user like a body part, expanding and extending the physical abilities of users, such that the user experiences empowerment without experiencing the technology that is enabling the empowering. The classic example of an embodiment relation—other than Heidegger's hammer example—is wearing a pair of glasses, as glasses enhance eyesight while disappearing from view. The better the glasses, the less likely it is that the glasses wearer will take notice of them, for which reason we say, "I see you," rather than, "My glasses and I see you." We do not mention the glasses in everyday conversation because the "I" has come to include the glasses. To make this relationship more clear, Ihde formalizes such embodiment relations as:

(I-Technology) → World[46]

We perceive the world through embodiment technologies, but this perception is achieved, as Heidegger described, by such technologies withdrawing from concern so that we can be concerned instead with the world that these technologies help to reveal. While such technologies can easily be listed—such as binoculars, ear buds, microphones, hammers, and shoes—because of the multistable nature of technologies it is important to recognize that we can potentially experience embodiment relations with almost any technology, like when we use a book as a hammer or when we use a smartphone to move something just out of reach. The specific technology is not therefore what defines an embodiment relation but rather the specific technology's dynamic of revealing and withdrawing in the form of the *amplification* of our perception and the *reduction* of our awareness of the technology mediating our perception.[47]

Hermeneutic relations occur when a technology functions for a user like a translator, expanding and extending the interpretive abilities of users, such that the user feels informed without thinking about the technology that is enabling the informing. An example of a hermeneutic relation is reading a book, as a book conveys information while the lines that make up the letters and the letters that make up the words and the words that make up the sentences are all absorbed into the experience of reading. Again, the better the book, the less likely it is that the reader will take notice of the lines, words, and sentences, for which reason we say, "I read a story," rather than, "I read a collection of various lines that combine to form a story." Ihde formalizes hermeneutic relations as:

I → (Technology-World)[48]

The world that we learn about through hermeneutic technologies is a world that we only have access to through hermeneutic technologies, technologies that merge with the world we are attempting to learn about such that the technology and the world become indistinguishable. Again, thanks to multistability, what is important here is not the particular technology involved in a hermeneutic relation—whether it be an artifact, a map, a website, or an app—but rather the particular technology's dynamic of revealing and withdrawing in the form of the *presence* of the world we are given access to and the *absence* of our awareness of the technology mediating that access.[49]

Alterity relations occur when a technology functions for a user like an *other*, like a person or animal, acting independently of the user, expanding and extending the interactive abilities of users, such that the users experience the presence of a seemingly autonomous being without thinking about the technology that is enabling the semblance of autonomy. An example of an alterity relation is playing a game against a computer, as the computer opponent challenges us and entertains us, leading us to feel inferior to the computer when we lose and to feel superior to the computer when we win, as if the computer opponent could likewise feel inferiority or superiority toward us. Once more, the better the game, the less likely it is that the user will take notice of the programming operating behind the computer opponent, for which reason we say, "I beat the computer," rather than, "I beat the programming that determined the moves made by the computer." Ihde formalizes alterity relations as:

I → Technology-(-World)[50]

Unlike embodiment and hermeneutic relations, alterity relations focus our attention on technologies rather than on the world. Yet with the disappearance of the world from our concern so too does the nature of the specific technology disappear, leaving us feeling that we are in the presence of a living being rather than a technology created by living beings to simulate the behavior of living beings. Multistability plays a role here too, such that the particular technology—whether a toy, a robot, a game, or a Siri—is less important than the particular technology's dynamic of revealing and withdrawing in the form of *fascination* with the liveliness of the technology and *obliviousness* with regard to the world.[51]

Background relations occur when a technology functions for a user like a part of the environment, operating unnoticed, expanding and extending the attentive abilities of users such that users can pay attention to the world without having to pay attention to the technologies working behind the scenes to enable the user's attentiveness. An example of a background relation is a refrigerator, as the refrigerator keeps food edible for us, through a process that we need not understand and that we likely would prefer not to think about. Hence the better the refrigerator, the less likely it is that we will think about the refrigerator, for which reason we say, "This food is good," rather than, "This food, which was kept fresh in the refrigerator, is good." Ihde does not formalize background relations, however we could imagine that if he had, it would look something like the following:

I → World-(-Technology)

Background relations are thus the reverse of alterity relations, as our attention is focused on the world rather than on technologies even though, as with alterity relations, our attention's focus is due to the automaticity of the technology, to the ability of the technology to function without our involvement. Yet the technologies that fade out of our awareness are still a vital part of our world, hence the world that we focus on in background relations is an incomplete world, a world where things work but in a taken-for-granted way. It is for this reason that multistability operates even in background relations, making the particular technology—such as lighting, heating, plumbing, electricity, or Wi-Fi—less important than the particular technology's dynamic of revealing and withdrawing in the form of the *absent presence* of the technology and the *present absence* of the world.[52]

Following Heidegger, Ihde not only focuses on the dynamics of revealing and withdrawing at work in human-technology relations in optimal situations but also focuses on how such dynamics work in suboptimal, or "breakdown,"[53] situations. Embodiment technologies have the ability to *empower* us, but they also have the ability to *belittle* us, revealing when they break how dependent on technologies we have become. Hermeneutic technologies have the ability to *enlighten* us, but they also have the ability to *betray* us, revealing when they misinform us how much faith we put into technologies. Alterity technologies have the ability to *entertain* us, but they also have the ability to *enrage* us, revealing when they impede us how much emotional investment we have put into technologies. Background technologies have the ability to *enliven* us, but they also have the ability to *incapacitate* us, revealing when they malfunction how reliant on technologies we have become.

For Ihde, these breakdown situations show that whereas Heidegger was right that we do not have a merely instrumental relationship with technologies, Heidegger was wrong that we have a merely deterministic relationship with technologies. Ihde writes:

> In extending bodily capacities, the technology also transforms them. In that sense, all technologies in use are non-neutral. They change the basic situation, however subtly, however minimally; but this is the other side of the desire. The desire is simultaneously a desire for a change in situation—to inhabit the earth, or even to go beyond the earth—while sometimes inconsistently and secretly wishing that this movement could be without the mediation of the technology. [. . .] In the wish there remains the contradiction: the user both wants and does not want the technology. The user wants what the technology gives but does not want the limits, the transformations that a technologically extended body implies. There is a fundamental ambivalence toward the very human creation of our own earthly tools.[54]

Technologies mediate our experience of the world, and mediate our experience of ourselves. That this mediation occurs in a "non-neutral" way does not mean that technologies *determine* our experiences but rather that technologies *give us exactly what we want*, fulfilling our "desire for a change in situation." The problem, according to Ihde, is that, while we want the situational changes that technologies provide, we do not necessarily want technologies to have to provide these changes for us.

3.4 NIETZSCHE AND NIHILISM-TECHNOLOGY RELATIONS

Technologies reveal who we are and, most importantly, technologies reveal that we have a "fundamental ambivalence" toward technologies, simultaneously wanting and not wanting technologies in our lives. We know we want what technologies do; we also know we do not want technologies to do what they do, at least insofar as technologies reveal that we want and often *need* technologies to do what we are incapable of doing on our own. Rather than the Heideggerian concern that we are enslaved to technologies, Ihde points toward a much greater concern, the concern that we are not blindly delivered over to technologies but are well aware of what technologies do, what technologies do to us, for us, and with us, yet we continue to use technologies nevertheless. And it is this *nevertheless* that we must investigate.

If we focus less on Being and more on Capitalism, we can see how we have come to be aware of technologies in ways that Heidegger did not think possible. Technologies have not only become increasingly prevalent in our everyday lives, they have also become increasingly likely to break, to misinform, to impede, to malfunction during their everyday use. Whereas in Heidegger's day it may have been a rare occurrence for a hammer to break, and thus a rare occurrence for someone to experience in such a breakdown situation the role that a hammer plays in our experience, today it is in no way a surprise for a hammer, or for any technology, to break. Thanks to the drive to max-imize profits by minimizing the costs of production, mass production and cheap materials have combined to surround us with technologies that are made not to last but to be replaced, providing us ample oppor-tunities to discover the roles that technologies play in our everyday lives.

It is here that we can begin to see the role that nihilism can play in human-technology relations. We continue to use technologies that have the ever-present possibility to belittle us, to betray us, to enrage us, and to incapacitate us, and yet this continued use is done not blindly but willingly. Or, to be more precise, we willingly make ourselves blind to these possibilities by taking them for granted, by treating them as just the price we must pay in order to be empowered, enlightened, enter-tained, and enlivened. Technologies have not, as Heidegger predicted, led us to feel like we are masters of the universe but rather something closer to middle management. We are forever in negotiations with our technologies, treating them as partners in a bad relationship, trying to make ourselves comfortable with the idea that even though technologies are not always good for us, we just cannot seem to live without them. So we settle for what we have, we enjoy the good and try to ignore the bad, while we wait for a newer, younger model to come along to hopefully provide what we are missing.

In this way, through our ambivalence toward technologies, we continue to come closer and closer to Heidegger's determinism. We relate to technologies *as if* they were our destiny, *as if* we were blind to their effects on us, *as if* we had no freedom to change our situation. By bringing Nietzsche and Ihde together to investigate this way of relating to technologies, we can discover a new type of human-technology relation, a type of relation I call *nihilism relations*. Nihilism relations can be formalized as:

Technology → World-(-I)

Whereas in alterity relations the world fades from our concern, and in background relations the technology fades from our concern, in nihilism relations the I fades from our concern. To put it another way, in nihilism relations, it is our concern that fades from our concern, which is what takes place whenever we use technologies while trying to conceal from ourselves the dangers of using technologies, for which reason we say, "I can't believe I spent all day on my computer," rather than, "I can't believe I am not taking responsibility for having spent all day on my computer."

As with the human-technology relations Ihde identified, here too multistability is operative, making the particular technology involved in a nihilism relation less important than the particular technology's dynamic of revealing and withdrawing. However, this dynamic can take several forms, as Nietzsche already indicated in his investigations into what I have called *human-nihilism relations*. In order to investigate our ambivalence toward technologies, we must bring together the insights from Nietzsche's analyses of human-nihilism relations with the insights from Ihde's analyses of human-technology relations and begin a new research program into what I call *nihilism-technology relations*.

In the chapters that follow I will try to show how this research could be carried out, and to make clear why this research *should* be carried out, by providing case studies of various technologies. These case studies will explore not only how technologies in our everyday lives are already being used nihilistically but also how using technologies nihilistically can be dangerous. Yet in the end these dangers will lead us in the final chapter not toward a Heideggerian pessimism, not toward a deterministic view of the destiny of Being, but rather toward a Nietzschean optimism, an optimism focused on moving from the understanding of what it means to be human that arises from reckoning with *the death of God* to forging a new understanding of what it means to be human from reckoning with *the death of Google*.

NOTES

1. Martin Heidegger, "The Question Concerning Technology," in *The Question Concerning Technology and Other Essays*, trans. William Lovitt (New York: Harper & Row, 1977), 3.
2. Heidegger, "Question," 4.
3. Heidegger, "Question," 5.
4. Heidegger, "Question," 12.
5. Heidegger, "Question," 13.
6. Heidegger, "Question," 14.
7. Heidegger, "Question," 15.
8. Heidegger, "Question," 17.
9. Heidegger, "Question," 19.
10. Heidegger, "Question," 18.
11. Heidegger, "Question," 28.
12. Heidegger, "Question," 24.
13. Heidegger, "Question," 35.
14. Heidegger, "Question," 7.
15. Heidegger, "Question," 8.
16. J. A. Symonds, "Twenty-three Sonnets from Michael Angelo," *The Contemporary Review* 20 (1872): 513.
17. Heidegger, "Question," 18.
18. For more on this thematic continuity in Heidegger see for example Raffoul's discussion of Heidegger in François Raffoul, *The Origins of Responsibility* (Bloomington and Indianapolis: Indiana University Press, 2010). As Raffoul points out, to make this theme more clear in his work, "after *Being and*

Time, Dasein will be referred to more and more as 'the called one' (*der Geru-fene*), having to answer for the very openness and givenness of being and be its 'guardian'" (Raffoul, *Origins of Responsibility,* 244).

19. Heidegger, "Question," 18–19.

20. Martin Heidegger, *The Essence of Human Freedom,* trans. Ted Sadler (London and New York: Continuum, 2002), 94.

21. Martin Heidegger, "Letter on 'Humanism'," in *Pathmarks,* ed. William McNeill, trans. Frank A. Capuzzi (Cambridge: Cambridge University Press, 1998), 250.

22. Heidegger, "Letter," 252.

23. Heidegger, "Letter," 268.

24. Heidegger, "Letter," 271.

25. Heidegger, "Letter," 272.

26. Nietzsche, *Will to Power,* 297.

27. Nietzsche, *Will to Power,* 299. See also Nietzsche, *Will to Power,* 59–60, where Nietzsche criticizes Schopenhauer for having succumbed to the "nineteenth century" search "for theories that seem to justify its fatalistic submission to matters of fact," for "determinism," and for "the denial of will as an 'efficient cause'."

28. Nietzsche, *Genealogy,* 17.

29. Martin Heidegger, "The Word of Nietzsche: 'God is Dead,'" in *The Question Concerning Technology and Other Essays,* trans. William Lovitt (New York: Harper & Row, 1977), 53–112.

30. Heidegger, "Question," 62–63.

31. Don Ihde, *Technology and the Lifeworld* (Bloomington and Indianapolis: Indiana University Press, 1990), 224.

32. Ihde, *Technology and the Lifeworld,* 21.

33. Peter-Paul Verbeek, *What Things Do,* trans. Robert P. Crease (University Park: Pennsylvania State University Press, 2005), 129–30.

34. Ihde, *Technology and the Lifeworld,* 44–46.

35. Ihde, *Technology and the Lifeworld,* 144.

36. Don Ihde, *Technics and Praxis* (Dordrecht: D. Reidel, 1979), 125.

37. Martin Heidegger, *Being and Time,* trans. John Macquarrie and Edward Robinson (New York: Harper & Row, 1962), 78.

38. On this distinction between Heidegger's earlier and later works see also Verbeek, *What Things Do,* 80.

39. Heidegger, *Being and Time,* 98.

40. Heidegger, *Being and Time,* 99.

41. Heidegger, *Being and Time,* 105.

42. Ihde, *Technology and the Lifeworld,* 72.

43. Ihde, *Technology and the Lifeworld,* 80.

44. Ihde, *Technology and the Lifeworld*, 97.

45. Ihde, *Technology and the Lifeworld*, 108.

46. Ihde, *Technology and the Lifeworld*, 86.

47. Ihde, *Technology and the Lifeworld*, 76.

48. Ihde, *Technology and the Lifeworld*, 86.

49. Ihde, *Technology and the Lifeworld*, 84. Though Ihde discusses the concept of "hermeneutic presence," he does not explicitly pair this with a concept of "absence," thus this pairing is my interpretation of his analysis.

50. Ihde, *Technology and the Lifeworld*, 107.

51. Ihde, *Technology and the Lifeworld*, 103. Again while Ihde discusses the concept of "fascination," he does not explicitly pair this with a concept of "obliviousness," thus this pairing is my interpretation of his analysis.

52. Ihde, *Technology and the Lifeworld*, 109. This conceptual pairing, like the previous two, is my invention, an invention based on my interpretation of Ihde's analysis.

53. Ihde, *Technology and the Lifeworld*, 32–33, 86–87.

54. Ihde, *Technology and the Lifeworld*, 75–76.

4

ECCE HULU

4.1 SELF-HYPNOSIS

The first human-nihilism relation that Nietzsche describes is that of "self-hypnosis":

> This dominating sense of displeasure is combated, first, by means that reduce the feeling of life in general to its lowest point. If possible, will and desire are abolished altogether; all that produces affects and "blood" is avoided (abstinence from salt: the hygienic regimen of the fakirs); no love; no hate; indifference; no revenge; no wealth; no work; one begs; if possible, no women, or as little as possible; in spiritual matters, Pascal's principle *il faut s'abêtir* is applied. The result, expressed in moral-psychological terms, is "selflessness," "sanctification"; in physiological terms: hypnotization—the attempt to win for man an approximation to what in certain animals is hibernation, in many tropical plants estivation, the minimum metabolism at which life will still subsist without really entering consciousness. An astonishing amount of human energy has been expended to this end—has it been in vain?[1]

According to Nietzsche, we have spent a lot of time and energy trying to put ourselves to sleep. The purpose of this self-hypnosis is to avoid having to feel, for feeling can make us vulnerable, can open us up to experiences of fear, of regret, of dread. Seeing, smelling, hearing, tasting, touching, desiring, caring, all of these experiences can be burdens, burdens that we try to avoid at different times and in different ways, but always with the same goal: separating the parts of life that we like from the parts of life that we hate. In other words, we have put a lot of blood, sweat, and tears into not experiencing blood, sweat, and tears.

The part of life that we are most interested in avoiding is pain. We may spend a lot of time talking about death and talking about how much we fear death, yet, as several Ancient Greek philosophers pointed out, we do not experience death. Or at least we do not experience death except indirectly, through the death of others, or through pain. Pain we do experience directly. Pain is an experience of powerlessness. Pain is a little taste of death. Pain is the realization that we are not invincible, that we are not immortal, that we are not gods. Pain can therefore make us suffer not only physically but existentially.

It is this evasion of pain through evading any experience that could make us vulnerable to pain—an evasion which ultimately entails an evasion of experience itself—that Nietzsche saw in both the growing cultural interest in Buddhism and in the persistent philosophical interest in mind/body dualism. To meditate is to try to empty the mind, to try to lose oneself, to try to become one with everything so that one can become nothing. Dualism is to try to empty the body of meaning, to try to isolate the body as an inessential part of oneself, to try to identify one's true self with one's immortal soul while the mortal body is reduced to nothing but a prison we must escape. What both Buddhism and Dualism share for Nietzsche then is the evasion of not only pain and feeling but of what it means to be human. It is for this reason that Nietzsche classified self-hypnosis as a form of nihilism, as an example of both how we are sick of being human and of how we attempt to cure ourselves of this sickness.

4.2 FROM SELF-HYPNOSIS TO TECHNO-HYPNOSIS

Techno-hypnosis is my name for the phenomenon of our increasingly turning to technological means to carry out our self-hypnosis. This evasiveness of our humanity, of our frailty, of our finitude, is still with us today and has, in keeping with Nietzsche's predictions, only grown stronger since Nietzsche's time. Today we are perhaps less interested in the spiritual aspects of Buddhism or the metaphysical aspects of Dualism, but we are still very much interested in self-hypnosis and have given ourselves a vast array of technological means to achieve putting ourselves to sleep, to achieve what today we might instead describe as procrastination or, even more commonly, as "zoning out."

The idea of using technologies for the purposes of zoning out is perhaps most associated with watching television. The TV may have begun as a luxury item, intended to entertain, to inform, and, most importantly, to advertise products to viewers, but it has steadily grown into a ubiquitous piece of furniture, something we turn on and leave on not unlike a light we may or may not be using.

Wake up, turn on the TV, and instantly become surrounded with sound, something, anything, to occupy what might otherwise be a space filled with nothing but silence and your own thoughts. Turn off the TV, leave. Return, turn the TV back on. In between, watch TV on the bus, on the train, on the plane, in the mall, on the billboard, on your computer, on your phone, or even on your watch.

The world is filled with screens. This is not, from a Nietzschean point of view, a shocking development. Screens occupy our time, our space, our thoughts, our feelings. What is perhaps shocking is that we are aware of the zombifying effects of staring at screens and yet continue to spend hours on end staring at screens regardless. We have long derided TVs as "boob tubes" and "idiot boxes" and have derided TV watchers as "couch potatoes" but that has not stopped us from putting screens everywhere and staring at them as much as possible. Indeed a regular fixture of local evening TV news programs are stories about how watching TV is bad for us, and again this irony does little to turn us off TV.

If anything it would appear that we like screens precisely *because* of their zombifying effects. We are exhausted—whether it be from our jobs, from our kids, from our political leaders—and thus we see zoning out in front of a screen for a few hours as something we have earned, as a right as well as a privilege. In other words, we know that to watch TV is to *escape reality*, and that is precisely *why we like it*.

That we know technologies can hypnotize us and that we see this hypnotization as not only pleasurable but as justified is important for understanding the proliferation of techno-hypnotic devices, websites, and apps. We are perfectly capable—thanks to the *multistable* nature of technologies—of turning almost any technology into a tool of techno-hypnosis whether it was intended to be used that way or not. However, because techno-hypnosis is not something that we are ashamed to admit as a pursuit, designers can view techno-hypnosis as a *feature* rather than as a *fault* of their creations.

"Netflix and chill" began as a euphemism that quickly became a meme. Netflix did not initially market itself as a tool for hooking up but, once the meme went viral, Netflix capitalized on this newfound success and turned the meme into a marketing campaign. What was important for Netflix to emphasize to potential subscribers was no longer the size of its library but rather the algorithmic ability of the streaming service to find what you would want to watch and to continue playing it for you with as little user intervention as possible so that you could, well, "chill."

And thus "binge-watching" was born. Again, like being a "couch potato" in front of an "idiot box," this description sounds negative. Streaming television nonstop, episode after episode, hour after hour, is here being likened to "binge-drinking," to an older form of self-hypnosis, one that can result in vomiting, blacking out, and death. Of course, when one criticizes another for being a couch potato, the implicit or explicit suggestion being made is that one should instead go outside, meet people, have a conversation, or, in other words, go to a bar. The criticism being made therefore is not that one is engaging in self-hypnosis but rather that one is engaging in the *wrong type* of self-hypnosis, that one should instead be more social with their self-hypnosis.

This criticism, not of zoning out but of zoning out *alone*, helps to explain why streaming services and binge-watching have become so popular. Again, screens are everywhere. Because of the ubiquity of screens we are able to watch a streaming service on one screen while simultaneously tweeting about what we are watching on another screen. Watching TV need no longer be a lonely escapist pastime as streaming services and social media have together turned zoning out into a social and engaged activity.

It may be argued here that if watching TV has become a social and engaged activity then it should not be thought of as zoning out, as techno-hypnosis, as nihilistic, but rather as a meaningful part of life. Of course, the same could be said about Buddhism. Yet in both cases what is important is not whether one derives meaning from the activity but rather that the activity can be used as a form of escapism.

Indeed for Nietzsche self-hypnosis is nihilistic precisely *because* we derive meaning from our escapism. The meaning that we find in seeking Nirvana or binge-watching Netflix points to our ability to devalue the world we live in and reinvest that value into another world, an imaginary world, a world that we create that would allow us to no longer have to be who we are.

4.3 TUBE LIFE

In his 1954 essay "How to Look at Television,"[2] Theodor Adorno makes clear the importance of "analyzing the implications and mechanisms of television"—and in particular television's "false realism"—because television can have "nefarious effects"[3] on society. What Adorno is especially concerned with is, on the one hand, how popular "popular culture" has become because of its increasing ability to consume all forms of culture and impact all classes of society and, on the other hand, how the medium of television tends to produce an audience of obedient conformists.

By focusing on what he takes to be the fundamental characteristics of television, such as the consistent use of longstanding genres and of well-known tropes, Adorno argues that television is, in its essence, *predictable*. It is this predictability which allows the audience to feel not only relaxed while watching thanks to the lack of tension that television produces (for example, main characters are never actually going to die, that's what "Red Shirts"[4] are for) but also guides the audience to identify with the characters and the situations of television shows to such a degree that the effect is that the audience's "very capacity for life experience may be dulled."[5] Echoing the concerns about how television-watching can make people violent, Adorno suggests that the "false realism" of television seeps into our daily lives such that we begin to see the world through the lens of television, molding not only our actions and our values but even our expectations.

We should hate our boss, but continue to work while making snarky comments to coworkers. We should let attractive people get away with anything. We should mistreat ugly people for choosing to be ugly since anyone could be attractive if they tried hard enough. We should be suspicious of foreigners. We should know that teenagers hanging out on the corner are up to no good. We should recognize empty warehouses as likely crime dens. We should think it normal for a belligerent and unattractive man to be loved by an attractive but bossy wife. We should expect everything to turn out all right in the end. We should expect society to be fundamentally stable and also be glad that it is.

In other words, according to Adorno, television teaches us how to be good citizens, citizens who worship the status quo, citizens who try to use humor and sex—or situational comedy and adult situations—to resolve any problems with the status quo rather than doing anything to upset it. And of course, if we do not get the message on our own, television provides musical cues and laugh tracks to make sure we feel what television is supposed to make us feel, which, if not actual happiness, is at least pleasure and contentment. In this way entertainment for the masses creates a society of the masses, a society where individuality becomes untenable, since everyone is supposed to be watching what everyone else is watching, and everyone is supposed to be talking about what everyone else is talking about, especially since that is of course what the characters we are watching on television are doing too.

In answer to the imagined question of whether television is designed to be this way, if it is the intent of the creators or "authors" of television shows to produce audiences of captivated conformists, Adorno argues that the effects of television are rather more a product of the medium than of the maker. Adorno writes:

> Although the authors' motivations certainly enter the artifact, they are by no means so all-determining as is often assumed . . . [T]he total set-up here tends to limit the chances of the artists' projections utterly. Those who produce the material follow, often grumblingly, innumerable requirements, rules of thumb, set patterns, and mechanisms of control which by necessity reduce to a minimum the range of any kind of artistic self-expression. The fact that most products of mass media are not produced by one individual but by collective collaboration—as happens to be true with most of the illustrations so far discussed—is only one contributing factor to this generally prevailing condition. To study television shows in terms of the psychology of the authors would almost be tantamount to studying Ford cars in terms of the psychoanalysis of the late Mr. Ford.[6]

For Adorno, television shows are not unlike cars coming off an assembly line. The demands of mass production, of producing on schedule, in accordance with a formula, and by committee rather than by oneself, entails that television not only produces conformity in its audience but also in its creators.

Such an analysis is of course likely to invite criticism, as Adorno is practically begging readers to play the "whataboutism" game and come up with numerous examples of television shows and of television creators that could counter Adorno's analysis. Indeed at the time when Adorno wrote this article the most popular show in America was *I Love Lucy*, a show that was so unique and so inventive that it required hiring the famous cinematographer Karl Freund to even get it on air.[7] Yet Adorno would likely point out that such examples only strengthen his argument rather than weaken it. Any television show, including *I Love Lucy*, quickly turns from "groundbreaking" to "genre-defining," as the elements of the show found to be successful become repackaged and recycled by other television shows, expanding rather than destroying the formulaic and predictable nature of television. Furthermore, television shows, even those that are unique and inventive, still repackage and recycle their own successful elements from episode to episode, giving the show its own formulaic and predictable nature.

It should not be surprising therefore that the arrival of YouTube in 2005 was welcomed with immediate and overwhelming success. For if audiences wanted to watch programs without being programmed and if creators wanted to make programs without turning into assembly line workers, then a new programming medium was necessary, a medium not bound by the demands of mass production. And this is precisely the opportunity that was presented to audiences and to creators in the medium of YouTube, a medium where audiences could *be* the creators.

YouTube was started in 2005 by three PayPal coworkers who were trying to find a way to share videos with each other online and discovered to their surprise that no such method already existed. Operating initially out of a San Francisco garage, Steve Chen, Chad Hurley, and Jawed Karim channeled their do-it-yourself attitude directly into You-Tube, making the site not only free to use but also free of "intrusive advertising." As Richard Alleyne wrote in his 2008 profile of YouTube for the *Telegraph*:

> The need to buy ever more powerful computer hardware soon outstripped the founders' credit cards and they sought backing from outside investors.

But they were determined to do it on their own terms and were
adamant there would be no intrusive advertising on their site.

Ultimately it was a stroke of genius, immediately setting them apart
from their fledgling competitors whose sites were dominated by
sponsors, pop-up adverts and mini commercials.

Once when they imposed on users with a small text ad on the site
they jokingly apologised, explaining they needed the cash to fix the
office sink.

Users flocked to their website, considering it to be anti-establishment and independent. [8]

The "anti-establishment and independent" nature of YouTube made it
incredibly popular, so popular in fact that YouTube required more resources than the three founders could provide on their own and so in
2006 they sold YouTube to Google for $1.65 billion in stocks.

And yet YouTube has only become more popular since Google acquired it and since Google altered it so that YouTube became "dominated by sponsors, pop-up adverts and mini commercials." YouTube
launched on February 14, 2005. By August of 2005, it had 2.8 million
users, and by August of 2006, it had 72 million users. [9] As of August of
2017, YouTube has 1.5 billion active users, making it the second most
popular social network after Facebook. [10] And these users are indeed
active. As YouTube's vice president of engineering Cristos Goodrow
posted on YouTube's official blog on February 17, 2017, "people
around the world are now watching a billion hours of YouTube's incredible content every single day!" [11] To helpfully "put that in perspective,"
Goodrow further pointed out that that is equivalent to YouTube users
cumulatively spending "100,000 years" consuming content, *every single
day!*

The key to the explosive success of YouTube has indeed been its
freedom, but not its freedom to create as much as its freedom to pirate.
Providing a platform for people to freely upload and to freely watch
copyrighted content from television, movies, music videos, and sports
brought millions of users to YouTube, but it also brought numerous
lawsuits from content owners. Google's response was to work with content owners by turning them into YouTube users themselves. Combining its already-existing advertising platforms with its newly acquired
video platform, Google created over the years a variety of ways to monetize YouTube for itself, and for content providers, through advertis-

ing.[12] One such way was a "YouTube Partner Program," a program to share revenue from advertisements on YouTube in exchange for uploading popular content to YouTube, a partner program that, when started in 2007, was invite-only but in 2009 became available to anyone whose content could be regularly uploaded and regularly popular.

For media corporations, monetizing YouTube meant that YouTube went from being a threat to their revenue to being a new opportunity for revenue. But for individuals, monetizing YouTube meant that YouTube went from being a place to fight the power of media corporations to being a place where one could try to become a media corporation. The YouTube Partner Program allowed individual users to turn creating content for YouTube into a career, a career that could potentially pay thousands, if not millions, in advertising revenue. As Jefferson Graham described the program in a 2009 USA *Today* article:

> You, too, could make a living producing videos for YouTube, but you'd need to devote massive hours (figure about 75 hours a week) making videos and spreading the word. You must stay in constant contact with the community, via the comments left on your work.

> And once you finish the video, you'll need to top it with another. And another. And another.

> "You're only as good as your last video," says McQuivey. "But in the traditional TV world, you produce a pilot, wait to sell the show and then premiere nearly a year later. In the YouTube model, you make a video, post it and hear back from your audience immediately. You get instant feedback. For a producer, that's got to be addictive."[13]

In other words, YouTube has become a challenge to television, not by freeing audiences and creators from the constraints of mass production but rather by expanding who could be constrained by the demands of mass production, so that now not only studios could churn out predictable conformist content but so too could individuals. Indeed, YouTube explicitly states as a demand for joining the Partner Program, as a demand for monetizing content through advertisements, that content must be "advertiser-friendly," that content must avoid not only "violence," "inappropriate language," and "sexually suggestive content" but also avoid "controversial and sensitive events."[14]

The *content* of the genres and the tropes may have changed in the move from television to YouTube, but the reliance on the *form* of genres and tropes, the reliance on *formula* for producing content, for producing content that could be regularly scheduled and regularly popular enough for advertisers and for audiences, has not changed in the move from television to YouTube.[15] Viewer statistics and viewer comments are not only publicly available on YouTube, they are placed immediately alongside content, making it overwhelmingly clear to everyone—including creators and those who want to be creators—both what content is popular on YouTube and which specific elements of the content are popular. Such "instant feedback" invites creators to focus on repeating what makes their audience happy, and invites others to copy what those creators are repeating so that they can build their own happy audiences. YouTube thus does not exist as a refuge from the assembly-line model of television production but is, rather, the perfection of this model, as it has become a world of assembly lines within assembly lines, where each individual can be an assembly line unto themselves while also working for the worldwide assembly line that is YouTube.

Not unlike *I Love Lucy*, YouTube was "groundbreaking" but has since become "genre-defining," only now the genre is not anything as specific as situational comedy but is rather the genre of pop culture itself, the genre that Adorno found to be centered on *false realism*. For if it is identifiable characters in identifiable situations that help television programming to create audiences of obedient conformists, then nowhere can one find more identifiable characters and more identifiable situations than on YouTube, a place where people only need a camera and an internet connection to upload their lives for others to voyeuristically consume. The most famous example of this is Felix Kjellberg—better known as "PewDiePie"—whose videos of himself playing video games led to him not only having the most subscribers of anyone on YouTube ever but also to him becoming, thanks to the YouTube Partner Program, the first YouTube millionaire.[16]

Such videos, known as "Let's Play" videos, are now a staple of YouTube, a genre with its own tropes, its own formula, its own production studios, and its own dependably returning audience, an audience of millions of people who watch hours and hours of someone else playing a video game. What is said to make PewDiePie and other Let's Players like him so popular is the "usually funny and profane"[17] commentary they provide while playing the video games, and the time they spend interacting with their fans. Indeed Kjellberg's commentary was so "funny and profane" that he was often forced to apologize for his commentary, commentary that was frequently misogynistic, racist, and anti-Semitic but all of which he defended as jokes that were taken too seriously. YouTube, a site known for its trolling comments,[18] made a millionaire out of someone famous for his trolling comments. In other words, the content that is most popular to consume on YouTube is watching someone else (PewDiePie) through a screen (YouTube) while trolling (user comments) watching someone else (video game avatar) through a screen (video game console) while trolling (PewDiePie commentary). The most popular content to consume on YouTube is *watching a YouTube user be a YouTube user*.

But why, out of everything we could watch on YouTube, out of the unfathomable hours of content available on YouTube, would we most want to *watch ourselves*? The answer would appear to be, in keeping with the analysis of television provided by Adorno, and with the analysis of self-hypnosis provided by Nietzsche, that watching ourselves is what is most *comforting*. It is comforting in two ways. First, it is comforting in the sense of confirming that how we are living is the right way to live, for if we are watching people on television watch television and we are watching people on YouTube use YouTube then surely there is nothing wrong with spending so much time watching television or using YouTube, surely there is nothing wrong with the status quo, with the status quo to which we are obediently conforming. Second, it is comforting in the sense of relaxing us, of helping us to avoid feeling, of helping us to feel only that which is not too extreme, that which is not too unexpected, providing instead only provocations that are not too provocative, and novelties that are not too novel. In other words, we watch ourselves watching ourselves so that we can feel comfortable with lives spent *watching* rather than feeling uncomfortable, uncomfortable enough to *stop watching*.

4.4 BINGE LIFE

In March of 2016, the consulting firm Deloitte put out a press release announcing the completion of their tenth annual "Digital Democracy Survey," which began:

> Has America become a marathon nation when it comes to video content consumption? Indications point to "yes." Seventy percent of US consumers now binge watch an average of five episodes at a time, and almost one-third (31 percent) binge on a weekly basis according to Deloitte's 10th "Digital Democracy Survey." In addition to binge watching, nearly half (or 46 percent) of Americans now subscribe to streaming video services, with millennials aged 14–25 spending more time streaming video content than watching live television. [19]

YouTube ushered in an era of entertainment focused not only on comfort, on maximizing the comfort of television, on consuming content of ourselves for ourselves by ourselves, on consuming content that reassured us that there is nothing wrong with *watching as a way of life*, but also on maximizing the comfort of being able to watch whatever we wanted, whenever we wanted, wherever we wanted. With such comfort maximization we shook off the shackles of traditional admonitions against *watching too much television* and instead developed an ethos of *never-not-watching*. This is the ethos that we now frequently see proudly championed in advertisements for new gadgets and for new data plans that enable us to ceaselessly watch videos while away from the living room, while outside, while at work, while on the bus, while on a plane, even while walking through streets filled with cars, cars that drive themselves so the drivers can keep watching too.

The idea of designing cars that can drive themselves so that we never have to stop watching is a development that parallels the idea of designing streaming services that can play themselves so that we never have to stop watching. YouTube, Netflix, and Hulu all not only have the ability to recommend videos but also have the ability to automatically play videos, to play videos one after the other, after the other, a process which, given the lifetimes of content available, could continue long after the watcher had lost the ability to watch. In the classic *Twilight Zone* episode "Time Enough at Last," bespectacled book-lover Henry Bemis is delighted to discover that humanity was wiped out while he was reading safely in a bank vault, leaving him alone so that he can finally read, that is, of course, until he accidentally breaks his glasses. From the perspective of YouTube, Netflix, and Hulu, the lesson of this episode is not that we need to appreciate how much we need other people but rather that we need better glasses, that we need more dependable technologies to mediate our entertainment.

While it is clear why companies trying to monetize streaming video services would want to keep us watching as many advertisements as possible for as long as possible, it is less clear what motivates our own desire to let these streaming video services keep us watching. For unless we truly all are like Henry Bemis, viewing others less as people and more as distractions interfering with our misanthropic pursuit of solitary entertainment, it would seem that the imperative to never stop watching—an imperative that, again, these video services, and the gadgets and the data plans they spawn, proudly champion in advertisements—would worry us rather than delight us. In the era of streaming video, movies like David Cronenberg's *Videodrome* and John Carpenter's *They Live* seem less like dire warnings about the rise of an entertainment-industrial complex and more like advertisements for all that the entertainment-industrial complex has to offer. Today a television that could tell us what to do is not seen as horror but as *smart*, just as "Obey" is no longer a hidden message we need to decode but instead just a shorter version of the command: "Netflix and chill."

The meme-turned-marketing campaign of "Netflix and chill" suggests that there is a quid pro quo relationship between streaming services and audiences, a relationship where we pay to stream content in exchange for being able to "chill"—whether, as initially meant, in the form of solitary relaxation or, as it has come to mean, in the form of "hooking up."[20] It is indeed quite odd how the literal idea of watching Netflix to relax, to relax on one's own, has come instead to mean quite the opposite. The initial meaning of "Netflix and chill" suggested a Henry Bemis–like interest in being entertained alone without the distraction of going out and seeing other people, whereas the meaning the phrase has come to take on suggests the opposite, a desire to be with someone else, and to use entertainment not as an end but as a means to an end. We still want to be alone, but we want to be alone together, just as we still want to watch, but we want to also do more than mere watching.

Wanting to be alone together and wanting to do more than mere watching are both representative of our current binge culture. The idea of "appointment television" has largely been replaced with the idea of "competitive television," as we now race through episodes of television at a time and place of our choosing, rather than having to schedule our lives around weekly programming. Hulu, having been started as a joint venture by NBC and FOX, has been more resistant to the binge-watching model than Netflix. Yet even though Hulu maintains the traditional weekly release of its own content while Netflix dumps entire seasons all at once, multiple seasons of content are still available on Hulu. Subsequently, television networks have followed suit and begun to create their own streaming services, making available to subscribers multiple seasons of old and new content to be binged. So it is no surprise that television programming increasingly has aesthetic sensibilities that have more in common with YouTube than with traditional television.

YouTube content is created with the understanding that viewers are unlikely to be sitting at home on a couch in front of a television. The content is designed to be short and simple, to be watched quickly, easily, on any device, at any time, one video after another, after another. Given that streaming services like Netflix and Hulu began after YouTube rose to prominence—and were likely begun in response to YouTube's prominence—television programming is increasingly *designed to be binged.* Streaming services not only make entire seasons of television available all at once but television episodes themselves appear more and more to be produced with the expectation that audiences will watch multiple episodes at a time. This is not an accident, of course, since streaming services not only provide content to their audiences but also provide television studios new means to study their audience's content consumption habits. In a 2016 survey of its global users, Netflix found that the "very fast binger" finishes a season in "four days" while watching "two hours and 30 minutes" each day, while "the slightly more relaxed binger" finishes a season in "six days" while watching "one hour 45 minutes" each day, findings that left Netflix to conclude that "the binge model is what viewers want."[21]

The standalone episode, once the standard of television programming, has become a rarity. Programming in the streaming era is instead increasingly focused on season-long arcs existing within series-long arcs, making use of storytelling devices that dare audiences to only watch one episode at a time. Multiple characters and multiple plot-threads are introduced and explained in trickles of information spread over multiple episodes and multiple seasons. Every episode ends in a cliffhanger, and every season ends in a cliffhanger, cliffhangers that are often never fully resolved but instead returned to as needed, giving episodes the feeling of having been created by dramatic masterminds while having the underlying effect of maintaining audience captivity. Binge programming thus combines the never-to-be-resolved plot-pacing and character-development of soap operas with the never-to-be-finished content availability and algorithmic curation of YouTube.

The incomprehensibility-by-design of episodes, of episodes that always refer back to previous episodes while yet pointing forward to subsequent episodes, has not only helped to give programming in the binging era the feel of high-minded artiness, it has also helped to give social media a key role in binging. Just as we can no longer watch solitary episodes in isolation in order to make sense of them neither can we any longer be solitary individuals watching episodes in isolation in order to make sense of them. Instead we live-tweet and live-post about episodes with friends and with strangers on Twitter and on Facebook, and we read episode reviews on the A.V. Club or on Collider or on HitFix or on Vulture or on Entertainment Weekly or even on the website of the business magazine Forbes.

It may seem odd at first that a business-focused site like Forbes would review television episodes, that is until one realizes how much television viewing has come to feel like a job. The "false realism" of television has become less about art imitating life in the sense of identifiable characters in identifiable situations and more about art imitating life in the sense that watching television feels increasingly like a duty. A 2015 survey of TiVo subscribers found that 31 percent of respondents said they "lost sleep due to binging," 37 percent said they "spent entire weekends binging," and 52 percent said they "felt sad after finishing a show they binge watched."[22] Similarly, in an article for the *New York Times* entitled "The Post-Binge-Watching Blues: A Malady of Our Times," Matthew Schneier writes:

> I felt anxious, wistful, bereft in advance; I'd eaten up nine episodes in only a few days, liking them more than I'd expected to. Once finished, there'd be no more until the next season—if there was a next season, which has still not been officially announced. Unlike on net-

work TV, where my fix would be parceled out week by week over the course [of] a season, I had binged.

It turns out, I was not alone. Social media teemed with fellow sufferers.

"Think I have post-Netflix binge depression," @_PhilippaRose posted on Twitter, with a weepy emoji.

"The struggle of having nothing left to binge watch is real," @FicholasNoster wrote.

Some have wondered whether there is a term for this post-binge separation. Allow me to suggest one: We have, to tweak a term from the glum in winter, Unseasonal Affective Disorder: post-binge malaise.[23]

This "post-binge malaise," this sadness that comes from having completed a binge marathon, is a sadness that is both like what Alexander felt after discovering he had no worlds left to conquer and like what Sisyphus felt after discovering his labor was without purpose and without end. For as a 2016 survey of "binge viewers in the United States" conducted by the Gesellschaft für Konsumforschung (GfK) found, while 40 percent of respondents said they felt a sense of accomplishment after binge watching, 36 percent felt "sad it ended," and 18 percent felt "regretful/lazy."[24] Perhaps these post-binge feelings of sadness and regret help to explain why "Netflix and chill" went from a literal to a euphemistic statement, as binge-watching has left us in need of sex to help keep our minds off of television, now that television has itself become work, which is of course what television was supposed to help keep our minds off of in the first place. In other words, binge-watching has left us in need of distractions from our distractions.

4.5 VIRTUAL LIFE

Yet perhaps another reason we are left saddened and regretful after each binge marathon is because binging is a way to be immersed in another world, a world that disappears when we have nothing left to binge, forcing us to return to the world of reality, the world that led us to binge in the first place. It is this desire to find worlds different from our own, better than our own, that leads us to seek out new worlds in books, in television, in film, and in video games. Each of these sources of entertainment is limited though, lasting only as long as there remains content to keep us entertained. Thankfully, scientists and engineers have spent decades trying to solve this problem by developing technologies that can either alter reality itself—through what is commonly referred to as augmented reality (AR) devices—or even allow us to fully immerse ourselves in an alternate reality—through what is commonly referred to as virtual reality (VR) devices.

In a 1965 essay entitled "The Ultimate Display," Ivan Edward Sutherland—"one of the godfathers of computer graphics"[25]—describes what he sees as the future of human-computer interaction. He concludes:

> The ultimate display would, of course, be a room within which the computer can control the existence of matter. A chair displayed in such a room would be good enough to sit in. Handcuffs displayed in such a room would be confining, and a bullet displayed in such a room would be fatal. With appropriate programming such a display could literally be the Wonderland into which Alice walked.[26]

Sutherland never specifies whether by "ultimate" he means the "best" display or the "final" display. Given the speed with which Sutherland imagines someone using this display would move from creating a chair, to creating handcuffs, to creating a bullet, moving from what is "good," to what is "confining," to what is "fatal," such ambiguity is perhaps not an accident. And considering the number of episodes of *Star Trek: The Next Generation* devoted to both the dreamlike and nightmarish elements of their version of the "ultimate display"—the "Holodeck"—maybe it is simply impossible to avoid a certain amount of ambivalence about such a technology.

This ambivalence is further suggested by Sutherland himself, who invented "the first AR display," but also gave the head-mounted display (HMD) the name "Sword of Damocles."[27] According to Cicero, the Sword of Damocles was used by King Dionysius to teach Damocles, the man jealous of his power, that with greater power comes not greater happiness but greater danger. As Cicero puts it, the lesson was that "happiness is out of the question if you are menaced by some terror."[28] The terror experienced by King Dionysius was due to the combination of knowledge and power, due to the knowledge of what he had done in his youth with his power, and it was just such a terror-inducing combination of knowledge and power that the King shared with Damocles through giving him the sword, the sword the first AR device was named after.

Such ambivalence leads us to the essential question of why we would want such an "ultimate display" to begin with, particularly as the world seems to have no problem creating more than enough chairs, handcuffs, and bullets already. While we might be tempted to answer that it would simply be fun, that, like the Holodeck, the purpose of such a technology would be to provide us with a new form of entertainment, early in the essay Sutherland makes clear that the answer to this question is rather that such a technology would bring us new ways to solve problems. Sutherland writes, "A display connected to a digital computer gives us a chance to gain familiarity with concepts not realizable in the physical world. It is a looking glass into a mathematical wonderland."[29] In other words, the purpose of such a technology is that it allows us to *think outside the box*, though with the important caveat that in this case the *box* we are trying to escape is "the physical world."

For Sutherland, the purpose of technologies that augment reality or that create a virtual reality is to allow us to perceive that which we could otherwise only imagine. Our imaginations invite us to explore "wonderlands" in our minds, but Sutherland points to our desire to go beyond such limitations, to merge the mental with the physical, to make lands of *wonder* into lands of *reality*. This desire is what we find motivating a particular trajectory of innovation, the trajectory that turns thinking into speaking, speaking into writing, writing into drawing, drawing into animating, animating into film-making, film-making into video games, video games into AR, and AR into VR. In other words, this desire to bring the mental into the physical, to bring fantasy into reality, is not a new desire, rather what is new, what is changing, is the technological capability to realize this desire.

To suggest a trajectory of innovation such as this is to be seen as suggesting an evolutionary dimension to innovation, to be suggesting that innovation is tantamount to a struggle for survival, that new innovations must necessarily endanger all previous innovations by making them obsolete. Such an argument is then easily waved away by pointing out that these worries recur with each new innovation, and that, as older innovations continue to exist alongside the new, such worries are necessarily reactionary rather than realistic. However the issue here is not whether AR and VR will replace the innovations that preceded them. Rather what is at issue here is what is signified by this trajectory of innovation itself, what it means that our imaginations again and again lead us to try to find ways to turn what we imagine into reality, and what this trajectory reveals about our relationship both to imagination and to reality. For what should concern us is not whether AR and VR will make reading and writing obsolete but whether our desire to create AR and VR is a desire to make imagination and reality obsolete.

In a 1964 episode of *MIT Science Reporter* focusing on the work of Sutherland and his colleagues at MIT's Lincoln Laboratory, professor Steven Coons pointed out that the computer-aided design program (CAD) that they were developing—a program called "Sketchpad"—would not only expand the possibilities for imagining *through* a computer but would for the first time make it possible to imagine *with* a computer. As Coons described this new human-computer relationship:

> You will see a designer, effectively, solving a problem step by step, and he will not at the outset know precisely what his problem is, nor will he know exactly how to solve it, but little by little he will begin to investigate ideas, and the computer and he will be in cooperation, in the fullest cooperation, in this work . . . [T]he old way of solving problems with the computer has been to understand the problem very, very well indeed, and moreover to know at the very outset just exactly what steps are necessary to solve the problem. So the computer has been, in a sense, nothing but a very elaborate calculating machine, but now we're making the computer be more like a human assistant. And the computer will seem to have some intelligence. It doesn't really, only the intelligence that we put in it, but it will seem to have intelligence. [30]

Previous versions of computer programming required the programmer to create a program independently of a computer, using punch cards for example to correctly write and to correctly input a program in order to have a computer carry out the program. While such requirements limited both who could program and what could be programmed, at the same time, such requirements also entailed that the expertise necessary to be a programmer compelled an elevation of the skills necessary to program, an elevation of not only the programmer's proficiency and knowledge but also of the programmer's creativity and imagination.

What Sutherland and his colleagues made possible was a way to "investigate ideas" with computers, to work "in cooperation in the fullest" with computers in order to form a *unit* rather than working independently of each other, rather than one serving the role of *programmer* and the other only of *programmed*. Sketchpad and the programs that would follow in its wake not only lowered the level of expertise required to program, thus opening the door for more people to participate in programming, but also raised the level of expertise required of the program itself, thus opening the door for computers to participate more in programming, to participate more like "a human assistant," participating to such a degree that computers would "seem to have intelligence." In other words, Sutherland and his colleagues made it possible for computers to move from helping us to turn imagination into reality to helping us with the act of imagination itself, making it possible for computers to imagine *with* us, and possibly even to imagine *for* us.

Central to postphenomenological investigations of technologies is, as we have seen, the idea that the technological amplification of human abilities comes at the price of having a reduced awareness of the mediating role of technologies in those abilities. In their analyses of AR, Rosenberger and Verbeek describe what they call "augmentation relations"[31] as a combination of embodiment and hermeneutic relations, as AR devices augment both our ability to perceive the world and our ability to interpret the world. This double amplification then entails a double reduction, as AR not only makes it possible to experience the world in increasingly augmented ways, and to know the world in increasingly augmented ways, but also makes it possible to become increasingly unaware of the role that AR plays in mediating what we can experience and what we can know.

The dynamic of amplification and reduction that AR makes possible was well demonstrated by Niantic in July of 2016 with the release of their AR game Pokémon GO. In August of 2016, Shiva Kooragayala and Tanaya Srini, researchers at the Urban Institute, published a report detailing how even though Pokémon GO had become an instant success—in only three weeks after its release both becoming more popular than Twitter and receiving recognition for providing a new way to motivate people to go outside and explore—Pokémon GO was not appealing to all users in all places equally. As Kooragayala and Srini write:

> Even when accounting for population density and the percentage of millennials at the neighborhood level, we find that as the share of the white population increases, PokéStops and gyms become more plentiful. How stark is the difference? In neighborhoods that are majority white, there are 55 portals on average, compared with 19 portals in neighborhoods that are majority black. [. . .] These disparities are not unique to Pokémon GO, but they do highlight a central challenge of placemaking, the process of collaboratively creating public spaces that are meaningful to a community and that enhance people's quality of life. Pokémon GO facilitates virtual placemaking, as players are finding new meaning in their daily commutes, exploring new areas of their neighborhoods in hopes of discovering rare Pokémon, and perhaps forming relationships they never would have otherwise. But it also points to a problem: placemaking can only be as inclusive as the population engaged in the process.[32]

While AR games like Pokémon GO create opportunities for users to engage with the world in new and exciting ways, they also create opportunities to redefine how users experience the world. AR shapes what aspects of the world are to be considered worthy of experiencing, subtly directing users *toward* certain parts of the world and *away* from other parts of the world.

As Kooragayala and Srini indicate, this engagement is determined by the biases of the game programmers, biases that result in the exclusion of particular users and particular places in ways that the programmers might not even realize. Yet, as Coons pointed out with regard to Sketchpad, because we interact with AR programs to such a degree that the program can seem to be intelligent, AR not only reduces our awareness of how our engagement with the world is mediated by AR, AR also reduces our awareness of the role that programmers, and not the AR itself, play in shaping these mediations. In other words, the more we act not *through* AR but *with* AR, the more likely we are to let ourselves be directed by AR, to *trust* AR, since we take for granted that AR cannot be biased, that AR cannot be untrustworthy, since, after all, it is a program, not a person, and only people are biased and untrustworthy. Or, to put it in postphenomenological terms, the embodiment relations of AR can amplify our perception of the world and reduce our awareness of the role of AR programmers in shaping what we perceive, while the hermeneutic relations of AR can amplify the information we have about the world and reduce our awareness of the role of AR programmers in shaping that information.

The power of this amplification of perception and reduction of awareness was even recognized by Niantic itself. In September of 2016, Niantic posted a "Safety Tips" page on the Pokémon GO website, a page which has several warnings for users, including:

> ° When you're out and about playing Pokémon GO, stay aware of your surroundings at all times—especially when traveling alone or in areas you're not familiar with. Whenever you start the app, you'll see a reminder to help you keep this precaution in mind.

> ° To make sure you and those around you are safe, do not play Pokémon GO while riding a bike, driving a vehicle, operating heavy machinery, or doing anything else that requires your full attention.

> ° Schedule regular breaks while you're out exploring. This will help you remain alert and energized during your Pokémon GO adventures. [33]

The first warning alerts users to the immersive nature of the game, that the game so commands our attention that we lose sight of where we are and what we are doing. The second warning, reading not unlike the warnings found on alcohol and on prescription medication, alerts users to the addictive nature of the game, of our inability to stop playing the game even when it is dangerous to keep playing. The third warning alerts users to the hypnotic nature of the game, to the zombifying effect of the game, that the game reduces our awareness of not only our environment but of ourselves. In other words, Pokémon GO is so immersive, so addictive, and so hypnotic that the game itself has to remind users of reality, of the reality that AR amplifies and reduces.

Based on what we have already seen in the analyses of television, of YouTube, and of streaming services, it appears that the immersive, addictive, and hypnotic nature of AR is a feature rather than a bug. AR allows us to experience certain aspects of the world while cutting us off from other aspects of the world, making the reality that we experience more fascinating, and making the reality that we do not experience, that we perhaps *do not want to experience*, more easily forgettable. AR thus functions like a daydream, but a daydream that we can remain in, that we can share with others, that we can have control over. Or, to be more precise, AR provides us with the *illusion* of control, for while AR oversteps the bounds of the imagination, bringing fantasy into the world of reality, the fantasy is not of our own creation but rather a creation of others, of programmers and computers working together to reshape reality such that we get lost in a new reality and lose sight of both the old reality and of the *shaped* nature of the new reality.

But of course if losing ourselves was what we were hoping to achieve in reading, in watching, in binging, in the modes of entertainment that we happily call our "diversions" and our "guilty pleasures," then it would make sense that we would pursue the "ultimate display," that we would seek not only to augment reality but to create virtual reality. Living virtual lives in virtual worlds represents the culmination of the desire, the Henry Bemis–like desire, to exist in realities of our own choosing and to escape from realities not of our own choosing. This is a desire for freedom, a freedom that before AR and VR we could only imagine, a freedom that, with the rise of AR and VR, we will no longer need to imagine, a freedom that makes the imagination itself something we would no longer need. For the freedom of AR and VR is a freedom to escape—not a freedom to create—a freedom that is made *for* users, not *by* users. Yet just as we have sought refuge in offers of better realities, so too have we sought refuge in offers of better imaginations, preferring the imaginations of writers, of artists, of programmers to our own, for which reason the version of freedom offered by AR and VR might be the only freedom we ever truly wanted: the freedom to be hypnotized. As the "San Junipero" episode of *Black Mirror* illustrated, we might even call this freedom *Heaven*.

4.6 THE DANGERS OF TECHNO-HYPNOSIS

Sleep is a necessary part of life. It is a part of our lives that is so important that it consumes almost a third of our lives. Sleep is normal, it is natural, for which reason we do not find it abnormal or unnatural that people would want to sleep, to sleep for just five more minutes, to repeatedly hit the snooze button, to view the alarm clock as an enemy. And yet we buy ourselves alarm clocks, we set our own alarm clocks, we even surround ourselves with alarm clocks, with notifications, updates, and alerts, with apps and devices that allow anyone, anywhere, to wake us up at any time. We want to be asleep; so much do we want to be asleep that we keep creating new ways to wake ourselves up, ways to be awake that in turn lead us to keep creating new ways to put ourselves to sleep.

This dynamic of innovating ways to both keep us awake and to keep us asleep, to make us alert and to make us distracted, to command our attention and to divert our attention, suggests a tug-of-war within ourselves, that we both do and do not want to spend our lives sleeping. This fight within ourselves between the urge to sleep and the urge to awaken has led us to find ways to satisfy both urges simultaneously, whether by finding a dream job, by finding time to daydream while on the job, or by finding ways to enter into dream-like states in order to forget our jobs, states we can enter into through such means as drinking, taking drugs, or watching TV.

Traditionally, the danger with our desire to enter into dream-like states, with our desire to achieve self-hypnosis, has been our inability to moderate this desire—to drink, but not too much; to take drugs, but not too many; to watch TV, but not for too long. While the worry with alcohol and with drugs is that of poisoning our bodies and atrophying our minds, the worry with TV is that it will poison our minds and atrophy our bodies. Yet with the rise of new technologies to mediate our hypnotic desires, and with the rise of new technologies to moderate our hypnotic desires, we have sought to overcome these traditional dangers and have in the process created new dangers. We have moved from drinking ourselves into a stupor to designing stupors to enter into soberly, trying to experience the best of both worlds, but such achievements have made us vulnerable to taking for granted that being sober, that being active, that being outside, is the same as being healthy, as being engaged, as being alive.

The trajectory of innovation that has enabled us to move from self-hypnosis to techno-hypnosis, from the boob tube to YouTube, from watching to binge-watching, from imagination to augmentation, has at the same time enabled us to move from the nihilism of trying to evade reality to the nihilism of trying to replace reality. As Adorno argued, the danger represented by technologies like television, technologies that hypnotize us, is that they provide us not only comfort but induce in us complacency. Or, to be more precise, what is comforting about watching television is precisely that which induces complacency in the watcher. For familiar tropes, familiar characters, and familiar storylines lead us to associate comfort with familiarity, to increasingly feel comfortable only with what is familiar, with what is presented to us as normal, with the status quo, with the idea that there is nothing wrong with watching television, that there is nothing wrong with having one's ideas shaped by watching television.

The danger here is not merely that watching television can shape our ideas, but—as Adorno pointed to and as postphenomenology helps to reveal—that techno-hypnotic technologies can reduce our awareness of the role they play in shaping our ideas. To worry only about specific content, about specific content creators trying to convert us to their specific ideologies, is to have already accepted the ideology that only humans have biases, that only humans can mislead other humans, that technologies are merely neutral tools, tools made liberal or conservative, radical or reactionary, solely in accordance with the intentions of the tool user. What should especially worry us here is that such a worldview is precisely the worldview that techno-hypnotic technologies lead us to accept, by reducing our awareness that techno-hypnotic technologies could even present us with a worldview rather than merely a view of the world. To be unaware that there is a worldview present, a worldview that could be accepted or rejected, is to tacitly accept the worldview, to take for granted that what is being presented to us as reality is actually reality and not a version of reality shaped by the technologies through which we view reality.

From a Nietzschean perspective, reduced awareness is precisely what we were seeking in the development and use of techno-hypnotic technologies in the first place. Thus our taking for granted that the world presented to us by techno-hypnotic technologies simply is the world, is the world as it *is* rather than the world as it has been *shaped to appear to be*, is not a result of our being misled, of our being manipulated into shutting off our skepticism, but rather a result of our desire to shut off our skepticism, to let our guard down, to *relax*. For Nietzsche,

the concern surrounding self-hypnosis is that, on the one hand, it represents a desire to resign from the world, a desire to be free of desire, to
live without living, and, on the other hand, that it enables priests who
recognize in us such desires the ability to convert us to asceticism, to
believe that ascetic ideals are the only ideals, that selflessness is the
virtue of virtues.

Yet techno-hypnosis is more dangerous than self-hypnosis insofar as
it similarly leads us toward self-denial, but a self-denial that we are led
to, not by priests who can take advantage of our desire for reduced
awareness but by technologies that can reduce our awareness for us.
Techno-hypnotic technologies can reduce our awareness of our reduced awareness, reducing our awareness further than we realize, and
perhaps even further than we desire. TV can make us comfortable, but
it can also make us complacent, leading us to believe TV shows are like
reality and reality is like a TV show. YouTube can let us create our own
content, but it can also let us turn ourselves into production studios and
turn our lives into content to be staged, recorded, and uploaded for
mass consumption. Streaming services like Netflix can make us feel like
we are at an all-you-can-eat buffet of content, but they can also make us
feel like we are at a pie-eating contest of content to race through, not
leisurely but competitively, and with no end in sight. AR can help us to
engage with the world, but AR can also help us to ignore the world we
are not engaging with, the world not displayed through AR, the world
not made more fascinating by AR, the world not yet upgraded by AR,
the world perhaps not worthy of being upgraded by AR.

What VR will provide us with is not yet clear as VR is still in its
nascent stage. What is clear, at least from the billions of dollars companies like Facebook are pouring into VR companies like Oculus, is that
VR is believed to be the way of the future. VR represents the culmination of the promises made by the preceding techno-hypnotic technologies. VR promises to provide the comfort of TV, the personal content of
YouTube, the content variety of Netflix, and the engagement of AR.
The question then is to what degree VR will also represent the culmination of the threats of techno-hypnosis, whether VR will also threaten to
provide the complacency of TV, the person-as-content of YouTube, the
content consumption of Netflix, and the obfuscation of AR. Again what
should concern us more here though is not what VR will do to us but
what we will do with VR, what our nihilistic desire for reduced aware-

ness could achieve when combined with the awareness-reduction capabilities of a technology like VR. In other words, technologies are hypnotic, not only because we are *capable* of being hypnotized but also because we *want* to be hypnotized.

NOTES

1. Nietzsche, *Genealogy*, 131.

2. Theodor Adorno, "How to Look at Television," in *The Culture Industry*, ed. J. M. Bernstein (London and New York: Routledge Classics, 2001), 158–77. For more on Adorno's views on the "culture industry" and how they apply to contemporary technologies such as YouTube, see Babette Babich, *The Hallelujah Effect: Philosophical Reflections on Music, Performance Practice, and Technology* (Farnham: Ashgate, 2013).

3. Adorno, "Television," 158. On this point, see also Günther Anders, "The World as Phantom and as Matrix," *Dissent* 3, no. 1 (Winter 1956): 14–24.

4. TV Tropes, "Red Shirt," *TV Tropes*, http://tvtropes.org/pmwiki/pmwiki.php/Main/RedShirt.

5. Adorno, "Television," 171.

6. Adorno, "Television," 168.

7. Ted Eldrick, "I Love Lucy," *Director's Guild of America Quarterly*, July 2003, https://www.dga.org/Craft/DGAQ/All-Articles/0307-July-2003/I-Love-Lucy.aspx.

8. Richard Alleyne, "YouTube: Overnight Success Has Sparked a Backlash," *Telegraph*, July 31, 2008, http://www.telegraph.co.uk/news/uknews/2480280/YouTube-Overnight-success-has-sparked-a-backlash.html.

9. BBC News, "Google Buys YouTube for $1.65bn," *BBC News*, October 10, 2006, http://news.bbc.co.uk/1/hi/business/6034577.stm.

10. Statista, "Most Famous Social Network Sites Worldwide as of September 2017, Ranked by Number of Active Users (in Millions)," *Statista*, https://www.statista.com/statistics/272014/global-social-networks-ranked-by-number-of-users/.

11. Cristos Goodrow, "You Know What's Cool? A Billion Hours," *YouTube Official Blog*, February 27, 2017, https://youtube.googleblog.com/2017/02/you-know-whats-cool-billion-hours.html.

12. YouTube, "History of Monetization at YouTube," *YouTube 5 Year Anniversary Press Site*, https://sites.google.com/a/pressatgoogle.com/youtube5year/home/history-of-monetization-at-youtube.

13. Jefferson Graham, "YouTube Keeps Video Makers Rolling in Dough," *USA Today*, December 16, 2009, https://usatoday30.usatoday.com/tech/news/2009-12-16-youtube16_CV_N.htm.

14. YouTube, "Advertiser-Friendly Content Guidelines," *YouTube Help*, https://support.google.com/youtube/answer/6162278?hl=en&ref_topic=1121317.

15. For more on the genres, tropes, and false realism of YouTube, see for example Dan Olson, "Vlogs and the Hyperreal," *Folding Ideas*, July 6, 2016, https://www.youtube.com/watch?v=GSnktB2N2sQ.

16. Christopher Zoia, "This Guy Makes Millions Playing Video Games on YouTube," *The Atlantic*, March 14, 2014, https://www.theatlantic.com/business/archive/2014/03/this-guy-makes-millions-playing-video-games-on-youtube/284402/.

17. Zoia, "This Guy."

18. See chapter 8.

19. Deloitte, "70 Percent of US Consumers Binge Watch TV, Bingers Average Five Episodes per Sitting," *Deloitte Press Releases*, March 23, 2016, https://www2.deloitte.com/us/en/pages/about-deloitte/articles/press-releases/digital-democracy-survey-tenth-edition.html.

20. Kevin Roose, "'Netflix and Chill': The Complete History of a Viral Sex Catchphrase," *Splinter*, August 27, 2015, http://splinternews.com/netflix-and-chill-the-complete-history-of-a-viral-sex-1793850444.

21. John Koblin, "Netflix Studied Your Binge-Watching Habit. That Didn't Take Long," *New York Times*, June 8, 2016, https://www.nytimes.com/2016/06/09/business/media/netflix-studied-your-binge-watching-habit-it-didnt-take-long.html.

22. Statista, "Reasons for Binge Viewing TV Shows among TV Viewers in the United States as of September 2017," *Statista*, https://www.statista.com/statistics/620114/tv-show-binging-reactions-usa/.

23. Matthew Schneier, "The Post-Binge-Watching Blues: A Malady of Our Times," *New York Times*, December 6, 2015, https://www.nytimes.com/2015/12/06/fashion/post-binge-watching-blues.html.

24. Statista, "Reasons for Binge Viewing."

25. Frank Steinicke, *Being Really Virtual: Immersive Natives and the Future of Virtual Reality* (Cham, Switzerland: Springer International, 2016), 19.

26. See article by Bruce Sterling in *Wired* reproducing an essay by Ivan Sutherland, "Augmented Reality: 'The Ultimate Display'," citing the *Proceedings of IFIP Congress*, 1965, 506–508, available online at: https://www.wired.com/2009/09/augmented-reality-the-ultimate-display-by-ivan-sutherland-1965/

27. Steinicke, *Being Really Virtual*, 27.

28. Cicero, *On the Good Life*, trans. Michael Grant (London: Penguin Books, 1971), 85.

29. Sutherland, "AR: 'The Ultimate Display'."

30. bigkif, "Ivan Sutherland : Sketchpad Demo (1/2)," *YouTube*, November 17, 2007, https://www.youtube.com/watch?v=USyoT_Ha_bA.

31. Robert Rosenberger and Peter-Paul Verbeek, "A Field Guide to Post-phenomenology," in *Postphenomenological Investigations: Essays on Human-Technology Relations*, eds. Rosenberger and Verbeek (London: Lexington Books, 2015), 22.

32. Shiva Kooragayala and Tanaya Srini, "Pokémon GO Is Changing How Cities Use Public Space, But Could It Be More Inclusive?," *Urban Wire*, August 1, 2016, http://www.urban.org/urban-wire/pokemon-go-changing-how-cities-use-public-space-could-it-be-more-inclusive.

33. The Pokémon Company, "Pokémon GO Safety Tips." *Pokémon GO*, http://www.pokemongo.com/en-us/news/pokemon-go-safety-tips.

5

AMOR FITBIT

5.1 MECHANICAL ACTIVITY

The second human-nihilism relation that Nietzsche describes is that of "mechanical activity." Nietzsche writes:

> Much more common than this hypnotic muting of all sensitivity, of the capacity to feel pain—which presupposes rare energy and above all courage, contempt for opinion, "intellectual stoicism"—is a different training against states of depression which is at any rate easier: mechanical activity. It is beyond doubt that this regimen alleviates an existence of suffering to a not inconsiderable degree: this fact is today called, somewhat dishonestly, "the blessings of work." The alleviation consists in this, that the interest of the sufferer is directed entirely away from his suffering—that activity, and nothing but activity, enters consciousness, and there is consequently little room left in it for suffering: for the chamber of human consciousness is small! [1]

Instead of making the effort required to actively avoid ourselves through self-hypnosis, we can simply use repetitive tasks to so occupy our time that we cannot have even a moment of self-reflection. What Nietzsche appears to have in mind here is the Protestant work ethic, "the blessings of work," the belief that it is through vigorous and constant effort that we find salvation. This work ethic has grown beyond Protestantism, grown beyond the world of work, and has come to instead regulate the entirety of our daily lives. For it is precisely through the regulation of our daily lives that we can best avoid the *daily-ness* of our daily lives, the fact that our existence consists of so many minutes, days, hours, years, needs, wants, desires, burdens, pains, birthdays, anniversaries, holidays, deaths, hellos, goodbyes, thank yous, you're welcomes, I love yous, I hate yous, and, most importantly, decisions, decisions, decisions.

Though we don't like to admit it, we live by habits, crave routines, and tend to avoid any spontaneity that does not fit into our preconceived plans of what can count as safely spontaneous. We often complain about these habits, routines, and lack of spontaneity, yet when these habits are challenged, when our routines are interrupted, and when true spontaneity presents itself, we get defensive, confused, and anxious, demanding a return to the comforts of normalcy. In this way we are not only able to make ourselves feel at home in the world, we are also able to prevent ourselves from having to make choices, make decisions, or in any way have to struggle with the burden of accountability.

It is here that we find the Nietzschean counterargument to the "leisure-as-liberation" model of innovation that I discussed in the first chapter. Again, for Nietzsche it is not the case that we are too busy to find ourselves, and thus are in need of being liberated from mind-numbing chores in order to have the leisure necessary to rediscover our humanity. Rather, Nietzsche is here suggesting that we busy ourselves with chores precisely *because they are mind-numbing*, which perhaps might explain why Marx's predicted revolution has not taken place—for fear that we would then indeed have no one else but ourselves to blame for our not finding ourselves, for our not rediscovering our humanity.

5.2 FROM MECHANICAL ACTIVITY TO DATA-DRIVEN ACTIVITY

Data-driven activity is my name for the phenomenon of our increasing willingness to let technologies regulate and control our daily lives. Whereas in the nineteenth century we were in need of other humans to order us around and give us chores to occupy us, today, as Apple might say, "there's an app for that." Netflix can tell us what to watch, Amazon can tell us what to buy, and eHarmony can even tell us who to love.

In order words, we have replaced the mechanistic unthinking regularity of clockwork with the algorithmic unthinking regularity of data-driven predictions, options, and commands. Though these algorithms may seem invasive to some (such as the United States Federal Trade Commission[2])—as algorithms attempt to develop profiles of us by keeping track of all of our activities both online and offline—technological progress appears to be measured more and more not by the protection of our privacy but by the accuracy of the algorithms' predictions.[3] Or as *trendwatching.com* puts it:

> Convenience. Seamlessness. Relevance. Customer expectations around these intertwined basic needs will reach new heights in 2017. And while in George Orwell's *1984* Big Brother was a dystopian overlord, the relentless desire for (what would have only recently been) magical levels of personalized service will meet new intelligent technologies and lead to a new generation of BIG BROTHER BRANDS. But now we'll willingly be watched.[4]

"Big Brother" is no longer a forewarning of the rise of the surveillance state—a forewarning that exists only to those reading the novel, not to those living in the surveillance state of the novel—but rather an ideal of technological progress, of "intelligent technologies" that we will "willingly" invite into our homes, our devices, our bodies. The vital question here is whether such "magical levels of personalized service" are achieved by *learning* who and what we are, or by *shaping* who and what we are.

5.3 FIGHTING FREEDOM WITH FITBIT

Wearable activity trackers are increasingly flooding the market. For example, currently we can find such health and fitness trackers, and related apps, as: Apple Health, Microsoft Health, MyFitnessPal, Garmin, Jawbone, UA Record, Moves, RunKeeper, Foursquare, Withings, RunDouble, Strava, Fitbug, Daily Mile, LifeFitness, iHealth, Expresso, A&D Connect, Qardio, One Drop, MapMyFitness, MapMyRun, MapMyRide, MapMyWalk, and MapMyHike.

For my purposes here I will focus only on the top-selling tracker: Fitbit. Fitbit was released in 2009. In 2010, Fitbit had a revenue of just over 5 million USD. In 2015, Fitbit had a revenue of over 1.85 billion USD. In that timespan Fitbit sold more than 38 million devices world-wide.[5] And, according to data scientist Luca Foschini, "Fitbit users are actually really engaged," as only "5 percent stop using their device with-in a week of buying it, and 12.5 percent stop within a month."[6]

These health and fitness trackers such as the Fitbit are used not only to monitor the steps we are taking and the calories we are burning but are increasingly becoming wearable gym trainers, pushing us to take more steps, to burn more calories, and even uploading our data for others to see in order to shame us into increased activity.

On the face of it, this does not seem like a negative thing. Staying healthy is desirable, and it is simpler and more cost-effective to have a device rather than a person serve as your personal trainer. Or, as Fitbit puts it on their "Why Fitbit" web page:

> Every moment matters and every bit makes a big impact. Because fitness is the sum of your life. That's the idea Fitbit was built on—that fitness is not just about gym time. It's all the time.
>
> How you spend your day determines when you reach your goals. And seeing your progress helps you see what's possible.
>
> Seek it, crave it, live it.[7]

In other words, the Fitbit is not merely a device, it is a way of life. If you care about your health, then you should care about fitness, and if you care about fitness then you should care about maximizing your time—all of your time—as time for fitness. Time spent not moving is time spent not improving one's fitness.

The key to maximizing fitness is monitoring—"And seeing your progress helps you see what's possible"—as monitoring is what guaran-tees your awareness of how you have spent your time, how you are spending your time, and of how you *could* be spending your time. Because fitness is a goal that can never be completed, how many steps you have taken and how many calories you have burned are always simultaneously a measure of how many steps you *have not* taken and of how many calories you *have not* burned.

However, Fitbit's monitoring does more than just count steps and calories. As Fitbit Help explains:

> Fitbit trackers use a 3-axis accelerometer to understand your motions. An accelerometer is a device that turns movement (acceleration) into digital measurements (data) when attached to the body. By analyzing acceleration data, our devices provide detailed information about frequency, duration, intensity, and patterns of movement to determine your steps taken, distance traveled, calories burned, and sleep quality. The 3-axis implementation allows the accelerometer to measure your motion in any way that you move, making its activity measurements more precise than older, single-axis pedometers.[8]

The Fitbit is not merely counting and calculating as it is instead attempting to "understand your motions," all of your motions, even those occurring while you are asleep. This *understanding* is achieved by translating acceleration into data, data into patterns, and patterns into judgments. Or, to be more specific, one judgment: *Move!*

You have walked 5,000 steps. Why not 10,000? Now you have walked 10,000 steps. Why not 15,000?

This quantification of life represents the severing of *action* from *purpose*. One moves, not in order to go somewhere but merely for the sake of moving. Motion is not a means-to-an-end, it is now an end-in-itself. "Fitness," it is true, is the stated end, what one claims to be the purpose of this ceaseless ceaselessness, but "fitness" is not only a never-attainable goal, it is an indefinable, relativistic concept, a concept sufficiently vague to serve as an explanation to others, but more importantly to oneself, as to why one must never stop moving.[9] The Fitbit says "Move!" and you move, not because the Fitbit told you to move—that would be ridiculous—but because *you* want to be more fit.

But who is the "you" that the Fitbit is monitoring, motivating, and attempting to "understand"? Quantification does not only sever *action* from *purpose*, it also severs *action* from *actor*. Moving for the sake of moving, or even for the sake of "fitness," means that it is the numbers that matter, not the person behind the numbers. In fact, *there is no person behind the numbers.* At least not to the extent that "person" means anything other than what is measurable, what is translatable into data. Acting for the sake of acting divests action of personhood, of individuality, of meaningfulness. And it is precisely this *action without an actor* that led Nietzsche to define this behavior—whether performed mechanistically or algorithmically—as nihilistic, as allowing one to reduce oneself to simply that, a *oneself*, a self who is anyone, the *any one* who carries out the action without the burdens of decision-making and responsibility that would require that the anyone become again a *someone*.[10]

5.4 THE GAMIFICATION OF EVERYDAY LIFE

Another important aspect of having one's life reduced to a set of data points—number of steps, number of calories, number of minutes spent looking at numbers—is that these data points come more and more to look like scores in a video game. One moves, not only for the sake of chasing the ever-elusive goal of "fitness" but for the sake of the seemingly less real and yet much more familiar goal of "points."

Calories are, for most people, vague quantities. But points are well known. Points everyone understands. Points are a way of knowing where we stand, of where we stand as compared to others, to others who have similarly been reduced from persons to points.

Collecting data about ourselves can thus not only be useful, it can be addictive. Like pumping quarters into arcade games in the pursuit of higher and higher scores, we check our statistics endlessly. Of course measuring ourselves against others is nothing new, but the quantification of all action provides us constant feedback, feedback that allows us to compare ourselves against others without having to go to a gym or an arcade, feedback that allows us to feel like professional athletes. This feeling extends beyond ourselves, for if we can be made to feel like athletes at any time, then the world around us can always feel like an arena.

The Fitbit is not the only example of a technology that enables us to turn life into a game and the world into an arena. With the advent of augmented reality (AR) technology, AR games such as Pokémon GO allow users to separate video games from video game consoles, to score points anywhere at any time rather than only while on the couch in front of the TV.

Like all such wireless innovations, the selling point for AR games is precisely this liberation. Rather than being chastised for spending too much time indoors, AR allows users to go outside without having to stop playing. AR users can further claim that they are not "wasting their time" in "fantasy" worlds, as instead AR offers the user the ability to explore the "real" world in new and exciting ways.

I have already discussed in the previous chapter the nihilistic qualities of AR through the lens of techno-hypnosis, and in particular the question of why AR users feel the need to have devices augment reality in order to find it worth exploring. Here, with regard to data-driven activity, the question again—like that raised by the Fitbit—is rather: who is the "you" who is playing the AR game? In other words, is the AR user the one who is *playing* the AR game or is the user the one who is being *played by* the AR game?

In traditional video games, the player is the one who operates the controller, making the avatar navigate the world of the game. In AR games, while the user's smartphone can serve as a controller, the user is not operating the controller but is rather being operated by the controller, as the smartphone tells the user where to go. In AR games, it is thus the user, not an avatar, who is the one navigating the world of the game, a navigation that takes place not in accordance with the decisions made by the user but with the decisions made by the game. Just as an avatar cannot move until the player directs the avatar, the AR user cannot move until the AR game directs the player to do so.

Furthermore, the world being explored by the user is a flattened world, a world closer to that of a board game than that of a video game. In a video game, the avatar explores not only on the x- and y-axes of the game world but also on the z-axis, moving in and out as well as side to side. But in an AR game, the user is constrained by the laws of physics in ways that video game avatars are not, for which reason AR users are only ever directed to move left, right, or straight. The AR user is also constrained by having to always see the world through the AR device, for which reason AR users are only ever directed to look down, not at the world, but at the device.

A recent study conducted by researchers from San Diego State, University of California San Diego, Johns Hopkins, University of Southern California, and the AAA Foundation for Traffic Safety found—over merely a ten-day span—that "more than 110,000 discrete instances where drivers or pedestrians were distracted by Pokémon GO, and some crashed."[11] This included one user who "almost got hit by a car" and another user who "drove his car into a tree." Similarly, the Baltimore Police Department tweeted a video of a Pokémon GO user crashing his car into one of their police cars, along with the message: "Poké-mon GO is not all fun and games."[12]

Not only researchers but also criminals discovered that users of Pok-émon GO will blindly go wherever the game commands. Taking advantage of both the geolocation features of AR and of the avatar-like obedi-ence of AR users, criminals were able to trick Pokémon GO users to walk into traps, traps where they were assaulted,[13] traps where they were robbed at gunpoint,[14] or traps where they were met by a sex offender.[15]

Again what we find here is data-driven nihilism not unlike that found with Fitbit users, the data-driven nihilism of *action without an actor*. Millions of people obey the Fitbit's command to "Move!" Millions of people obey Pokémon GO's command to "Play!" In both cases the blind obedience can be covered over with the apparent meaningfulness of either seeking fitness or seeking points, but what appears to truly underlie such obedience is the meaninglessness of mindlessness, the mindlessness achieved by letting devices, apps, and algorithms make decisions for us.

5.5 IN ALGORITHMS WE TRUST

Yet the most common and the most pervasive example of this data-driven blind obedience is our increasing reliance on algorithms. Google algorithms not only predict what we are searching for, they tell us when we have found it. Amazon algorithms not only predict what we want to buy, they tell us when we should buy it. Facebook algorithms not only predict who we want to be friends with, they tell us when and with whom we should want to keep in touch.

What is at issue here is not that these algorithms claim to know us but that we believe them. Algorithms make recommendations, recom-mendations that are claimed to be tailored to us—"The more you watch, the better Netflix gets at recommending TV shows and movies you'll love"[16] —to our preferences, our profiles, and our past actions. But we have no way of knowing whether, and to what extent, such claims are true.

Often we are not even aware of the algorithms acting behind the scenes of the technologies we are interacting with. One researcher attempting to study how people behave online due to algorithms ran into the problem that the research participants did not know that their behavior was being influenced by algorithms. The researcher found that "62% of people didn't know that their [Facebook] News Feeds were being filtered. When the algorithm was explained to one subject, she compared the revelation to the moment when Neo discovers the artificiality of The Matrix."[17]

Even if we are aware of such algorithms, we still are not aware of what the algorithms know about us and how this data is being used. In 2014, the United States Federal Trade Commission published a report entitled "Data Brokers: A Call for Transparency and Accountability," which included the following discovery:

> Data brokers collect and store a vast amount of data on almost every U.S. household and commercial transaction. Of the nine data brokers, one data broker's database has information on 1.4 billion consumer transactions and over 700 billion aggregated data elements; another data broker's database covers one trillion dollars in consumer transactions; and yet another data broker adds three billion new records each month to its databases. Most importantly, data brokers hold a vast array of information on individual consumers. For example, one of the nine data brokers has 3000 data segments for nearly every U.S. consumer.[18]

While the Federal Trade Commission has the power to discover this information, the average consumer does not. There are, however, companies that do offer to help individuals track down what data has been collected about them, such as Acxiom, which runs the website About-TheData.com. Simply give them your name, email address, and the last four digits of your social security number, and Acxiom will tell you what data brokers have discovered about you. Of course the reason Acxiom will tell you this is because Acxiom is itself a data broker which not only "has some 3,000 data segments for nearly every U.S. consumer" but is also "shar[ing] with marketers the info you provide during registration."[19]

In other words, algorithms are able to learn about us, but we are not able to learn about them, and this is an arrangement that we not only accept but actively participate in daily, even when we do try to fight back against it. Yet more often than not we do not try to fight back. The argument that data brokers use to defend such massive data collection is that they are trying to learn about us in order to *help us*, in order to provide us better Google search queries, better Amazon recommendations, better Facebook News Feeds.

Many, such as Cass Sunstein, have argued against the presumption that "better tailored results" and "better for you" are in fact the same thing. As Sunstein writes:

> In 1995, MIT technology specialist Nicholas Negroponte prophesied the emergence of "the Daily Me"—a communications package that is personally designed, with each component fully chosen in advance. Negroponte's prophecy was not nearly ambitious enough. As it turns out, you don't need to create a Daily Me. Others can create it for you. If people know a little bit about you, they can discover, and tell you, what "people like you" tend to like—and they can create a Daily Me, just for you, in a matter of seconds.[20]

While Sunstein's worry is that such algorithmic curation is dangerous for the proper functioning of a democracy—as filtering leads to echo chambers, group polarization, extremism, and "making America great again"—my interest here is rather in the question of what leads us to desire a "Daily Me" in the first place. Pointing out the dangerous consequences of living a life of algorithmic curation will not change anything if we do not first understand why we are increasingly driven to lead such lives.

Algorithms are nothing more than computer programs containing a series of instructions. The instructions are designed such that computer programs can sort through massive amounts of data in order to profile and judge, to determine, for example, "what 'people like you' tend to like." The embodiment of such algorithms is Sherlock Holmes, or at least the incarnation of Sherlock Holmes by Benedict Cumberbatch in the recent BBC series *Sherlock*. Cumberbatch's Holmes—let's just call him   Cumber-
Holmes—immediately profiles any individual he meets, a profile that he creates by making "deductions" based on all of the information he has gathered over the years from other individuals he has met or studied.

CumberHolmes does not focus on what people say but rather focuses on what they wear, how they smell, the way they walk, etc., as the operating assumption of CumberHolmes is that people cannot be trusted, only data can. CumberHolmes so believes in his data processing abilities that he revels in showing them off, rapidly reading back the results of his data processing to the very individual being processed. The individual on the receiving end of these results is often shown to experience a mix of anger, confusion, and astonishment, an experience based not on CumberHolmes reducing a human being to a set of data points but rather based on CumberHolmes being correct in the deductions he makes based on those data points. CumberHolmes is *always* correct.

Indeed CumberHolmes is so accurate that his services are requested by people who have been the victims of mysterious crimes as well as by the police and the government. Yet, from the very beginning of this series, it is suggested that the police and government call on him both because of how his powers can be used for good and because of how his powers can be used for evil. Not unlike a computer program, Cumber-Holmes is presented as incapable of turning off his data processing abilities, for which reason his "deductions" can be, and often are, both life-saving and life-destroying.

CumberHolmes is immensely clever, immensely useful, and immensely dangerous. And yet he is the hero, he is who we root for, who we perhaps even wish would make "deductions" about us. In much the same way that 24's Jack Bauer helped to not only normalize but champion torture, making it look like it was both heroic and effective,[21] CumberHolmes has helped to normalize and champion the algorithmic equivalent of "Big Brother" that has come to be known as "Big Data."

So what is it about the predictive power of either CumberHolmes or of algorithms that we find so appealing? Predictive algorithms are everywhere, not only working behind the scenes of decisions made using Google, Amazon, and Facebook but increasingly behind the scenes of seemingly all decisions made:

> For wines or films, the stakes are not terribly high. But when algorithms start affecting critical opportunities for employment, career advancement, health, credit and education, they deserve more scrutiny. U.S. hospitals are using big data-driven systems to determine which patients are high-risk—and data far outside traditional health records is informing those determinations. IBM now uses algorithmic assessment tools to sort employees worldwide on criteria of cost-

effectiveness, but spares top managers the same invasive surveillance and ranking. In government, too, algorithmic assessments of danger- ousness can lead to longer sentences for convicts, or no-fly lists for travelers. Credit-scoring drives billions of dollars in lending, but the scorers' methods remain opaque. The average borrower could lose tens of thousands of dollars over a lifetime, thanks to wrong or un- fairly processed data. [22]

Algorithms offer a promise of safety and security, of being able to make reliable predictions that can help us to save time and energy, or in the case of businesses, to save resources, or in the case of governmental institutions, to save lives. But why are the predictions of algorithms, or of CumberHolmes, so reliable? Or, to be more precise, why are they so relied upon?

What one has done in the past, even what all of humanity has done in the past, need not be capable of predicting what anyone will do in the future. Algorithms and CumberHolmes both reach their conclusions by reasoning inductively, not deductively, as deductive reasoning from past events to future events is, as David Hume famously argued, impossible. Algorithms and CumberHolmes are yet nevertheless treated as if they were making deductions, as if they were making knowledge claims about the future rather than merely educated guesses.

These educated guesses are of course made based on mountains of data. However, according to Nietzsche, such knowledge claims are pos- sible, not because of the *amount* of information that has been gathered on human behavior but because of *who* the information is being gath- ered about. Nietzsche writes:

> That is precisely what constitutes the long history of the origins of *responsibility*. That particular task of breeding an animal with the prerogative to promise includes, as we have already understood, as precondition and preparation, the more immediate task of first *mak- ing* man to a certain degree necessary, uniform, a peer amongst peers, orderly and consequently predictable. The immense amount of labour involved in what I have called the 'morality of custom' [see *Daybreak*, I, 9; 14; 16], the actual labour of man on himself during the longest epoch of the human race, his whole *prehistoric* labour, is explained and justified on a grand scale, in spite of the hardness, tyranny, stupidity and idiocy it also contained, by this fact: with the

help of the morality of custom and the social straitjacket, man was *made* truly predictable.[23]

If algorithms can predict human behavior it is because humans have *become predictable*. This *becoming predictable* is for Nietzsche something that we do to each other, and to ourselves, through customs ("the morality of custom") and through civility ("the social straitjacket"), through teaching each other how to behave *properly*, *normally*, *responsibly*.

The extent to which we have become predictable through our proper, normal, responsible behavior was brilliantly captured in Steven Soderbergh's 1996 film *Schizopolis*, which is filled with surreal exchanges such as:

Fletcher Munson: [sunnily, on homecoming] Generic greeting!

Mrs. Munson: [warmly] Generic greeting returned!

[they kiss and chuckle at each other]

Fletcher Munson: Imminent sustenance.

Mrs. Munson: Overly dramatic statement regarding upcoming meal.

Fletcher Munson: Oooh! False reaction indicating hunger and excitement![24]

Algorithmic predictions are reliable because we are reliable, so reliable that, as Soderbergh shows, we can map out in advance what our conversations with others will be, almost as if our conversations have themselves become algorithmic in nature. And this is true not only of our conversations with others whom we know intimately but also with strangers whom we have never met, strangers who, because of the situation in which we are meeting, are nevertheless as predictable as lifelong friends. The "Daily Me" can ensure that I hear only what I want to hear, and yet, as Sunstein suggests, it is others, not I, who make this "Daily Me" for me. Our fascination with CumberHolmes further suggests that what I want to hear is the answer to the question: Who am I? Sunstein worries that we use algorithms to filter the world in our own image. But that would require that we know who we are, that we know who the "Me" of the "Daily Me" is, and it is precisely this lack of self-knowledge that is at issue here.

The cost of our making ourselves so predictable is, as Nietzsche suggests, that we have become not only "calculable" but also "necessary, uniform, like among like, regular," that we have become deindividualized. Individuality is dangerous to the degree that it is unpredictable, for which reason there is safety in conformity and regularity, as the more predictable we become, the more trustworthy we become. This trade-off of personal identity for social acceptance helps explain why we are so willing to live lives of algorithmic determination. For if algorithms claim to know us, then there is the hope that we can learn from algorithms who we are. The use of the "Daily Me" curation, the faith put in "people like you" recommendations, all of this data-driven activity is mindlessness, mindlessness in search of a mind, in search of the mind that the data processed by these algorithms proves not only exists but is knowable. The medieval nihilism of trying to prove that God exists has been replaced with the modern-day nihilism of trying to prove that *I exist*. If Big Brother, or now Big Data, is watching me, then there must still be a *me* who exists, a me who is *worth watching*.

5.6 THE DANGERS OF DATA-DRIVEN ACTIVITY

What we have found in the previously analyzed cases of data-driven activity—much as Nietzsche found with mechanical activity—is activity without an aim, activity without an actor, activity without accountability. In other words what we have found here is activity designed to free us from the oppressiveness of life and, in particular, from the oppressiveness of decision-making or, as Sartre described, from the oppressiveness of our having been "condemned to be free."

We have become predictable, according to Nietzsche, because we have made ourselves predictable. Our having become predictable is the result of a process of manipulation, indoctrination, conditioning, and torture, of "harness, tyranny, stupidity, and idiocy," but it was at least a *human* process, something that we did to each other and to ourselves. But what if this "labor performed by man upon himself" is no longer being directed by humans alone? What if, as postphenomenology would suggest, algorithms are not only the *means* by which we achieve our data-driven nihilism but are also *actively shaping* our data-driven nihilism? In replacing Big Brother with Big Data we have perhaps lost the one glimmer of hope we could still cling to, that even if humans have been reduced to mere puppets, there were still some humans who were not puppets, some humans who were capable of pulling the strings.

Nevertheless, even if we are today driven by data and algorithmic obedience rather than by priests and mechanical obedience, our current situation need not be all that different from what Nietzsche described. Though the tools used behind-the-scenes and the beliefs covering over the manipulation and indoctrination have changed, still we are describing how knowledge becomes power. And still *someone* must be collecting the data, *someone* must be writing the algorithms, *someone* must be benefiting from this obedience.

As I pointed out earlier, it is almost impossible to find out what algorithms know and how they work. But there was nonetheless the assumption that this lack of knowledge was due to secrecy, that if there is a "black box" containing our algorithmic infrastructure, it is because designers, engineers, lawyers, and CEOs constructed such a black box out of a mix of mathematical, legal, and bureaucratic complexity. As Frank Pasquale, in his book *The Black Box Society*, argues:

> In his book *Turing's Cathedral*, George Dyson quipped that "Facebook defines who we are, Amazon defines what we want, and Google defines what we think." We can extend that epigram to include *finance*, which defines what we have (materially, at least), and *reputation*, which increasingly defines our opportunities. Leaders in each sector aspire to make these decisions without regulation, appeal, or explanation. If they succeed, our fundamental freedoms and opportunities will be outsourced to systems with few discernible values beyond the enrichment of top managers and shareholders.[25]

In other words, knowledge of what is inside the black box is possible, the issue is that we—those whose daily lives are being driven by what is inside this black box—do not have access to this knowledge, or at least we do not have access to this knowledge *yet*.

But perhaps this is not the case. Perhaps the assumption that there is always a human "in the loop" is outdated. As Andrew Moore, a former vice president at Google and current dean of computer science at Carnegie Mellon University, put it in a recent interview:

You might be overestimating how much the content-providers understand how their own systems work . . . You might want to say, "Why did you recommend this movie?" When you're using machine-learning models, the model trains itself by using huge amounts of information from previous people . . . Everything from the color of the pixels on the movie poster through to maybe the physical proximity to other people who enjoyed this movie. It's the averaging effect of all these things . . . One of the researchers at Carnegie Mellon just launched a new machine-learning system which can handle putting together tens of billions of little pieces of evidence.[26]

When the interviewer asked Moore about Facebook's patent for "a tool that lenders could use to consider the credit ratings of a person's Facebook friends in deciding whether to approve a loan application," Moore added:

That is a really difficult problem . . . You're asking a computer that's obviously not that smart in the first place to predict whether this person is a risk based on what we know about them—but [you're telling it], "Please exclude these features that, as a society, we think would be illegal." But it's very hard or impossible for the engineers to know for sure that the computer hasn't inadvertently used some piece of evidence which it shouldn't.

Coders write algorithms. Algorithms produce results. How these results were produced is unclear, not only to those who the results are about but to the very authors of the codes producing the results. This is the paradox of what has come to be known as "machine learning":

In a 'Big Data' era, billions or trillions of data examples and thousands or tens of thousands of properties of the data (termed 'features' in machine learning) may be analyzed. The internal decision logic of the algorithm is altered as it 'learns' on training data. Handling a huge number especially of heterogeneous properties of data (i.e. not just words in spam email, but also email header info) adds complexity to the code. Machine learning techniques quickly face computational resource limits as they scale and may manage this, using techniques written into the code (such as 'principal component analysis') which add to its opacity. While datasets may be extremely large but possible to comprehend and code may be written with

clarity, the interplay between the two in the mechanism of the algorithm is what yields the complexity (and thus opacity).[27]

As machines learn more and more about us, we learn less and less about
the machines. This is not the result of the machines outsmarting us for,
as Moore makes clear, these machines are "obviously not that smart," as
they are still *just following rules*. The problem is that it seems to increasingly be the case that no one knows *how* these machines are following the rules, no one knows *what* information is being included or
excluded in following the rules, no one knows *why* these decisions
about inclusion and exclusion are being made in following the rules.

The deeper problem here however is that, though no one knows
how these algorithms work, we still trust them. The Nietzschean response to this problem is that we trust algorithms *because no one knows
how these algorithms work*. The greater the opacity, the greater the
mystery, the greater the faith. Humans are fallible; hence, the less of a
role that humans play in algorithms, the more the aura of infallibility
surrounding algorithms grows.

Of course algorithms make mistakes all the time, but this is attrib-
uted to human, not machine, error.[28] If an algorithmic prediction leads
to someone being wrongly recommended a product, wrongly denied a
loan, or wrongly targeted by a drone, then this is believed to be the
result of either human bias in designing the algorithm or of a lack of
information given to the algorithm. While the former excuse can be
used to further justify replacing humans with machines, the latter excuse can be used to further justify replacing human values (for example,
privacy) with machine values (such as efficiency).

Human values being replaced by machine values was precisely the
worry that motivated the French sociologist and theologian Jacques
Ellul. As Ellul writes:

> Herein lies the inversion we are witnessing. Without exception in the
> course of history, *technique belonged to a civilization* and was merely
> a single element among a host of nontechnical activities. Today *tech-
> nique has taken over the whole of civilization* . . . [T]he necessity of
> production penetrates to the very sources of life. It controls procrea-
> tion, influences growth, and alters the individual and the species.
> Death, procreation, birth, habitat; all must submit to technical effi-
> ciency and systematization, the end point of the industrial assembly

line. What seems to be most personal in the life of man is now technicized. The manner in which he rests and relaxes becomes the object of techniques of relaxation. The way in which he makes a decision is no longer the domain of the personal and voluntary; it has become the object of the techniques of "operations research." As Giedion says, all this represents experimentation at the very roots of being.[29]

Already in 1963, Ellul saw the rise of "efficiency" as the dominant value in society due to the rise of "technique" as the dominant rule of society. For Ellul, "technique" is not synonymous with "technology" but rather is defined as "the *totality of methods rationally arrived at and having absolute efficiency* (for a given stage of development) in *every* field of human activity."[30] In other words, "technique" represents the strategies employed in the drive to, as Nietzsche put it, make all of human life uniform, calculable, and, as a result, predictable. To the extent that *efficiency* comes to supplant all other ends as *the end*, more and more of human life comes under the rule of *technique*. If efficiency is what we want, then technique is the way to get it.

What really worries Ellul is the question of whether efficiency is actually what *we* want, or if it is what we have been led to *believe we want*, what we have been led to believe because of the rule of technique. We may have begun from the standpoint that, say, efficiency is the best way to maximize profit by minimizing waste, and have thus "technicized" all profit-seeking activities. But of course, as Marx realized, this is a self-defeating strategy, a strategy that leads to the destruction of the consumer class, of the class of those who are minimized because the employment of people rather than programs is increasingly seen as wasteful. That we are becoming more and more aware of the problem of maximum efficiency leading to maximum unemployment and are yet nevertheless continuing to seek maximum efficiency is what led Ellul to argue that efficiency has become an end-in-itself, an end-in-itself driven not by the bourgeoisie behind this technicization but by the technicization behind the bourgeoisie.

It is this worry that has led Ellul to be labeled as a "determinist" and thus relegated to the techno-dystopic, techno-phobic dustbin of history. And yet the present-day issues surrounding the lack of regulation and the lack of understanding of algorithms, algorithms that we nevertheless continue to allow to drive our decision-making, are perfectly described by Ellul's analyses of technique and efficiency. For, as Ellul predicted, even if we did wish to extricate ourselves from our data-driven ways, even if governments did wish to regulate algorithms, this would only be possible through the help of those who are capable of understanding the algorithms. Technique is thus for Ellul as much of a challenge to democracy as efficiency is a challenge to morality. As algorithms become more complex, more opaque, and more embedded in society, it becomes increasingly likely that we will be left with no alternative but to try to have "good" algorithms fight "bad" algorithms.

Yet even such a doomsday scenario as this is only going to occur if we actually decide to stop trusting algorithms. But of course such a decision would require that we not only make a decision without an algorithm telling us to do so but that we would be willing to again take on the burden of decision-making that drove us to embrace data-driven nihilism in the first place. The question then is not whether we can understand and regulate algorithms but whether we can understand and regulate nihilism.

NOTES

1. Nietzsche, *Genealogy*, 134.

2. Federal Trade Commission, "Data Brokers: A Call for Transparency and Accountability," *Federal Trade Commission*, May 2014, https://www.ftc.gov/system/files/documents/reports/data-brokers-call-transparency-accountability-report-federal-trade-commission-may-2014/140527databrokerreport.pdf.

3. Nolen Gertz, "Autonomy Online: Jacques Ellul and the Facebook Emotional Manipulation Study," *Research Ethics* 12, no. 1 (2016): 55–61.

4. Trend Watching, "5 Consumer Trends for 2017," *Trend Watching*, http://trendwatching.com/trends/5-trends-for-2017/.

5. Statista, "Fitbit—Statistics & Facts," *Statista*, https://www.statista.com/topics/2595/fitbit/.

6. Stephanie M. Lee, "How Many People Actually Use Their Fitbits?," *BuzzFeed News*, May 9, 2015, https://www.buzzfeed.com/stephaniemlee/how-many-people-actually-use-their-fitbits.

7. Fitbit, https://www.fitbit.com/us/whyfitbit.

8. Fitbit, "How Does My Fitbit Device Count Steps?," *Fitbit Help*, https://help.fitbit.com/articles/en_US/Help_article/1143.

9. See also Zygmunt Bauman, *Liquid Modernity* (Cambridge: Polity Press, 2000), 77–80.

10. The increasing *one-ness* of everyday life is also a vital theme in Heidegger's *Being and Time*, encapsulated in his distinction between *Dasein* and *das Man*.

11. J. W. Ayers, et al., "Pokémon GO—A New Distraction for Drivers and Pedestrians," *JAMA Internal Medicine* 176, no. 12 (December 1, 2016): 1865–1866.

12. Mary Bowerman, "Driver Slams into Baltimore Cop Car While Playing Pokemon Go," *USA Today*, July 20, 2016, http://www.usatoday.com/story/news/nation-now/2016/07/20/driver-slams-into-baltimore-cop-car-while-playing-pokemon-go-accident/87333892/.

13. Alonzo Small, "Pokémon Go Player Assaulted, Robbed in Dover," *USA Today*, July 20, 2016, http://www.usatoday.com/story/news/crime/2016/07/19/pokemon-go-player-assaulted-robbed-dover/87304022/.

14. Ryan W. Miller, "Teens Used Pokémon Go App to Lure Robbery Victims, Police Say," *USA Today*, July 11, 2016, http://www.usatoday.com/story/tech/2016/07/10/four-suspects-arrested-string-pokemon-go-related-armed-robberies/86922474/.

15. Vic Ryckaert, "Sex Offender Caught Playing Pokémon Go with Teen" *USA Today*, July 14, 2016, http://www.usatoday.com/story/news/nation-now/2016/07/14/indiana-sex-offender-caught-playing-pokemon-go-teen/87083504/.

16. Netflix, "How Does Netflix Work?," *Netflix Help Center*, https://help.netflix.com/en/node/412.

17. Victor Luckerson, "Here's How Facebook's News Feed Actually Works," *TIME*, July 9, 2015, http://time.com/collection-post/3950525/facebook-news-feed-algorithm/.

18. Federal Trade Commission, "Data Brokers," *iv*.

19. Adrienne LaFrance, "Why Can't Americans Find Out What Big Data Knows About Them?," *The Atlantic*, May 28, 2014, https://www.theatlantic.com/technology/archive/2014/05/why-americans-cant-find-out-what-big-data-knows-about-them/371758/.

20. Cass Sunstein, *Republic.com 2.0* (Princeton, NJ: Princeton University Press, 2007), 4.

21. Nolen Gertz, *The Philosophy of War and Exile* (Basingstoke: Palgrave Macmillan, 2014), 67–71.

22. Frank Pasquale, "Digital Star Chamber," *Aeon*, August 18, 2015, https://aeon.co/essays/judge-jury-and-executioner-the-unaccountable-algorithm.

23. Nietzsche, *Genealogy*, 36.

24. IMDb, "Schizopolis (1996) Quotes," *IMDb*, http://www.imdb.com/title/tt0117561/quotes?ref_=tt_ql_trv_4.

25. Frank Pasquale, *The Black Box Society: The Secret Algorithms that Control Money and Information* (Cambridge, MA: Harvard University Press, 2015), 15.

26. Adrienne LaFrance, "Not Even the People Who Write Algorithms Really Know How They Work," *The Atlantic*, September 18, 2015, https://www.theatlantic.com/technology/archive/2015/09/not-even-the-people-who-write-algorithms-really-know-how-they-work/406099/.

27. Jenna Burrell, "How the Machine 'Thinks': Understanding Opacity in Machine Learning Algorithms," *Big Data & Society* 3, iss. 1 (January–June 2016), 5.

28. Pasquale, "Digital Star Chamber."

29. Jacques Ellul, *The Technological Society*, trans. John Wilkinson (New York: Vintage Books, 1963), 128–29.

30. Ellul, *The Technological Society*, xxv.

6

THE UBER MENSCH

6.1 PETTY PLEASURES

The third human-nihilism relation that Nietzsche describes is that of the "petty pleasure." Nietzsche writes:

> An even more highly valued means of combating depression is the prescribing of a petty pleasure that is easily attainable and can be made into a regular event; this medication is often employed in association with the previous one. The most common form in which pleasure is thus prescribed as a curative is that of the pleasure of giving pleasure (doing good, giving, relieving, helping, encouraging, consoling, praising, rewarding); by prescribing "love of the neighbor," the ascetic priest prescribes fundamentally an excitement of the strongest, most life-affirming drive, even if in the most cautious doses—namely, of the will to power. The happiness of "slight superiority," involved in all doing good, being useful, helping, and rewarding, is the most effective means of consolation for the physiologically inhibited, and widely employed by them when they are well advised: otherwise they hurt one another, obedient, of course, to the same basic instinct.[1]

Nietzsche here makes the audacious claim that we help others in order to help ourselves. This claim seems less audacious however if we remember that Kant similarly worried that it was impossible to disentangle the duty to help others from the desire to receive pleasure from helping others. For Nietzsche, to be able to help another is to be both less in need of help than someone else and to be capable of helping someone else. In other words, helping others is an indication of one's own power. And the more we can help, the more powerful we must be.

For example, when a man holds a door open for a woman, she says, "Thank you," he says, "You're welcome," and they both walk through the door. But when a woman holds a door open for a man, he might not say, "Thank you," but rather grab the door and say, "Oh please after you." The unwillingness of the man to let the woman hold the door open for him—or pull out his chair for him, pay for his meal, or drive him home—is an indication of the recognition of the power dynamics at play in even such a seemingly mundane act.

For another example, think of the expression, "Kill them with kindness." The idea here is of course not meant to be taken literally, as it describes when we attack someone with false smiles and eye rolls rather than through more traditional forms of violence. And yet, as this expression reveals, we are indeed—in even such nontraditionally violent acts as baking cookies for someone we hate—still seeking to (metaphorically) kill someone, to reduce them, to reveal that they are beneath us, that they are not even worth traditional forms of violence. The ultimate aim of such actions is to "win them over," to, in other words, manipulate them, bend them to our will, turn them from an enemy into a friend, which is of course also the ultimate aim of war. That we are aware of the Nietzschean insight into what such behavior truly means is clear in our describing these actions as "passive-aggressive," for the heart of nihilism is precisely our ability to be destructive while being passive.

As with the previous two human-nihilism relations, there is here too a sense of selflessness. However while the selflessness sought in the previous two forms of nihilism was based on escapism, an escape into mindless activities, with petty pleasures we instead find a selflessness in the form of altruistic activities. Yet for Nietzsche these seemingly altruistic activities are still escapist in nature, though what we are escaping is not reality, nor accountability, but rather impotency.

Before death, we are powerless. Before nature, we are powerless. Before time, we are powerless. Before most things really, we are individually powerless. But before those whom we can help, we are powerful. Or at least we can have a momentary experience of what being powerful feels like. Helping others does nothing to change our situation with regards to death, nature, time, or any of the other countless things in life that make us feel like we are nothing more than the playthings of fate. But it is for precisely this reason that we cling to this momentary experience, returning to it again and again by finding new and grander ways to help more and more people.

Of course, seeking new and grander ways to help more and more people does not seem like something bad, let alone nihilistic. For even if we have ulterior motives, even if we take the most cynical view of the selflessness of altruism as being secretly motivated by the selfishness of the will to power, the fact still remains that people in need are being helped. Yet what is at issue here is not only how helping others makes us feel powerful but also how helping others makes us view others as powerless. The nihilistic replacement of our own impotency with an artificial superiority is at the same time a nihilistic replacement of the others' humanity with the others' artificial inferiority. Helping people in need becomes helping *needy people*, and helping needy people becomes helping *the needy*.

6.2 FROM PETTY PLEASURES TO PLEASURE ECONOMICS

Pleasure economics is my name for the phenomenon of our using technologies to expand our abilities to help and support others—and to expand the elevation of ourselves and the reduction of others lurking beneath such supportiveness—in ever newer and ever grander ways.

Whereas in Nietzsche's time we could only help those near to us, today we can go online and help people all over the world. On "crowdfunding" sites such as Kickstarter, GoFundMe, and Indiegogo, billions of dollars are being sent all over the world to help artists, musicians, filmmakers, and designers in exchange for small gifts of gratitude. Similarly "gig economy" sites such as Airbnb, Uber, and Lyft are allowing people to rent out their homes and their cars, while sites such as TaskRabbit are allowing people to rent out their bodies.

In all such cases we find the ability to, as Nietzsche would put it, expand the range of our will to power to undreamt-of heights, allowing us to experience the superiority of helping those in need not only through charitable donations but also through letting strangers have the gift of spending time in our homes, of driving us around, and even of doing our chores.

6.3 THE OBJECTIFICATION ECONOMY

According to Nietzsche's aforementioned definition of petty pleasure, there is a connection between mechanical activity and petty pleasure, as he believes the "medication" of the latter is "often employed in association with the previous one." The question of whether there is a similar association to be found between data-driven activity and pleasure economics can be answered if we return again to the Fitbit.

As I mentioned in the previous chapter, the Fitbit's information about calories burned, steps taken, and heartbeats per minute are more readily understood by users if seen not as markers of the abstraction we call fitness but as scores in a video game. Having already turned our bodies into avatars and our lives into games, it is easy to see how quickly we can take the further step of turning these scores into monetary values, our bodies into commodities, and our lives into businesses. For once we have turned health into a competition, it only makes sense to turn that competition into a profit.

This idea of health-as-profit is precisely what we find in Achievement. Achievement is a website that turns fitness tracking into fitness money-making:

> Get Points for Being Healthy
> We've awarded over 100 million Activities. Here's the most common ways to earn:
>
> > Walking/daily steps
> > Any form of exercise
> > Sleeping
> > Logging food/calories
> > Weighing yourself daily
> > Tweeting healthy Tweets
> > Taking a survey
> > Participating in research[2]

On the face of it, this seems too good to be true. Who wouldn't want to make money just for walking or sleeping? As Achievement says, we're doing these activities anyway, we might as well get paid for them.

But of course Achievement gets something out of this too. As is hinted at by the last listed way to make money—"Participating in research"—Achievement is operated by the medical research company

Evidation Health. To make money for walking and sleeping one must first register with Achievement, a process which includes giving Evidation access to data from your wearable fitness tracker. In other words, whether you explicitly choose to participate in research, simply by signing up you are already implicitly choosing to participate in research. So while it might seem like this arrangement is too good to be true for you, it is really too good to be true for Evidation. They are not giving away free money, *you are*, in the form of your data, data which is worth far more than the relatively paltry amount of money they give you for walking and sleeping.

What is at issue here, however, is not that Evidation is tricking people into giving away their data. What should instead concern us is that Evidation is *not* tricking people, that Evidation makes it quite clear on the Achievement website what this arrangement is, and yet people—according to their website, over one million people—still use it. As is explained on Achievement's homepage:

> We've paid out over $500,000 so far. Here's how it works:
>
>> Earn $10 for 10,000 points. There's no limit to how much you can earn.
>> In addition, earn up to hundreds of dollars for contributing health research.
>> We've partnered with leading health companies to make these rewards possible. [3]

Such arrangements like this are of course not new. Medical research companies have always paid participants for data, for data which they profit off of many times over. Indeed one—say, for example, a Marxist—could argue that this arrangement is nothing more than the Capitalist arrangement between the bourgeoisie and the proletariat, between those who *control* the means of production and those who *are* the means of production.

Yet what is new here is that Achievement is aimed neither at the traditional members of the proletariat nor at the traditional participants of medical research. To use Achievement one must own and use a wearable fitness tracker like a Fitbit. The proletariat is made up of manual laborers, medical research is made up of college students, and what both have in common is that they *need money*, money that they are less likely to spend on a Fitbit than on food.

Achievement is therefore aimed at the population of people who have enough money to buy a Fitbit but who do not have enough money to see something like Achievement as beneath them. And it is precisely this lack of *beneath-ness* that is at issue here. Making money off of our bodies is no longer seen as a form of prostitution, as something sad, desperate, morally depraved, but is instead seen as simply good business sense. Why let *pride* stand in the way of *profit*? Just as there is the argument that prostitution is not about sexual debasement but about sexual liberation, is not about weakness but about strength, not about powerlessness but about empowerment, so too can we find in these new ways to make money off of our bodies a sign of the will to power.

Providing data to a medical research company in exchange for rewards is not about manipulation, about being tricked into thinking we are getting something for nothing, it is about empowerment. Medical researchers want our data, *need* our data, thus giving them our data is a sign of our power, of our power to give what others need, of our power not to reduce others but to reduce ourselves. The paltriness of the reward we receive in exchange for our data is not a sign of our being taken advantage of, a sign of our naïveté about how much our data is worth, but is instead a sign of willingness to reduce our bodies to data and our data to a gift. The reward therefore is not compensation for a transaction but a "thank you" for a present, a present willingly, freely, *proudly* given. Taking pride in what we can say "No" to is outdated. Today we take pride in what we can say "Yes" to instead. But that does not mean that our *pride* is not still about our *power*.

6.4 SHARING IS CARING

Taking pride in what we can say "Yes" to is what the "sharing economy" is all about. Rather than being obsessed with consumerism and ownership, with having access to only that which we can afford to own, the internet makes it possible to have access without ownership. What matters from this perspective is not whether something *belongs to* someone but rather whether something is currently being *used by* someone. Something not being used is something that is being wasted.

And this waste comes in the form of not only the opportunity to make money but in the form of the opportunity to meet people. As the *Economist* described this phenomenon in its early stages in 2013:

> Such "collaborative consumption" is a good thing for several reasons. Owners make money from underused assets. Airbnb says hosts in San Francisco who rent out their homes do so for an average of 58 nights a year, making $9,300. Car owners who rent their vehicles to others using RelayRides make an average of $250 a month; some make more than $1,000. [. . .] For sociable souls, meeting new people by staying in their homes is part of the charm. Curmudgeons who imagine that every renter is Norman Bates can still stay at conventional hotels. For others, the web fosters trust. As well as the background checks carried out by platform owners, online reviews and ratings are usually posted by both parties to each transaction, which makes it easy to spot lousy drivers, bathrobe-pilferers and surfboard-wreckers. By using Facebook and other social networks, participants can check each other out and identify friends (or friends of friends) in common.[4]

The sharing economy is not only about sharing commodities and services, it is about sharing experiences. From the perspective of the sharing economy, it is not only unused products that are wasted if not shared, time is wasted if not shared.

While websites like Amazon and eBay have made it possible for people to buy and sell products directly rather than through a store, they do not afford the opportunity to meet people in the way that websites like Airbnb and TaskRabbit do. Intermediaries like Amazon and eBay inform potential buyers and sellers about the other, but only with regard to their transaction history (that is, can the buyer be trusted to pay and can the seller be trusted to deliver). However intermediaries like Airbnb and TaskRabbit operate through face-to-face transactions, for which reason much more than one's transaction history is shared in advance.

The sharing economy not only requires the sharing of products and the sharing of time but also the sharing of *trust*. The sharing economy was supposed to be about bringing people together, about nurturing a new sense of community on the basis of trust. Indeed, according to Benita Matofska, founder of The People Who Share, "Trust is the secret of the Sharing Economy."[5] But because we do not actually have the level of trust demanded by the sharing economy, we have asked the internet intermediaries that drive the sharing economy to run background checks, verify social media accounts, and prevent anonymity. What is revealed by such security measures is that the trust that the sharing economy is built on is not trust *of each other* but trust *of technology*. Trust here comes not from strangers meeting and developing a relationship but from uploading personal information onto a website. In other words, trust comes from *data*. What is further revealed by how we use this technology is that we lack not only the trust demanded by the sharing economy, we lack even *the desire to share* demanded by the sharing economy.

In the previous chapter I discussed the relationship between trust and data from the perspective of data-driven activity, of how, on the one hand, we trust data more than we trust each other and, on the other hand, of how we become trustworthy by becoming capable of being reduced to data. Here, from the perspective of pleasure economics, what should concern us is not what data does to us but what data allows us to do to each other.

In order to participate in the sharing economy one must create a profile, a profile that other participants in the sharing economy are able to peruse, use, and abuse. We find something we want to share, we place a request to share it, and then we wait. We have something we want to share, we post it online to be shared, and then we wait. In both cases what we are waiting for is to be judged, to be judged worthy of sharing.

That sharing is less about *caring* and more about *judging* became clear in the recent controversy over the discovery that users of Airbnb were racially discriminating against potential guests who were African American. As researchers from the Harvard Business School write in their study "Racial Discrimination in the Sharing Economy: Evidence from a Field Experiment":

> We find widespread discrimination against guests with distinctively African-American names. [. . .] Our results are remarkably persistent. Both African-American and White hosts discriminate against African-American guests; both male and female hosts discriminate; both male and female African-American guests are discriminated against. Effects persist both for hosts that offer an entire property

and for hosts who share the property with guests. Discrimination persists among experienced hosts, including those with multiple properties and those with many reviews. Discrimination persists and is of similar magnitude in high and low priced units, in diverse and homogeneous neighborhoods.[6]

Requiring that users post a picture of themselves, and use their real names, invites judgment, invites discrimination, invites the exercise of *power*. Introducing oneself online before introducing oneself in person does not help to build relationships between strangers, it helps to build inequalities between strangers, allowing users to pick and choose, to stereotype and avoid, more than to simply meet and greet.

That these researchers found this discrimination to occur so consistently, across all populations, only further points toward the role of the technology, of the common denominator, in enabling this discrimination. Similarly, in an op-ed in the *New York Times*, Kristin Clarke writes:

> While my fourth request was accepted, the overall experience was a sour one. I am African-American, and because Airbnb strongly recommends display of a profile picture (which I provided) and requires its users to display an actual name, it was hard to believe that race didn't come into play.
> That stay marked my last booking through Airbnb.
> My experience is hardly unique. This year, the issue of Airbnb discrimination has received considerable attention, especially after African-American users of the service began sharing stories similar to mine on social media using the hashtag AirbnbWhileBlack.[7]

Clarke, who is the president and executive director of the Lawyers' Committee for Civil Rights Under Law, concludes her op-ed with several suggestions for how Airbnb can help stop this discrimination. Aside from suggesting that Airbnb actively oppose the discrimination through auditing for, and banishment of, the hosts perpetrating the discrimination, Clarke adds, "Third, Airbnb should stop having users display an actual name or profile picture before booking; that information should be withheld until a reservation has been confirmed." In other words, to stop discrimination, Airbnb must not only start policing it, Airbnb must stop empowering it.

Importantly, Airbnb was not alone in the sharing economy in having researchers discover that its users were discriminating against other users. Uber and Lyft, the ridesharing internet companies that are supposed to be "disrupting" the taxi industry—and in particular the tradition of taxi drivers avoiding picking up people of color—were both found recently to be enabling discrimination. However, while researchers from the University of Washington, Stanford, and MIT found that Uber's drivers were more discriminatory than Lyft's drivers, this appears to have less to do with the differences between the drivers and more to do with the differences between the amount of information shared with the drivers:

> That Uber generated some of the most troubling data doesn't necessarily mean that Lyft is friendlier to black customers. Instead, it might reflect the ability of Lyft drivers to discriminate much earlier in the process of finding riders. When riders used Lyft—which allows drivers to see a prospective rider's name and photo before accepting a trip—it was harder to identify potential discrimination before and during rides, since drivers could simply choose never to confirm black passengers to begin with, the researchers note. But the prolonged wait times that did show up among black Lyft users, the authors say, might be consistent with drivers viewing and skipping over a pending request from a black customer. [. . .] The study found little evidence of discrimination among Flywheel drivers, a fact that the researchers say might be due to the fact that the service doesn't have users add photos to their profiles.[8]

The differences in discrimination between the users of Uber, Lyft, and Flywheel only further highlight the correlation between data and power. Uber does not share rider information with drivers until the driver accepts the rider's request, and driver discrimination becomes apparent. Lyft shares rider information with drivers before the driver accepts the rider's request, and driver discrimination becomes less apparent. Flywheel does not share rider information with drivers at all, and driver discrimination does not appear. The less data given, the less power to abuse.

Furthermore, the researchers found that ridesharing drivers were not only able to exercise power in the form of discrimination but also in the form of sexism and harassment. Female riders often experienced longer-than-necessary rides, even involving driving through the same intersection multiple times, which the researchers conclude "appears to be a combination of profiteering and flirting to a captive audience."[9] In other words, the sharing economy raises the question of whether being rejected is based solely on someone not liking your profile picture, as well as the question of whether being accepted is based solely on someone liking your profile picture *too much*.

Evidence of the role of the profile picture determining how and what one shares has also been discovered in that offshoot of the sharing economy known as "crowdfunding." In much the same way that the sharing economy was supposed to "disrupt" traditional economics by putting caring above consumerism, crowdfunding was supposed to "disrupt" traditional fundraising by putting the masses above the markets. Rather than trying to convince a hedge fund manager to make a large investment to get an idea off the ground, sites like Kickstarter, GoFundMe, Indiegogo, and many, many more, allow people to try to convince the masses to make small donations to get an idea off the ground. However, while there are many tips floating around on the internet about how to successfully crowdfund ideas, research suggests that "the best advice to those seeking money online might sound more like this: Be thin, fair-skinned, and attractive."[10]

Crowdfunding, like the sharing economy, appears to be something that simply should not work. The sharing economy requires that people would want to share their belongings with strangers, invite strangers into their homes, and ask strangers to be allowed to share their belongings and be allowed into their homes. Crowdfunding requires that people would want to give money to strangers, and would want to ask strangers for money. These are activities that traditionally we would see as imposing on others, as unbecoming of civilized society, as *beneath us*. And yet, as the evidence of the discrimination and sexism of users of sharing economy and crowdfunding websites suggests, we see these activities not as lowering us but as elevating us, not as a sign of weakness but of strength, or, as Nietzsche would put it, of *power*.

If one posts their home on Airbnb, they may be judged by others, by friends and family, as needy. But such judgments can be waved away by the ideology of the sharing economy—I am not a *needer*, I am a *sharer*, I am altruistic, I am part of a community, I am part of a movement. People peruse and judge the host's home. People peruse and judge the host. But while the host does not know how many people are looking at their home, rejecting their home, rejecting them, they do know how many are asking to be allowed into their home, asking to be approved by them, to be judged by them. Potential guests send at the very least a profile, a profile with a name, a photo, and past reviews. But Airbnb also invites potential guests to send hosts a message, to send a justification for judging them worthy, a justification based either on need (for example, "Your home is perfectly located for my needs!") or on desire (for example, "Your home looks great and I'd love to meet you!"). The host is invited to not only judge the potential guest but to judge the guest's needs and desires. Having received such justification, the host can ask for more, for more evidence of worthiness, of being sufficiently clean, trustworthy, dependable, interesting, exciting, etc. But of course what matters is not that one can prove such worthiness through a message but that the potential guest is willing to *try* to offer such proof, proving consequently that the potential guest is sufficiently *needy*. The host rents out their home. The potential guest rents out their dignity.

The guest deemed sufficiently needy gets to sleep on the host's couch or extra bed in addition to paying the host for such an honor, a payment that is made in an exchange of both money and power. This power exchange is expressed in the steps required to gain entry into the host's home—the home which, in being able to be made available to the guest, is already an indication of the power of the host, of the power to serve *as a host*—and in the steps required to obey the host's rules, rules which are often the first thing the host shares with the guest. The guest must respect the host's home. The guest must respect the host. The penalty for disrespect comes not only in the form of a fee but in the form of a negative review. For while Airbnb allows both guests and hosts to review each other, the guest is always asked to review first, allowing the host to not only review the guest but to review the guest's review. Dignity—measured in the neediness to be willing to jump through hoops, and in the reviews that show how well one jumped through hoops—is the true currency of the sharing economy.

This exchange of property for dignity is even more pronounced in crowdfunding. In crowdfunding, there is not the one-to-one relation of the sharing economy but rather a one-to-many relation, for which reason one does not jump through the hoops specified by another but rather through the hypothetical hoops of the hypothetical others of the crowd. The creator asking for money for their creation begins by anticipating the demands of the crowd and trying to fulfill them.

This attempted fulfillment comes primarily through the pitch. The pitch is where the creator shows they are worthy of the crowd, of the crowd's time and of the crowd's money. The crowd does not ask the creator for anything, the crowd makes no demands on the creator, the crowd does not communicate any desires to the creator. Those in the crowd consequently need not reveal themselves but can instead remain anonymous, watching the creator dance for them, watching the creator try to guess what dance the crowd wants.

The dance is often in the form of a personal photo, of an appeal, and, frequently, in the form of a video. The creator is not just selling their creation, the creator is selling the creator. And while in the sharing economy one can hide one's neediness behind ideology—behind the desire to share, to try something new, something different—in crowdfunding, there is nothing to hide behind. The creator needs money. The creator is asking for money. The crowd has money. The crowd has what the creator needs. The crowd is needed, but the crowd is not needy, for the crowd has the power, the power that comes from being in the position of being able to give, to give to the needy.

But there are many creators, there are many who are needy, and thus the crowd has the power not only to give but to judge, to judge who is not only sufficiently needy but sufficiently worthy. The crowd does not have the power of a god or of a Nietzschean "Master," but the crowd does have a taste of that power, for the crowd decides whose creation lives and whose creation dies. And yet, as the aforementioned research shows, the crowd ultimately judges not the attractiveness of the creation but the attractiveness of the creator.

It is almost as if what the crowd is buying with their donation is not a piece of the creation but a piece of the creator. For why else would the attractiveness of the creator matter, particularly when, unlike with the sharing economy, the crowd will never meet the creator? Yet just because the crowd will never meet the creator, that does not mean that the crowd cannot show off in front of the creator.

Again, the crowd has the power to give. Seemingly, this is not altruistic but rather an exchange, for while the creator asks the crowd for money, the creator offers perks in return. But these perks are, as we saw with Achievement, worth little compared to what the creator is hoping to receive. Members of the crowd each get a prototype, each get their name on a list of donors, each get a personalized "thank you," etc. Yet it is precisely the relative worthlessness of these perks that gives them their value. For it is the worthlessness of the perk received that allows the crowd to show off, that allows the crowd to show that the donation is less of an investment and more of a gift, not something one does with the hope of getting their money back but what one does *because one can*. And all one asks for in return is a "thank you," a very *public* "thank you," a "thank you" that, thanks to the internet—and in particular the integration of crowdfunding and social media websites— *the whole world can see*.

6.5 THE DATING GAME

While sharing economy and crowdfunding websites allow us to mask our uses and abuses of profile pictures, hiding our judgmental, discriminatory, power-seeking behavior beneath the cover of altruistic intentions, the world of online dating instead revels in letting users accept and reject each other over profile pictures. There are of course some dating websites that still seek the mask of noble intentions, of helping users to seek love rather than power, websites such as Match.com, eHarmony, and OkCupid. But Tinder is different. Tinder focuses not on romance but on transactions, on the nihilism of pleasure economics rather than on the nihilism of data-driven activity. And Tinder is not only the most popular dating app, it "has been ranked as the most downloaded lifestyle app in America for nearly two years."[11]

Whereas most dating websites offer the power of data-analytics, of algorithmic profile matchmaking, Tinder offers instead the power of accepting and rejecting, the power of "swiping right" and "swiping left," a power that has become so popular that it has entered the cultural lexicon as code for accepting and rejecting. The popularity of Tinder is also clear in its growth compared to its competition. While sites like Match.com, eHarmony, and OkCupid remained fairly consistent between 2013 and 2015 in their number of users, Tinder more than tripled its monthly active users over the same time period. One explanation for this success is that Tinder is "increasingly addictive":

After taking off on college campuses, Tinder now boasts 26 million matches a day, and its leaders have invested heavily in maintaining its reputation as a hook-up haven for young people. [. . .] Surrounded by rivals like Hinge, Zoosk and Wyldfire, Tinder has nevertheless tripled its user base since the start of 2014 and now reaches more than 3 percent of all active American cell-phone users, an analysis from 7Park Data shows. It's also become increasingly addictive: The average user checked the app 11 times a day, seven minutes at a time, the firm said in 2013. [12]

Data-driven dating sites operate by having users fill out questionnaires, and then waiting to be matched. Tinder however invites users to go shopping—or swiping—through profiles, through profiles that contain little more than pictures, pictures that are uploaded by users to be looked over and judged. And with so many millions of users, there is much to be looked over and judged.

Tinder is not only one of the most popular dating apps, it is one of the most popular apps of any kind. According to Tinder's website, the app is in 196 countries, and registers over 1.4 billion swipes per day. [13] Tinder's reported 26 million matches per day seems like a large number, but compared to the number of swipes per day it's actually quite small, meaning that only about 2 percent of swipes result in a match. It would appear then that what is perhaps so "addictive" about Tinder is not the possibility of finding a match but rather the ability to judge—the ability to swipe through thousands of profiles, profiles of people who Tinder's geolocation software found living near each other, of people who perhaps had just passed each other on the street, and judge them.

That Tinder users are more interested in judging than in matchmaking is further supported by the research of social psychologist Jeannette Purvis. As Purvis writes:

As a social psychologist, I've focused my research on exploring why Tinder—as one of my interview participants put it—is so "evilly satisfying." [. . .] Tinder's approach to romance is straightforward, yet brutally effective. Matches are made using sparse criteria: Looks, availability and location. Because people can gauge someone's attractiveness after just a one-second glance, Tinder users often churn through profiles at astounding speeds. In terms of psychological conditioning, Tinder's interface is perfectly constructed to encourage this rapid swiping. Since users don't know which swipe will bring the "reward" of a match, Tinder uses a variable ratio reward schedule, which means that potential matches will be randomly dispersed. It's the same reward system used in slot machines, video games and even during animal experiments where researchers train pigeons to continuously peck at a light on the wall. [14]

Tinder is not only "addictive," it is both "evilly satisfying" and "brutally effective." Matches occur on only 2 percent of swipes, suggesting that it is not the *match* but the *swipe* that is "satisfying" and "effective." Yet what is it that makes a swipe both "evil" and "brutal"?

Purvis appears to believe that the answer lies in the user not knowing "which swipe will bring the 'reward' of a match," thus presuming that the end that users on Tinder seek is the match, and that the swiping is only the means. But what if this is wrong? What if the match is not the end, not the "reward," but is instead something closer to a *bonus*? Users swipe through profiles, rapidly, deeming each profile as acceptable or rejectable, doing so in a matter of seconds. And this judgment is based on nothing more than "looks, availability, and location." In other words, users are reduced from persons to profiles, from profiles to pictures, and from pictures to *Hot* or *Not*.

Matches disrupt this process, not only serving as an interruption, but as a demand, as a demand for a *decision*, for a response, for a response that requires more than a mere swipe. On the one hand, a match is a reminder that the user is not only judging but being judged, not only reducing but being reduced, not only swiping but being swiped. On the other hand, a match is a reminder that the user is more than what they have been reduced to, that the user is a person, a person who is now put in a situation where they must choose whether or not to "chat" with another person who is also more than that to which he or she has similarly been reduced.

If the match was the desired result, then this moment of decision would presumably be a moment of delight. Yet as researchers from Queen Mary University of London, Sapienza University of Rome, and the Royal Ottawa Health Care Group discovered:

> Overall, we find that 21% of female matches send a message, whereas only 7% of male matches send a message. [. . .] The median message length sent by men is only 12 characters, compared to 122

from women. For men, 25% of messages are under 6 characters (presumably "hello" or "hi"). Consequently, it is clear that little information is being imparted in opening conversations. [15]

Only 2 percent of swipes result in a match and yet, of those matches, only 21 percent of women and only 7 percent of men who found a match sent a message. And when users did send a message, they appeared to not see it as an opportunity to be more than what they had been reduced to but rather as yet another medium for reduction, with women writing the equivalent of a tweet, and men writing the equivalent of bathroom stall graffiti.

While it is generally accepted that users of Tinder are not looking for love, such behavior suggests that users of Tinder are barely even engaged in pursuing casual flings. Instead it would appear that users of Tinder are engaged in *pursuing pursuing*, or again what Nietzsche would call *the will to power*. Of course we do this offline as well, scanning crowds in bars, looking people up and down, rejecting people as undesirable without ever saying a word. But the key here is the question of whether the technology of Tinder acts as more than a neutral medium for our power-seeking behavior, whether Tinder mediates—in a postphenomenological sense—our will to power, influencing and shaping the behavior of users on Tinder in a way that motivates, encourages, and even elicits such power-seeking behavior.

The invitation to swipe is, as we have seen, both "evilly satisfying" and "brutally effective," not because users hope to hook up but because users enjoy turning others down. Dragging someone's profile photo off of the screen, throwing someone's face onto a virtual reject pile, allows users to experience the power previously reserved for hiring committees and casting directors. For a moment, someone's fate is in your hands, literally, thanks to the ergonomic nature of the smartphone app.

This is not to say of course that such power does not also reside in approving as well as rejecting, in swiping right as well as swiping left, for what matters here is not how one feels about the other but about how one feels while swiping the other. Tinder reduces the complications of interpersonal relationships to a hand gesture, allowing users to decide the fates of others with their thumbs, not unlike the purported gestures of emperors in the gladiatorial arena. Whether one wants the other to live or die, whether one finds the other to be hot or not, all that Tinder requires is the swipe, the same activity that we also use when we speed through social media timelines, choosing in a similar fashion which of our "friends" are worth our time and which are not, which are worth a "like" and which are worth *nothing*.

But of course a "like," just as a swipe, is also worth *nothing*. Clicking here or clicking there, swiping left or swiping right—ultimately there is no difference. It is the same action either way. This is not to say that the actions are meaningless, far from it, for what should concern us is precisely the meaning that we do find in such actions. Unwilling to express ourselves in our daily lives, unable to confront people, to tell people how we feel or don't feel about them, we continue to passive-aggressively kill each other with kindness in person, and then feign aggressivity in cyberspace, playing out on our phones the fantasy of having real power, the fantasy of taking what we want and of destroying what we don't want.

It is here that we see the nihilistic danger of Tinder's addictiveness. For this fantasy has come to supplant reality. The pleasure that we can derive from Tinder, the pleasure that is "brutally effective" and "evilly satisfying," far outweighs the pleasure that we can derive from face-to-face interactions. For even when we do have the capacity to express power in our daily lives, even when we could be open and honest with someone standing before us, we have become so accustomed to retreating to our phone-based sources of power that we often pass over the face-to-face in favor of the swipe-to-swipe. Turning people down in person is *mean* and *complicated*, but turning people down in Tinder is *fun* and *fast*.

Of course we may question whether this is actually fun, whether reducing ourselves and others to swipeability is actually a pleasurable activity, and what indeed is the source of such pleasure, but Tinder is designed—"Tinder's interface is perfectly constructed to encourage this rapid swiping"—precisely such that we do not raise such questions. Tinder invites users to have the best of both the real and the cyber worlds: the users are real people whom one could meet face-to-face, and the users are avatars that one can swipe through like pictures of cats on Facebook or pictures of products on Amazon. Thanks to the former, users can feel like they are not wasting time but are engaging in human interaction. Thanks to the latter, users can feel like they are not hurting anyone's feelings but just having a good time. And because we can experience both perspectives simultaneously, we can *be* brutal and evil without *feeling* brutal and evil.

Dividing who we *are* from what we *do* is nihilism. We are what we do.[16] There is no "real world" different from the "cyber world" but only the world of experience. Maintaining the illusion of these dualisms is central to Tinder's success, for if we were forced to confront what we are actually doing to ourselves and to each other, we would be forced to recognize that what we find so *fun* about Tinder is—as I will discuss further in the next section—what Nietzsche describes as *the pleasure of cruelty*.

6.6 THE DANGERS OF PLEASURE ECONOMICS

In the preface to the *Genealogy*, Nietzsche warns that the dominant morality of contemporary society, the morality that provides us with our highest values and aspirations, the "morality of pity"[17] is "the great danger to mankind," and a "sinister symptom" of nihilism. To explain what Nietzsche is getting at here, let's use as an example a type of pity that we are perhaps all well aware of (and perhaps some of us are even the product of): pity sex.

You go out drinking with some friends, you see someone looking sad and alone at the bar, and being the good person that you are, you decide to join this person. After several rounds of drinks, you leave together, and the next morning you feel a strange mix of shame and pride. On the one hand you've been brought up to believe that one-night stands are wrong, but on the other hand you've been brought up to believe that offering someone a helping hand is doing a good deed. Whether thanks to reason or to rationalization, you're able to go home feeling like you've at least made someone feel better, which of course in turn makes you feel better.

Now imagine that you again go out drinking with some friends and again see that same person sitting at the bar. Would this person, would this recipient of your good deed, now be looking less sad and alone? No, of course not. Because what one learns from pity sex, what one is inspired to do thanks to pity sex, is not to become a more attractive person but a more unattractive person, a person who is sadder, more pathetic, more able to arouse the pity of those like you.

In pity sex you get to experience the power of pitying someone else, of helping someone whom you see as *beneath* you, but such help is for the other momentary at best or counterproductive at worst. At the same time, the power of pitying is won at the expense of having to reduce your time, your body, your sexuality, to *nothing*, to being things not that someone must *deserve* but that you will give away if someone else looks pathetic enough. This is likewise what occurs in pity grading (a student cries over a bad grade, so a professor raises the grade, disincentivizing the student from studying harder, while revealing that grades, that education, that one's profession, are worthless) and what occurs in all forms of pity, for what they all have in common is the reduction of the pitied, the pitier, and what is exchanged between them, to *nothing*.

In other words, when we help others out of pity, when we *selflessly* give to those who arouse our pity, we risk both degrading those we help—by seeing the other as *beneath* us, as nothing other than *needy*—and degrading ourselves—by trying to prove that we are *above* others by giving away our time, our energy, and our possessions as if they were worthless. This of course raises the question of why we engage in such behavior, a question which Nietzsche answers by suggesting that if we are cruel, it is because *we enjoy it*.[18] Cruelty was a right of the "masters" according to Nietzsche, and thus even though the masters no longer exist, we still yearn to experience the power of the masters, even if it means being cruel not only to others but to ourselves. This is how Nietzsche explains our equation of an unpaid debt with a payment in pain (for example, the classic "Give me my money or I'll break your legs!") since the pain of someone else cannot be considered equal to what was lost unless there is something that we gain from being able to cause someone else pain. This is also why guilt is so important to Nietzsche, as in guilt we can experience a double cruelty and a double pleasure, as we first get to experience the pleasure of being cruel to someone else, and then we get to experience the pleasure of being cruel to ourselves, punishing ourselves for having been cruel to someone else.

For Nietzsche, the seeming selflessness of helping others can be explained as the self-seeking behavior of those in pursuit of the pleasure of cruelty. One gives to someone else, asking for nothing in return, or at least that's how it appears. Think for example of even just the gesture of buying a round of drinks. The person who buys the drinks is quick to wave away attempts by others to pay, making it clear that this is an act of kindness. Yet the person who buys is now entitled to make jokes both about their own magnanimity and about the others' indebtedness. The debt can at any time be called upon, not for its repayment but for its acknowledgment. And indeed the attempts of the others to repay the debt are often avoided. The person who buys continues to buy, the debt continues to grow, the kindness continues to be joked about and called upon for acknowledgment. So long as there is a debt, there is a justification for the cruelty of the creditor, a cruelty not in the form of the breaking of legs but in the form of the breaking of egos, of making joke after joke, acknowledgment after acknowledgment, reminding the others, though always with a smile, who is the creditor and who is the debtor.

Though Nietzche was referring to the morality of the Europe of the late-nineteenth century, the cases that we have here analyzed provide a strong argument for claiming that the morality of pity is not only still with us, it has become even more pervasive online. From crowdsourcing to crowdfunding, from the sharing economy to the gig economy, we are giving to others more and more—others whom we have never met beyond an online profile—our time, our energy, our knowledge, and our money. What should concern us here is not just the Nietzschean question of whether such giving is driven by the pleasure of cruelty but also the postphenomenological question of to what extent such giving is driven by the technologies mediating our giving. In other words, the question we need to ask is not only *why do we give?* but also *who is truly doing the giving?*

To return to the example of Tinder, it may seem as though Tinder does not belong with the likes of Airbnb, Uber, and Kickstarter, since users of Tinder are not trying to connect in order to exchange goods and services but simply in order to meet each other. However, as I attempted to show, the behavior of users of Tinder appears to suggest that the aim of users is not necessarily to meet others, nor even to hook up with others, but rather to swipe others, to judge others as acceptable or rejectable. Hence what Tinder shares with Airbnb, Uber, and Kickstarter is that it provides users with an opportunity to exercise the power of judging and the pleasure of cruelty.

Tinder presents a perfect distillation of the power and cruelty of pleasure economics, allowing users to swipe with little to no pretense about their pleasure in accepting and rejecting others. Yet Tinder also presents the problem of accounting for why we *keep swiping*. For while swiping can provide quite a power rush, it must be recognized that it can also be quite tedious. Millions of users, millions of swipes, millions of photos judged, millions of thumb gestures. Sites like Airbnb, Uber, and Kickstarter at least offer the promise of receiving *something* (meeting someone new, making money, receiving a reward) in return for one's thumb gestures, but Tinder not only makes no such promise of a return on one's investment, it advertises, as we have seen, a less than 2 percent success rate. Can the pleasure of cruelty that one obtains while using Tinder really be enough to account for all of the hours spent on Tinder, for all of the hours spent doing nothing other than repeatedly sliding one's thumb from side to side?

It is here that the double pleasure of cruelty found in guilt may help us to better understand the time spent on Tinder. Another aspect of Tinder that connects it with the other examples of pleasure economics is that the profiles presented to users are presented in the form of a request, a request for help, for help in the form of a swipe. Swipe one and another takes its place, asking, just like the previous forced smile on the previous artificial profile, to be judged, to be swiped, to be spared the misery of not knowing if one is a *swipe left* or a *swipe right*. Just like how in Pokémon GO the user must "catch 'em all," in Tinder the user must *swipe 'em all*. For while it is cruel to reduce others to acceptable or rejectable, it is far crueler to reduce others to not even worth accepting or rejecting. Users of Tinder can therefore be made to feel guilty not only for reducing others to their swipeability but also for *not* reducing others to their swipeability.

If such guilt exists in a "brutal" and "evil" app like Tinder, then imagine how much more guilt must exist in altruism-preaching apps like Airbnb, Uber, and Kickstarter. Users present themselves as in need, in need of a home, of a ride, of a donation, and other users in turn present themselves as in need, in need of a guest, of a fare, of a cause. For every user whose needs are met, there are countless other users whose needs are not. In traditional economics we have no need to feel guilty for choosing one hotel over another, for choosing one cab over another, for choosing one investment over another, as it's not personal, *it's just business*. But in pleasure economics, *it is personal*. In pleasure economics, the motivation of users is not supposed to be business, it is supposed to be about "disrupting" business, about proving that people are willing to help each other rather than just trying to compete with each other.

And yet pleasure economics turns out to be even more competitive, even more brutal, than traditional economics precisely because of how personal it is. The ideology of pleasure economics, of pursuing communities based on trust rather than pursuing personal gains, is not only utopian but unrealizable. From a Nietzschean perspective, even in helping others we can still be pursuing personal power. From a post-phenomenological perspective, our communities are mediated not by trust but by identity-verifying security systems. In other words, pleasure economics simply guarantees that users will both pursue personal gains and feel guilty about it.

Pleasure economics allows users to feel the power of reducing others to their neediness, while at the same time allowing users to feel the double guilt of reducing others to their neediness and of not being able to live up to the ideological demands of altruism and of trust. It is easy to see then why the websites and apps of pleasure economics would so embrace and broadcast their guilt-inducing ideology, since guilt can keep users coming back for more and more. For if there is any way to atone for one's guilt it is surely by giving to others and by helping others or, in other words, by participating in pleasure economics. And because users will again fail to be altruistic and again fail to be trusting, the result will of course not be atonement but *more guilt*.

The danger of pleasure economics is precisely this vicious cycle of cruelty, of cruelty both to others and to oneself. Pleasure economics is indeed selfless—not selfless in the sense of altruism but in the sense of the self-destruction of the morality of pity, of reducing others and oneself to nothing while at the same time feeling guilty about it. What must be realized, what is revealed here by bringing Nietzsche and postphenomenology together, is how the technologies of pleasure economics are designed to keep this cycle going, to keep this cycle vicious.

Such design occurs not only in the creation and promotion of the ideology surrounding these technologies but in the technologies themselves. Whether by encouraging users to rate each other, by encouraging users to share pictures with each other, or by encouraging users to swipe each other, the websites and apps of pleasure economics encourage not sharing, not caring, but judging and discriminating. It is not community that is the aim here but superiority, the superiority, first, of being a sharer, of being a crowdfunder, of choosing the moral path of putting people over profit, and second, the superiority of being able to accept and reject, the superiority of having been accepted and not rejected, the superiority of having a higher rating than others who have also been accepted. And because what these apps encourage runs counter to the ideology they promote, one feels not only superior but also guilty for having felt superior, for having felt the pleasure of pursuing power.

But of course if users feel superior thanks to the apps and users feel guilty thanks to the apps, then the true power lies not with the users but with the apps. From a postphenomenological perspective, pleasure economics operates through embodiment relations, as these apps are designed around a dynamic of revealing and withdrawing designed to make us aware of the power of the apps without being aware of how much we rely on the apps to experience that power. The giver therefore is not the user, the giver *is the app*.

The question we must ask ourselves then is not whether we can better design apps to encourage true community-building in lieu of pleasure economics. Rather we must ask whether we have grown so dependent on apps for feeling superior, for feeling powerful, for feeling pleasure, that we can no longer experience community with others without the mediation of, and dependence on, the apps of pleasure economics.

NOTES

1. Nietzsche, *Genealogy*, 135.

2. Achievement, https://www.myachievement.com/ (accessed February 20, 2017).

3. Achievement, https://www.myachievement.com/ (accessed February 22, 2017).

4. The Economist, "The Rise of the Sharing Economy," *The Economist*, March 9, 2013, http://www.economist.com/news/leaders/21573104-internet-everything-hire-rise-sharing-economy.

5. Benita Matofska, "The Secret of the Sharing Economy," *TEDxFrankfurt*, November 29, 2016, available at: https://www.youtube.com/watch?v=-uv3JwpHjrw.

6. Benjamin Edelman, Michael Luca, and Dan Svirsky, "Racial Discrimination in the Sharing Economy: Evidence from a Field Experiment," *American Economic Journal: Applied Economics* (forthcoming), 2–3. Available online: http://www.benedelman.org/publications/airbnb-guest-discrimination-2016-09-16.pdf.

7. Kristen Clarke, "Does Airbnb Enable Racism?," *New York Times*, August 23, 2016, https://www.nytimes.com/2016/08/23/opinion/how-airbnb-can-fight-racial-discrimination.html.

8. Gillian B. White, "Uber and Lyft Are Failing Black Riders," *The Atlantic*, October 31, 2016, https://www.theatlantic.com/business/archive/2016/10/uber-lyft-and-the-false-promise-of-fair-rides/506000/.

9. White, "Uber and Lyft."

10. Joe Pinsker, "How to Succeed in Crowdfunding: Be Thin, White, and Attractive," *The Atlantic*, August 3, 2015, https://www.theatlantic.com/business/archive/2015/08/crowdfunding-success-kickstarter-kiva-succeed/400232/.

11. Jeanette Purvis, "Finding Love in a Hopeless Place: Why Tinder Is So 'Evilly Satisfying'," *Salon*, February 12, 2017, http://www.salon.com/2017/02/12/finding-love-in-a-hopeless-place-why-tinder-is-so-evilly-satisfying/.

12. Drew Harwell, "Online Dating's Age Wars: Inside Tinder and eHarmony's Fight for Our Love Lives," *Washington Post*, April 6, 2015, https://www.washingtonpost.com/news/business/wp/2015/04/06/online-datings-age-wars-inside-tinder-and-eharmonys-fight-for-our-love-lives/.

13. Tinder, https://www.gotinder.com/press(accessed March 5, 2017).

14. Purvis, "Finding Love."

15. Gareth Tyson, et al., "A First Look at User Activity on Tinder," *arXiv*, July 7, 2016, https://arxiv.org/pdf/1607.01952v1.pdf.

16. Nietzsche, *Genealogy*, 45.

17. Nietzsche, *Genealogy*, 19.

18. Nietzsche, *Genealogy*, 65.

7

THUS SPAKE ZUCKERBERG

7.1 HERD INSTINCT

The fourth human-nihilism relation that Nietzsche describes is that of the "herd instinct." Nietzsche writes:

> The "will to mutual aid," to the formation of a herd, to "community," to "congregation," called up in this way is bound to lead to fresh and far more fundamental outbursts of that will to power which it has, even if only to a small extent, aroused: the formation of a herd is a significant victory and advance in the struggle against depression. With the growth of the community, a new interest grows for the individual, too, and often lifts him above the most personal element in his discontent, his aversion to himself (Geulincx's "despectio sui"). All the sick and sickly instinctively strive after a herd organization as a means of shaking off their dull displeasure and feeling of weakness: the ascetic priest divines this instinct and furthers it; wherever there are herds, it is the instinct of weakness that has willed the herd and the prudence of the priest that has organized it.[1]

This relation, the most famous of Nietzsche's human-nihilism relations, shares with the previous relation the attempt to make the sick feel powerful rather than weak. However, rather than help others, here we join with others, for it is in joining with others, in merging our interests and actions with those of other people around us, that we can overcome our individual weaknesses and replace them with the newfound strength of the whole. In groups we are able to avoid not only our powerlessness, not only our burden of accountability, but our very individuality. To join a crowd, to "go with the flow," is to feel the freedom of letting go, of being carried off, of being able to act without thinking, without caring, and often without even being aware that we are acting.

Again following the logic of the will to power, the more we derive strength from those around us, the more we need others in order to feel powerful, and the less able we are to leave the others and risk losing that power. Consequently we identify ourselves more and more by our associations with the group and less and less by our differences with the group. This phenomenon has, since Nietzsche, become the basis of what has come to be known by fans of Orwell as "groupthink" or by rebellious high schoolers as acting like a "sheep."

7.2 FROM HERD INSTINCT TO HERD NETWORKING

Herd networking is my name for the phenomenon of our forming and joining herds technologically rather than in person. Previously we could only band together with those physically near us, but today we can connect to and form groups with anyone, anywhere, so long as they have an internet connection.

Social networking sites such as Facebook, Twitter, and Instagram have hundreds of millions of users, all of whom are people who—according to the Nietzschean language already inherent to social networking—are defined as "followers." Social networks operate by exploiting group psychology, leading users to "follow" the most popular accounts, and to in turn try to become more popular by following not just people but also "trends" or the topics of the day (or, more frequently, of the minute) that the majority of people online are also discussing.

Social networking may seem to privilege uniqueness rather than conformity, as it is those who stand out who get the most noticed. But once one has been noticed, once one has achieved an *online identity*, an identity *worth following*, then what becomes of that uniqueness? Can uniqueness exist in social networking? Can one preserve one's individuality even at the risk of losing one's followers? Or does the discovery of having followers create a gravitational pull, drawing the individual to cater to the demands of maintaining one's following, to preserve one's following at the risk of losing one's individuality, of losing one's uniqueness as a *person* by creating and curating one's uniqueness as a *brand*?

7.3 DISILLUSIONMENT KILLED THE RADIO STAR

In the beginning, there was the CB radio. The citizens band (CB) radio craze of the 1970s contained within it many of the elements that we today take for granted as having been invented by social networking. Or to put it another way, the CB radio was the original social network. Users communicated anonymously with other like-minded or similarly bored users, through slang designed to separate the authentic from the phony, in a technological medium that was defined by its lawlessness. As James Feron wrote in the *New York Times* in 1974:

> The five-watt community radio network, with a range of 15 to 25 miles, was developed in 1958 to fill a variety of commercial and private needs: two-way taxi transmission, truck dispatching, office use, emergency service and the like.

> It has developed, however, into a transcontinental hobby with millions of operators, many of them unlicensed, engaging in the "idle chitchat" that F.C.C. regulations strictly forbid. In some cases the violations are much worse.[2]

CB radios were initially designed and sold for commercial and emergency use, and were installed primarily in commercial trucks, taxis, police cars, ambulances, and fire trucks. The F.C.C. sold licenses to CB radio operators in order to ensure the radios were used properly; licensed users agreed to abide by regulations in using CB radios, which included not only banning personal use of the radio as a hobby or diversion but also prohibited swearing and whistling.

CB radios were made popular for their ability to be used in both personal and communal ways. So popular in fact that while in 1972 there were only 127,000 licensed users, there were 1.7 million license applications granted in 1975, 4.8 million applications granted in 1976, and 4.6 million applications granted in 1977.[3] 1977 marked the height of the CB radio's popularity, as by that time there were 14 million licensed users and an estimated 6 million unlicensed users.[4]

Yet, only a few years after the CB radio reached its peak popularity, applications for CB radio licenses would drop back down to the level of the CB radio's inception in 1958. As Ernest Holsendolph wrote in the *New York Times* in 1983:

> Citizens' band radio, a sociological phenomenon that turned the highways of the 1970's into a giant chattering social circle, is fading in popularity so fast that even the Federal Communications Commission is losing interest. The commission abolished the licensing process today, throwing CB open to all comers of all ages. [. . .] Boredom and disillusion among the once-enthusiastic CB users account for the decline, commission staff members say, but they insist that the craving for "personal communication" among people was probably undiminished.[5]

The CB radio was a fad, having become immensely popular for a time due to its novelty only to be killed off by its own success, with novelty turning to ubiquity turning to boredom. But the "craving" for social networking that the CB radio opened up is still with us to this day, jumping from novelty to novelty as each medium is reduced to a boredom-inducing fad in its turn. But why would the CB radio have led to not only an experience of boredom but also of "disillusion"?

The essential difference from today's social networking is that the CB radio required one to speak rather than to type, and to speak with people who were within the limited range of the CB radio transmitter. Hence while people used "handles" rather than real names, there was nevertheless an intimacy to the anonymity. To hear a voice over the radio, much like hearing a voice over the phone, is to be led to imaginatively fill in the blanks of the disembodied sounds, to picture the person we hear as if they were sitting beside us. And thanks to the range limitations, the opportunity to actually sit beside the person behind the voice was an ever-present possibility.

The medium of the CB radio thus gave users a space open enough to create and play with different identities, while at the same time giving users a space closed enough to offer the potential of being confronted by other users face to face. The allure of this dynamic of the risks and rewards of the CB radio was even a common theme in 1970s pop culture, both in movies (such as *Smokey and the Bandit*) and in music (for example, C. W. McCall's "Convoy").

Disillusionment stems from this allure, from this dream of the CB radio opening users up to new opportunities and new adventures. What one wants in joining a new community is to transcend oneself and to transcend one's reality, to be able to become someone else and to be somewhere else. Yet this someone else one wants to become is not a totally new person but rather the version of oneself one believes to be possible were the limitations of one's present circumstances removed. No longer constrained by geography, by socioeconomic status, by age, race, sex, or creed, CB radio users could just *be themselves* and find and join with others who liked them for who they *truly are*. For even if one invented a radio persona, that invention was still the product of one's creativity, and was thus still representative of one's *true* nature.

Yet as the CB radio slang suggests, and in particular the ability to create glossaries for this slang or "lingo,"[6] the CB radio did not turn out to be the tool for *self*-expression that users may have hoped for. Rules were imposed on CB radio users not only by the F.C.C. but by *other users*. The F.C.C. may have imposed a conformity to law, but users imposed on each other a conformity to language. One had to speak in a certain CB style, using certain CB words, or risk being shunned as either an intruder or an undercover police officer. The CB radio, therefore, started out by promising experimentation and expression but ultimately led to *compliance* and *repetition*. Made popular initially in order to escape the police, users of the CB radio simply became the police, monitoring each other's behavior not in an effort to learn about each other but to maintain and protect the group or, as Nietzsche would call it, *the herd*.

7.4 I EMOJI YOU

The CB radio may have died as a platform for herd networking, but it was reincarnated by CompuServe as one of the world's first computer-based chat rooms, which they named the "CB simulator." The culture of CB radio—wanting to evade the confines of one's culture only to create a new culture with new confines—became the culture of the CB simulator, and of chat rooms in general:

someone at CompuServe decided to replicate the experience on a computer network, and thus the CB simulator was born. If you joined one of the channels—which would later evolve into what we know today as chat rooms—you communicated with other people by typing in CB slang with a lot of 10-4s and other dumb lingo. People would form ersatz social networks, ganging up on interlopers or those not adhering to various policies set down by some boss within the group.[7]

Though chat rooms may have initially maintained the specific slang and rules of CB radio, new slang and new rules emerged:

Many of the structures, rules, and concepts developed by the CB simulator scene carried on into the later chat room concepts. This included the invention of the IM, or instant message, which was sometimes referred to as a PM or personal message. This would be a one-to-one conversation. Someone during this early era came up with an ad hoc rule that it was rude to IM someone without asking first in the larger chat room.[8]

One had to learn the culture of the chat room in order to participate in it as, just like with the CB radio, there was the constant policing of communication to weed out those who did not belong. Thus even though the computer, like the radio, created an atmosphere where users could feel liberated, such liberation nevertheless came through a medium that encouraged and empowered conformity.

Conformity was particularly encouraged in order to get noticed in a chat room. Whereas CB radio channels were an auditory medium, requiring that users take turns speaking and listening to avoid creating an incomprehensible cacophony, chat rooms were a visual medium, making it much easier for users to ignore each other. Chat room users could continuously talk, or type, over each other, creating an unstoppable scrolling screen of text, crushing message after message without a trace, unless of course other users responded and kept the message alive. Accordingly, in much the same way that users were coerced into learning the unwritten rules of chat rooms in order to avoid being shunned, users would consciously or unconsciously learn the habits and tricks of popular users and emulate them in order to avoid being ignored.

While it is painful to be ignored in one's everyday life, it is doubly painful to be ignored in one's chat room life. For the chat room was supposed to be a place where those who were overlooked and unappreciated by others at home, at school, or at work would come together and finally get attention and respect from their like-minded peers. To be ignored by people who one is forced to spend time with is hurtful, but to be ignored by people who one has sought out and chosen to be with is devastating. Though users want to be recognized as individuals, one must first be recognized at all, even if it means mimicking others in the chat room who have already achieved such recognition.[9]

It is no surprise therefore that the evolution of chat rooms tended not toward developing individuality but rather toward developing conformity. So long as chat rooms were text-based, users had to use words to communicate, and even if one did want to communicate through pictures, the pictures were creatively rendered through the ASCII art form of combining letters and symbols into intricate graphic patterns and designs. Yet, rather than encourage user creativity, chat room developers sought to undermine and replace it, turning text-based chatting into picture-based chatting, turning a canvas for ASCII art creation into a space to upload images created by others, resulting most notably in the replacement of user-made emoticons with developer-made emojis.

The creation of emoticons is credited to Scott Fahlman—a computer science professor at Carnegie Mellon—who, on September 19, 1982, sent an email to his colleagues suggesting that they make it more clear when someone was joking on their electronic bulletin board by using a colon, a dash, and a parenthesis.[10] Fahlman recognized that the medium of the electronic bulletin board led people to writing shorter and shorter messages, messages which in turn led to confusion about the intended meaning of the message.

Similarly, emojis were created by Shigetaka Kurita—an employee of a Japanese telecommunications company—who, in 1999, drew 176 cartoon-like images using a 12-pixel by 12-pixel canvas in order to make online communication easier to understand. As Kurita explained:

> Windows 95 had just launched, and email was taking off in Japan alongside the pager boom. But Kurita says people had a hard time getting used to the new methods of communication. In Japanese, personal letters are long and verbose, full of seasonal greetings and honorific expressions that convey the sender's goodwill to the recipient. The shorter, more casual nature of email lead to a breakdown in

communication. "If someone says *Wakarimashita* you don't know whether it's a kind of warm, soft 'I understand' or a 'yeah, I get it' kind of cool, negative feeling," says Kurita. "You don't know what's in the writer's head."[11]

Whereas we may have expected the Japanese letter-writing culture to have simply become translated into a similar email-writing culture, instead the new medium of emails replaced the letter-writing culture. The ensuing "breakdown in communication" did not, however, lead to a return to the more traditional form of text-based communication but instead to a new hybrid form of communication known as "emoji" (a neologism that roughly translates to "picture-word").

Though emojis may appear to be the natural result of the emoticon, Fahlman instead believes that the emoji has killed the spirit of the emoticon. As Fahlman argues, "I think they [emojis] are ugly, and they ruin the challenge of trying to come up with a clever way to express emotions using standard keyboard characters."[12] Emojis, like emoticons, attempt to fix the "breakdown in communication" created by replacing face-to-face communication with computer-to-computer communication. Yet whereas emoticons are a subspecies of ASCII art, created by users, emojis are a subspecies of cartoons, created by telecommunication companies.

Rather than users coming together to share their emoticon creations, emojis are created by corporations coming together in the form of the international corporate conglomerate known as the Unicode Consortium. Unicode created a standardized set of 722 emojis so that users could communicate across providers and across platforms.[13] In other words, Unicode created an emoji language, not to make it easier for users to communicate their individuality but to make it easier for Apple and Android to be able to profit off of users by helping them all to conform to the same ready-made, corporate-designed language.

Emojis have not replaced emoticons as a way to help clarify sentences. Rather, emojis have replaced sentences. According to Luminoso, in 2013 emojis became so popular that on Twitter they appeared in one out of every twenty tweets, more than once in every 600 characters; they were used more often than hyphens, the number 5, the letter V, and were half as common as the # symbol, the symbol which is central to how Twitter operates.[14] The website emojitracker.com shows the real-time use of emojis on Twitter, which occurs so rapidly that the site warns users that watching the real-time use of emojis may cause seizures.

According to emojitracker's stats page, as I am writing this emojis have been used on Twitter 18,585,748,389 times.[15] Currently the most used emoji is the "Face with tears of joy" emoji, also known as the "LOL" emoji, which has been used 1,653,960,266 times, and counting. In second place is the "Heavy black heart" emoji, which has so far been used 753,106,999 times. In other words, LOL is beating all other emojis on Twitter, and it is beating its closest competitor—the symbol for love—at a rate of more than two to one.

Emojis have come to have a power far beyond simply communicating user intentions, as they instead appear to have an intentionality of their own. Attempts have been made to translate *Moby Dick*, *Alice's Adventures in Wonderland*, and even the Bible into emojis.[16] In 2015, a teenager was arrested in New York for having made a "terroristic threat" by posting on Facebook an emoji of a police officer along with pistol emojis aimed at it.[17] In 2016, in response to such court cases, and to the "Disarm the iPhone" campaign of New Yorkers Against Gun Violence, Apple replaced the pistol emoji with a water gun emoji.[18] In other words, emojis have come to have literary, legal, and political significance.

However the most serious controversy surrounding the significance of emojis occurred when Oxford Dictionaries named the "Face with tears of joy" emoji its "Word of the Year" for 2015.[19] The idea that an emoji could not only be considered a word but the most important word for an entire year so incensed people that Oxford Dictionaries produced a very lengthy linguistic argument, defending emojis as comparable to onomatopoeias, pictograms, and sign language.[20] Sam Kriss took this argument one step further, using both Saussure and Derrida to claim that emojis are not only a language unto themselves but the "purest, perfected form"[21] of language. In other words, emojis are not just popular, they have led us to deconstruct our most basic assumptions about what constitutes a language.

Yet the question of whether emojis are meaningful units of communication is not what should concern us here. What should concern us is the question of *whose* meaning is being conveyed by emojis. We are born into languages not of our own making, whether the languages are comprised of words or of emojis. But whereas we individually have the power to remake our given languages through our ability to not only redefine words but to create new words (new words like "emoji"), no such power exists for individual emoji users. People cannot create emojis, only corporations can. Emojis are indeed a language, but they are a language of corporate logos.

In much the same way that "Netflix and chill" has become a euphemism, so too has the eggplant emoji, and both euphemisms reflect the fact that even when users do try to make a corporate language their own, the language nevertheless still refers back to, and ultimately serves to advertise for, the corporation. And indeed the eggplant emoji is actually a better advertisement than is "Netflix and chill," since one can say "Netflix and chill" without either the speaker or listener needing to be a Netflix subscriber, but both the sender and the receiver of the eggplant emoji must have an emoji-capable device. In other words, the emoji *demands conformity*, just as the CB radio and CB radio slang once did.

It should thus not surprise us that in a 2015 poll, while 49.7 percent of respondents said they use emojis because "they help create a more personal connection with the other person," 23.6 percent of respondents said they use emojis because "they are a more contemporary way to communicate," and 19.3 percent said they use emojis because "other people are using them, so I use them too."[22] Hence the experience of a "more personal connection" may result not from the capacity of emojis to convey a user's individuality but from their capacity to convey a user's conformity, conformity to what is "contemporary" and to what "other people are using." Even that users would describe the connection formed by emojis as "personal" may be due to corporations having categorized the apps related to emojis as "personalization" apps. And in 2015 these so-called personalization apps were the "fastest-growing category" of apps, having increased in use by 332 percent from the previous year (for comparison, the next-closest category—"News & Magazines"—increased by only 135 percent).[23] In other words, emojis may transcend the written word, but they do not transcend our *herd instinct* both to conform to whatever is *most popular*, and to justify such conformity by viewing it as what is *most personal*.

7.5 THE HERDBOOK

The best example of our seeking out what is most popular, while viewing what we are seeking as what is most personal, is Facebook. On August 27, 2015, Facebook founder Mark Zuckerberg posted the following status update on his personal Facebook page:

> We just passed an important milestone. For the first time ever, one billion people used Facebook in a single day.
> On Monday, 1 in 7 people on Earth used Facebook to connect with their friends and family.
> When we talk about our financials, we use average numbers, but this is different. This was the first time we reached this milestone, and it's just the beginning of connecting the whole world.
> I'm so proud of our community for the progress we've made. Our community stands for giving every person a voice, for promoting understanding and for including everyone in the opportunities of our modern world.
> A more open and connected world is a better world. It brings stronger relationships with those you love, a stronger economy with more opportunities, and a stronger society that reflects all of our values.
> Thank you for being part of our community and for everything you've done to help us reach this milestone. I'm looking forward to seeing what we accomplish together. [24]

In 2015, Facebook became the first social network to have one billion daily users. And yet, as Zuckerberg points out, this was "just the beginning of connecting the whole world." Indeed, with regard to monthly active users, Facebook passed the 1 billion user mark in 2012, the 1.25 billion mark in 2013, the 1.5 billion mark in 2015, the 1.75 billion mark in 2016, and the 2 billion mark in 2017 (it currently has 2.19 billion monthly active users). [25] In other words, Facebook is not only the most popular social network in the world (for comparison, Instagram has 600 million active monthly users and Twitter has 317 million actively monthly users), [26] its popularity has been, and continues to be, steadily increasing.

In fact, Facebook is so popular that a better comparison for its size and reach would not be contemporary social networks like Instagram and Twitter but rather more traditional social networks like Christianity (2.2 billion members), Islam (1.6 billion members), and Hinduism (1 billion members).[27] If we return to Zuckerberg's aforementioned status update, we can see that Facebook is like a world religion not only in *influence* but also in *purpose*. As Zuckerberg emphasizes, Facebook is more than a social network, it is a "community," a community that "stands for giving every person a voice, for promoting understanding and for including everyone in the opportunities of our modern world." What Zuckerberg is here preaching is simply the religion of Facebook, as it is through Facebook—and *only* through Facebook—that one can have a *voice* (status updates), achieve *understanding* (News Feed), and be *included* (friended).

To be a user of Facebook is to be an evangelist for Facebook, to be guided by, and a missionary for, its gospel. For as Zuckerberg makes clear, Facebook has a mission, the mission of "connecting the whole world" since "a more open and connected world is a better world." And it is precisely this mission that Facebook users are spreading, since one does not use Facebook without trying to get others to join Facebook, and one does not try to get others to join Facebook without promising them in some degree that joining will make their lives, their world, *better*. Though we of course do not often spread this gospel in words but rather in tone and facial expression, in the incredulity we express when we meet someone who is somehow *not on Facebook*.

To make this evangelizing point even clearer, Zuckerberg adds that the *better world* found through the light of Facebook is a world where users have not only "stronger relationships" and a "stronger economy" but "a stronger society that reflects all of our values." Yet 1.86 billion people spread all over the globe could not possibly have all of their values reflected in society, even if that society is Facebook. Though perhaps what Zuckerberg is suggesting is that either we must have values in common in order to be drawn to using Facebook in the first place or that, by using Facebook, we will all eventually come to have the same values, the values of Facebook, by Facebook, and for Facebook.

That Facebook is a source of values is clear in Zuckerberg wanting to create not only a "connected" world but a "more open" world. And it is indeed the *openness* that Facebook *demands* that is often the source of contention between users, nonusers, and Facebook. For while openness has been central to social networking from the start—from bulletin board systems (BBS) to AOL and Yahoo! groups to Friendster, LinkedIn, and Myspace—no other social network has *enforced* openness and *undermined* privacy to the degree that Facebook has. Or, as Zuckerberg would argue, no other social network has done more to *redefine* privacy by revealing to us how traditional notions of privacy constrain us, preventing us from connecting to the world, to a *better world*.

From its very beginning Facebook has operated from the presupposition that users want to be open with each other and with the world, a presupposition that has led Facebook to take an *opt-out* rather than an *opt-in* approach to privacy *modifications*. For example, in 2007, Facebook began reporting the online shopping habits of users on their News Feeds; in 2009, Facebook made public by default the name, profile picture, and gender of users; and in 2010, Facebook put its "Like" button on third-party sites, allowing those sites to have both instant access to user information and the ability to track users for the purposes of behavioral advertising.[28]

More recently, Facebook sought to redefine not only privacy but autonomy.[29] In 2014, Facebook's data scientists conducted an experiment to determine whether users could be "emotionally manipulated" by secretly changing the News Feed algorithm of 689,003 users such that they saw either only positive or only negative posts, with the aim being to see if those users then started sharing only positive or only negative status updates.[30] Zuckerberg wanted to know if Facebook had the power not only to make users more open, but whether it had the power to make users feel happy or sad. In other words, Zuckerberg wanted to know whether Facebook had the power of a god over its users. The true test of this godlike power, however, came not in the experiment itself but in informing the world about the experiment. By not only publishing the results of the experiment but by publishing them with a title so brazen—"Experimental Evidence of Massive Scale Emotional Contagion through Social Networks"[31]—one cannot help but wonder if the true experiment was not to see whether Facebook could emotionally manipulate its users but whether Facebook could tell the world its users were being emotionally manipulated and still continue to increase its number of users.

And indeed, even after all of these brazen attacks on privacy, attacks for which Facebook has been forced to retreat and apologize, the number of users continues to steadily increase. Considering how difficult it is to unfriend someone on Facebook, even someone who has become an enemy, it should be no surprise how much more difficult it is to unfriend Facebook itself. Facebook has become the medium through which we experience not only our friendships but the world. With functionalities that include searching the internet, private and group messaging, video streaming, planning events, playing games, uploading photos and videos, and hosting pages for celebrities and businesses, Facebook has sought to provide users more than a service on the internet, it has sought to provide users an internet within the internet, a one-stop shop for everything the internet has to offer. The aim of Facebook is to let users do everything on Facebook, or to put it another way, the aim of Facebook is to let users *do nothing without Facebook*.

Due to its success, Facebook operates not with a "customer is always right" mentality but with a "if you don't like it, then quit" mentality. Facebook dares individuals to not use Facebook. I say *individuals* because the nature of the dare is that either *everyone* quits Facebook or *no one* quits Facebook. So long as one's friends, family, coworkers, acquaintances, exes, former classmates, and political leaders are on Facebook, then to not have a Facebook account is to no longer be "connected," to no longer be part of the "relationships," "economy," and "society" of Facebook. And considering that users can post photos and status updates about anyone, one can be on Facebook (as content) without being on Facebook (as a user). Furthermore, as Facebook continues to expand, more and more services (for example, Tinder) require the use of a Facebook account as a form of authentication. In other words, it is increasingly becoming impossible to have an *individual identity* without first having a *Facebook identity*.

Another reason that people do not leave Facebook is that Facebook not only dares users to choose between having privacy or being connected, it dares users to join in the fun of invading the privacy of others. Of all the services that Facebook offers, none is more enjoyable, more enticing, more of a "guilty pleasure" than that of voyeurism. For while we decry Facebook as a threat to privacy, we are nevertheless using Facebook to peer into the lives of others, to gain access to a steady stream of the day-to-day experiences of others. By allowing users to sift through the timelines of other users undetected—since without a comment or a "Like" there is no trace of our snooping—Facebook is inviting users to not only spy on each other but to be confederates in Facebook's anti-privacy mission, for the more Facebook invades the privacy of its users, the more its users can invade the privacy of each other.

Hence to quit Facebook is to not only risk *exile*, it is to risk being a *hypocrite*.

Facebook has formed the world's largest herd, and maintained its herd, through the double-edged sword of the simple mantra: *Everyone is doing it*. Everyone is on Facebook, so to not be on Facebook is to be left out, to no longer be part of the *everyone*. Everyone is on Facebook, so whatever one does on Facebook is what everyone does on Facebook, so whatever one does on Facebook is no better and no worse than what everyone else does on Facebook. Facebook has in other words become what is *normal*. Posting personal opinions is normal. Posting intimate photos is normal. Posting your current whereabouts is normal. So normal in fact that to worry that these things should be kept private is to reveal oneself to have outdated and *abnormal* values.

In a world dominated by Facebook, a world dominated by *openness*, to want to maintain privacy is to be *closed*, to be suspiciously concerned more with *cutting oneself off* than with *sharing with everyone*. Due to this peer pressure, sharing with everyone has become a habit, a second nature, an instinct we experience so readily that it is impossible to determine if we post on Facebook because we want to share our experiences or if we want to have experiences *because we want to post on Facebook*. The nihilistic concern of this herd networking then is the question of whether Facebook has become a new place to live or a new *reason for living*.

7.6 THE DANGERS OF HERD NETWORKING

There is nothing inherently wrong with wanting to join a herd. Indeed there is much to be gained from joining a herd: community, strength, security. But these gains come with a price, the price of the communal identity replacing the individual's identity, the strength of the whole diminishing the need for the strength of the individual, and the security the herd provides becoming a threat against individuals ever taking the risk of leaving the herd.

To be in a herd is to lose oneself. The question then is whether losing oneself is necessarily an act of *self-destruction* or could instead be an act of *self-discovery*. For while Nietzsche argued that we wish to lose ourselves in the herd because we are sick of ourselves, others might argue that we wish to lose ourselves in the herd because it is through others that we find ourselves. To give oneself over to a group, a cause, a website, could be seen as a way of hiding from ourselves, as a form of *evasion*, but it could also be seen as a way of finding our purpose, as a form of *elevation*.

The worry here though comes from precisely this ambivalence, from this inability to determine what precisely our motivations are. As was seen in the previous analyses of herd networking, it is difficult to untangle not only the individual from the herd but the actions of the individual from the reasons given by the individual for those actions. Nietzsche points to this ambiguity by arguing that though it is our instincts that lead us to seek out others, to seek out a herd with which to join, it is the "priest" who forms and maintains the herd, it is the priest who "divines this instinct and furthers it."[32]

The question of whether the role of the priest is positive or negative, beneficial or dangerous, goes back at least as far as the debate between Socrates and Thrasymachus in Book I of Plato's *Republic*.[33] For while Socrates likens a leader to a doctor who works for the betterment of others rather than of himself, Thrasymachus instead likens a leader to a shepherd. From the perspective of the sheep, the shepherd is viewed precisely as Socrates describes a leader, as caring and protective. But from the perspective of the shepherd, the care and protection is merely a means to an end, the shepherd's end, the end of fattening the sheep for the slaughter. Socrates is not wrong therefore according to Thrasymachus, rather Socrates is simply naïve, too naïve to see the *bigger picture*.

Similarly what should concern us here is not whether the priests of herd networking—the Mark Zuckerbergs and the Jack Dorseys—are helping us or hurting us but rather whether we are able to see the bigger picture. Facebook and Twitter, much like the CB radio and chat room before them, certainly offer a space for people to find each other and to find themselves. But this is not all that such spaces offer. For, following Thrasymachus, what we should be on the lookout for here is not *what* herd networking provides for us but rather *how* and *why* herd networking is provided for us.

From the perspective of users, Facebook and Twitter are venues for self-expression, for creating and maintaining relationships, and for news and entertainment. But from the perspective of Zuckerberg and Dorsey, Facebook and Twitter are venues for *content* and for *advertising*. Self-expression is content. Relationships are content. News and entertainment are content. The more time users spend creating and consuming content, the more time users spend on the site consuming advertising. Since it is advertising and not users that generate profits for these "free" networks, these networks exist ultimately to serve advertisers, not users, as it is the advertisers who are the networks' paying customers, not the users. Or, as Zuckerberg and Dorsey would put it, since the advertising is increasingly targeted to users, serving the advertisers *is* serving the users.

If social networks operate like a religion, they are a religion whose holiest texts are blank. Facebook, Twitter, Instagram, Reddit are, like the CB radio, empty spaces, voids waiting to be filled by the content created not by them, not by the priests, but by users, by the herd itself. In other words, the herd consumes itself and the herd entertains itself. The job of the priests, of the networks, is then not to *provide* but to *preserve*. The challenge for any herd network priest therefore is to motivate the herd to continuously generate content for the network, and to continue to generate content for the network without being scared off by the increasing supply of content created by advertisers. For just as sheep might lose faith in the shepherd if they saw the shepherd's customers waiting hungrily nearby, so too might users lose faith in the networks if they saw the network's customers waiting greedily nearby.

The priests have discovered that the solution to this challenge is to make the distinction between user-generated content and advertiser-generated content *disappear*. This is achieved, on the one hand, through the use of targeted advertising, for the more that the advertisements appear to be *for you*, the more that the advertisements look like something *you chose* to have in your network rather than something merely *designed* to look like something *you would choose* to have in your network. This strategy is once more a cause of and justification for the privacy invasions of these networks, since in order to design advertisements for users the advertisers must know as much about the users as possible. The spirit of openness championed by Zuckerberg is thus not coincidentally also the spirit of targeted advertising.

The *better world* this creates is a world where not only users can find each other more easily but also where users and advertisers can find each other more easily. As has become increasingly common, to look up flights on one website is to have an advertisement for discount vacations instantly appear in your network. While this may have at first made users feel like they were being spied on, stalked, and hunted, over time users have grown accustomed to targeted advertisements, as is indicated by the seemingly unstoppable growth of social networks. This does not necessarily mean that users *want* these targeted advertisements, of course, particularly since the "If you don't like it, you can quit" dare of social networks makes users increasingly unlikely, and increasingly *unable*, to bother questioning whether these targeted advertisements are wanted or not.

Social networks erode the boundary between user-generated content and advertiser-generated content by using user data to help advertisers target users, to *help advertisers turn into users*, users who look and act just like the users with whom you would (or, based on your data, *should*) want to share a network. Aesop would perhaps call this the wolf-in-sheep's-clothing strategy. On the other hand, this erosion is also achieved by networks helping users to target each other, to *help users turn into advertisers*. Plautus would perhaps call this the man-is-wolf-to-man strategy.

As we saw with the CB radio, with the chat room, and with the emoji, there is not only a spirit of openness in herd networking but also a spirit of conformity. However, while the conformity of the CB radio and of the chat room was often a by-product of users policing each other in order to make sure they belonged, and of users trying to meet others through mimicking what was popular, emojis—and the contemporary social networks that breed them—take conformity much further, aided and abetted not only by peer pressure but by the networks themselves. For in the spaces provided by social networks we find not only users, advertisers, and the content that they generate but also algorithms, algorithms that determine which content is seen and which content is not.

Perhaps the most famous instance of the gate-keeping role that algorithms play in social networks occurred during the 2014 protests in Ferguson, Missouri. On Twitter, the top trending topic was the murder of Michael Brown by a Ferguson police officer, the ensuing protests by the community, and the militaristic attempts by the police to stop the protests. On Facebook, rather than Ferguson, one found cute uplifting posts about the ALS Ice Bucket Challenge. One BuzzFeed writer even went so far as to create a fake "life event" in the form of a wedding announcement on Facebook in order to comment on the Michael Brown story as a way to try to prevent discussion of the incidents in Ferguson from disappearing from Facebook News Feeds.[34]

The reason for this disparity was due to how differently the algorithms of the two networks operate. Facebook's News Feed algorithms promote certain posts but not others, and promote certain users but not others. The rationale for this promotion and demotion is, like the rationale of most algorithms (as was discussed in the chapter on data-driven activity), unknown, which simply leads users to speculate. But by promoting the ice bucket challenge and demoting Ferguson, Facebook did at least confirm that, in its quest to never give users a reason to leave, it promotes what is most likely to increase user engagement and demotes what is least likely to increase user engagement. In other words, users did "Like" the ice bucket challenge but did not "Like" Ferguson.

The effect of the News Feed's algorithmic arbiter is that users similarly post what is most likely to increase "friend" engagement and avoid posting what is least likely to increase "friend" engagement. Facebook is filled with baby photos and cat photos because users are most likely to "Like" baby photos and cat photos. The same goes for fun vacation photos, fun "night out" photos, and fun "life event" photos. In other words, Facebook promotes fun, and users post what is fun, because on Facebook *fun* equals *increased likelihood of engagement*.

Each day, Facebook tells users whose birthday it is, and provides a prompt to make it easy for users to wish each other a happy birthday, because remembering the birthdays of people who are supposedly your "friend" is difficult, but wishing each other a happy birthday is *fun*. And, as David Plotz discovered when he ran his own Facebook experiment,[35] users will even wish the same person—the same "friend"—a happy birthday *multiple times in the same month* because, on the one hand, Facebook algorithmically prompted them to do so and, on the other hand, because it's *fun*. Though *fun* means *increased engagement*, increased engagement does not appear to mean that we must actually *be engaged*. Not unlike when a cashier says, "Enjoy your meal!" and we respond with a mindlessly inappropriate, "Thanks, you too!", we can and do respond to prompts on Facebook without having to pay any attention to what we are being prompted to do. After all, if Facebook is prompting us to do it, it must be fun.

Twitter's algorithms, unlike Facebook's News Feed algorithms, monitor what topics users are tweeting about and prominently display a regularly updating list of these "trending" topics for all users to see. Because of the prominence of these trends, and because of the ability to gain visibility beyond one's followers by tweeting about these trends, it is difficult to determine whether these trending topics *reflect* what is currently being most discussed on Twitter or *create* what is currently being most discussed on Twitter. This ambiguity has even led to conspiracy theories about Twitter artificially promoting trending topics of one end of the political spectrum or censoring trending topics of the other end of the political spectrum.[36]

Such conspiracy theories are likely due in no small part to the confusion (and, from a postphenomenological perspective, the "hermeneutic faith") surrounding these algorithms. Twitter can give users the false impression that what one sees on one's timeline is what *everyone* (rather than only those one follows) is talking about. Twitter can also give users the false impression that what one sees trending is what *everyone* (rather than only those living in the same geographical area that the trend algorithm is set to monitor) is talking about. Lastly, Twitter can also give users the false impression that what is on one's timeline or what is trending on Twitter is what *everyone* (rather than only some percentage of the 313 million active users of Twitter) is talking about. And of course, if one leaves Twitter's herds-within-herds—even if only to enter Facebook's herds-within-herds—it can be quite disorienting to discover that somehow *no one* (in one herd) seems to know what *everyone* (in another herd) is talking about.

It is Twitter's ability to make users feel as though they are in touch with what *everyone* is talking about, and what everyone is talking about *right now*, that leads users to want to be part of *the conversation*. Just as advertisers follow what is trending in the pursuit of increasing clicks, so too do users follow what is trending in the pursuit of increasing followers. And because a trending topic shows what is being tweeted about the topic independently of the relevance of the tweet, users can increase their viewership, if not their following, by tweeting about *what* is trending whether or not they know *why* a topic is trending or have anything *meaningful* to tweet about the topic. Just as Facebook drives users to be *fun*, Twitter drives users to be *fashionable*, but in both cases, on both networks, users are simply trying to be *seen*.

Posting what is fun and what is fashionable in order to be seen is to post what has come to be known as *clickbait*. It has become commonplace to accuse corporations of posting mindless clickbait to get attention. It has likewise become commonplace for individual users to post mindless clickbait to get attention. We may have begun by simply engaging with clickbait, by taking personality quizzes in order to find out which Harry Potter school we would have been sent to or which *Sex in the City* character we are most like. But we have discovered that posting the results of these clickbait quizzes, these quizzes meant to increase user engagement with *corporations*, has led users to increase their engagement with *us*.

Rather than merely share the clickbait created by corporations, we have evolved to create our own clickbait, turning ourselves into mini-corporations in the process. Quizzes are popular, so we make our own quiz-like games with hashtags directing people to all make the same joke, such as by making the same puns (#CatTVShows) or by trying to reduce some aspect of life to three words (#MyPerfectDateIn3Words). Memes are popular, so we post memes, and use meme-making apps or websites to make our own memes. GIFs are popular, so we post GIFs, and use GIF-making apps or websites to make our own GIFs. Essayistic Facebook posts and threaded Twitter rants are popular, so we post essayist Facebook posts and threaded Twitter rants or, if that requires too much thought and effort, we simply repost someone else's post or rant (though of course, in order to make sure we get the engagement we're seeking, we add some useful bit of insight to the post or rant like a fire emoji or a "THIS" or a "SO MUCH THIS").

Conforming to what is popular in order to become popular oneself is of course nothing new. But in herd networking, is there even a *self* that is doing the conforming? Facebook recommends posts to us. Twitter recommends trends to us. Facebook and Twitter not only use algorithms to curate content for us, they use algorithms to *create* content for us. Facebook Messenger has even moved from recommending autocorrected words to recommending emojis and GIFs for us to use instead of words. Twitter bots allow users to create Twitter accounts that tweet for them. Increasingly there is little that is *social* about social networks. Or, to put it another way, the sociality of social networking is increasingly taking place between *algorithms*, not between *people*.

Herd networking is nihilistic because it is a technologically driven exploitation of our instinct for conformity, because it is a never-ending, emoji-fueled, individual-eroding pursuit of popularity. But herd networking is also nihilistic because it combines within it elements of techno-hypnosis, data-driven activity, and pleasure economics. We zone out on social networks. We post content on social networks because they tell us to. We reduce friends to "friends," humans to "followers," and ourselves to corporate-like "content" mills, all in the pursuit of having the *highest score* on our social networks. Nietzsche likened nihilism to a disease. And today, fittingly, we call this disease *going viral*.

NOTES

1. Nietzsche, *Genealogy*, 135–36.

2. James Feron, "Problems Plague Citizens Band Radio," *New York Times*, April 2, 1974, http://www.nytimes.com/1974/04/02/archives/problems-plague-citizens-band-radio-violations-abound.html.

3. Edwin McDowell, "C.B. Radio Industry Is More in Tune After 2 Years of Static," *New York Times*, April 17, 1978, http://www.nytimes.com/1978/04/17/archives/cb-radio-industry-is-more-in-tune-after-2-years-of-static-added.html.

4. Ernest Holsendolph, "Fading CB Craze Signals End to Licensing," *New York Times*, April 28, 1983, http://www.nytimes.com/1983/04/28/us/fading-cb-craze-signals-end-to-licensing.html.

5. Holsendolph, "Fading CB Craze."

6. See for example the appendix "Channel Jive (CBers Lingo)," in Bonnie Crystal and Jeffrey Keating, *The World of CB Radio* (Summertown, NY: Book Publishing Company, 1987), 223–31.

7. John C. Dvorak, "Chat Rooms Are Dead! Long Live the Chat Room!," *PCMag*, December 11, 2007, http://www.pcmag.com/article2/0,2817,2231493,00.asp.

8. Dvorak, "Chat Rooms."

9. However, the chat room's game of follow-the-leader does not mean that there actually *is* a leader, that there actually *is* at least *one person* in the chat room who is able to gain recognition by being authentic.

10. Paul Bignell, "Happy 30th Birthday Emoticon! :-)," *The Independent*, September 8, 2012, http://www.independent.co.uk/life-style/gadgets-and-tech/news/happy-30th-birthday-emoticon-8120158.html.

11. Jeff Blagdon, "How Emoji Conquered the World," *The Verge*, March 4, 2013, http://www.theverge.com/2013/3/4/3966140/how-emoji-conquered-the-world.

12. Bignell, "Happy 30th Birthday!"

13. Adam Sternbergh, "Smile, You're Speaking Emoji," *New York Magazine*, November 16, 2014, http://nymag.com/daily/intelligencer/2014/11/emojis-rapid-evolution.html.

14. Luminoso, "Emoji Are More Common than Hyphens. Is Your Software Ready?," *Luminoso Blog*, September 4, 2013, https://blog.luminoso.com/2013/09/04/emoji-are-more-common-than-hyphens/.

15. Emojitracker, http://emojitracker.com/api/stats (accessed April 8, 2017).

16. Beckett Mufson, "Author Translates All of 'Alice in Wonderland' into Emojis," *Vice*, January 2, 2015, https://creators.vice.com/en_uk/article/author-translates-all-of-alice-in-wonderland-into-emojis.

17. Vyvyan Evans, "Beyond Words: How Language-like Is Emoji?," *OUPblog*, April 16, 2016, https://blog.oup.com/2016/04/how-language-like-is-emoji/

18. Heather Kelly, "Apple Replaces the Pistol Emoji with a Water Gun," *CNN*, August 2, 2016, http://money.cnn.com/2016/08/01/technology/apple-pistol-emoji/.

19. Oxford Dictionaries, "Word of the Year 2015," *Oxford Dictionaries Blog*, http://blog.oxforddictionaries.com/2015/11/word-of-the-year-2015-emoji/

20. Evans, "Beyond Words."

21. Sam Kriss, "Emojis Are the Most Advanced Form of Literature Known to Man," *Vice*, November 18, 2015, https://www.vice.com/en_dk/article/sam-kriss-laughing-and-crying.

22. Statista, "Leading Reasons for Using Emojis According to U.S. Internet Users as of August 2015," *Statista*, https://www.statista.com/statistics/476354/reasons-usage-emojis-internet-users-us/.

23. Felix Richter, "The Fastest-Growing App Categories in 2015," *Statista*, January 22, 2016, https://www.statista.com/chart/4267/fastest-growing-app-categories-in-2015/.

24. Mark Zuckerberg, "We Just Passed an Important Milestone," *Facebook*, August 27, 2015, https://www.facebook.com/zuck/posts/10102329188394581.

25. Statista, "Number of Monthly Active Facebook Users Worldwide as of 3rd Quarter 2017 (in Millions)," *Statista*, https://www.statista.com/statistics/264810/number-of-monthly-active-facebook-users-worldwide/.

26. Statista, "Most Famous Social Network Sites Worldwide as of September 2017, Ranked by Number of Active Users (in Millions)," *Statista*, https://

www.statista.com/statistics/272014/global-social-networks-ranked-by-number-of-users/.

27. Pew Research Center, "The Future of World Religions: Population Growth Projections, 2010–2050," *Pew Research Center*, April 2, 2015, http://www.pewforum.org/2015/04/02/religious-projections-2010-2050/.

28. Richard A. Spinello, "Privacy and Social Networking Technology," *International Review of Information Ethics* 16 (12/2011), 43–44.

29. Nolen Gertz, "Autonomy Online: Jacques Ellul and the Facebook Emotional Manipulation Study," *Research Ethics* 12 (2016), 55–61.

30. Kashmir Hill, "Facebook Manipulated 689,003 Users' Emotions for Science," *Forbes*, June 28, 2014, https://www.forbes.com/sites/kashmirhill/2014/06/28/facebook-manipulated-689003-users-emotions-for-science/.

31. Adam D. I. Kramer, et al., "Experimental Evidence of Massive-Scale Emotional Contagion through Social Networks," *PNAS* 111, no. 24 (2014), 8788–90.

32. Nietzsche, *Genealogy*, 135–36.

33. Plato, *Republic*, trans. G. M. A. Grube (Indianapolis: Hackett, 1992), 17–23 (341c–348a).

34. Charlie Warzel, "How Ferguson Exposed Facebook's Breaking News Problem," *BuzzFeed*, August 19, 2014, https://www.buzzfeed.com/charliewarzel/in-ferguson-facebook-cant-deliver-on-its-promise-to-deliver.

35. David Plotz, "My Fake Facebook Birthdays," *Slate*, August 2, 2011, http://www.slate.com/articles/technology/technology/2011/08/my_fake_facebook_birthdays.html.

36. Laura Sydell, "How Twitter's Trending Topics Algorithm Picks Its Topics," *NPR*, December 7, 2011, http://www.npr.org/2011/12/07/143013503/how-twitters-trending-algorithm-picks-its-topics.

8

THE TROLLING OF THE IDOLS

8.1 ORGIES OF FEELING

The fifth and final human-nihilism relation that Nietzsche analyzes is that of "orgies of feelings," which Nietzsche describes as, unlike the previous four, a "guilty" form of treating our nihilistic sickness. Nietzsche writes:

> To wrench the human soul from its moorings, to immerse it in terrors, ice, flames, and raptures to such an extent that it is liberated from all petty displeasure, gloom, and depression as by a flash of lightning . . . Fundamentally, every great affect has this power, provided it explodes suddenly: anger, fear, voluptuousness, revenge, hope, triumph, despair, cruelty; and the ascetic priest has indeed pressed into his service indiscriminately the *whole* pack of savage hounds in man and let loose now this one and now that, always with the same end in view: to awaken men from their slow melancholy, to hunt away, if only for a time, their dull pain and lingering misery, and always under cover of a religious interpretation and "justification." Every such orgy of feeling has to be *paid* for afterward, that goes without saying—it makes the sick sicker; and that is why this kind of cure for pain is, by modern standards, "guilty."[1]

We can lose ourselves not only in mindless activities or in the presence of others but even in our own emotions. Since at least the time of the Ancient Greeks and their notion of the Furies we have had the idea that we can be overcome with emotion, so overcome that we have legally recognized this aspect of ourselves through the category of the "crime of passion." Blinded by love or by rage, what is important is that we are blinded, momentarily unable to experience any reality other than that of the pleasure of letting ourselves go—both in the sense of unleashing an emotional outburst and of evading any sense of the self behind the outburst.

In such orgiastic fever dreams we carry out actions that we would never carry out otherwise, for which reason this human-nihilism relation can be seen as combining elements of the previous four human-nihilism relations. Emotional outbursts allow us to avoid feeling the burden of consciousness, the burden of accountability, the burden of powerlessness, and the burden of individuality. In such a state we will likely do things that we will later regret, but what matters is that we will regret them *later*, for it is the moment that matters, and yet, in the moment, *nothing matters*.

8.2 FROM ORGIES OF FEELING TO ORGIES OF CLICKING

Orgies of clicking is my term for the phenomenon of our increasing tendency to express our orgies of feeling in and through technologies. While Nietzsche may have been describing the riots, uprisings, and revolutionary atmosphere of nineteenth-century Europe, today we have flash mobs, viral memes, and the ability to take down leaders, celebrities, and each other with little more than the click of a button.

Thanks to the multistability of technologies, no technology is inherently a tool for joy or a tool for rage. A megaphone, like the talismanic conch shell of *Lord of the Flies*, can be used to bring people together or to tear them apart. A soapbox on a street corner can be a gathering place around a performer or a gathering place around a reformer. And indeed often one does not know when one comes upon a crowd what precisely is in the center, what precisely has brought together the crowd, but seeing a crowd leads us to trust that there must be *something* in the center, something *worth gathering around*. To hear a megaphone, to see someone atop a soapbox, is to have one's attention piqued, is to have one's *herd instinct* aroused, is to be led to *react* to someone else having simply taken the initiative, the bold, *unherdlike* initiative, to *act*.

What we have seen thus far in our analyses of technology is that the megaphone and the soapbox do not merely serve to amplify the voice of the speaker; they do not merely serve as neutral devices for someone who has already made the decision to have their voice amplified. To see a megaphone or a soapbox is to be presented with the means, opportunity, and motive for amplifying one's voice, whether or not there is any *desire* or *decision* to be a speaker. In much the same way that passing a piano can lead us to stop and play it, whether or not we know how to play it, passing a megaphone or a soapbox can lead us to stop and speak, whether or not we have anything to say. In other words, a megaphone or a soapbox, like any other technology, can not only fulfill our intentions, it can also shape and even create our intentions. For this reason, given a *how* such as a megaphone or a soapbox, we can often find ourselves speaking without knowing necessarily *what* we are saying, or *why*.

From the listener's perspective however, there is no way of knowing whether and to what degree the *how* is leading the *what* and the *why*, as all that is known is *that* someone is making their voice heard, *that* someone has designated themselves as a speaker, *that* someone has determined that others *should listen*. This normative claim operating behind speaking, behind taking up a megaphone or a soapbox and constituting oneself as someone who *should* be heard and others as those who *should* listen, is what can lead a crowd to turn against a speaker, to want revenge against a speaker who did not live up to the other side of this normative claim, who did not live up to the implied promise that the speaker *would* be worth listening to.

Hence it should not surprise us that we often have no qualms against giving in to our herd instinct and forming a crowd around anyone holding a megaphone, around anyone atop a soapbox. For if the speaker is worth listening to, then we can be led to participate in an orgy of feeling, and if the speaker is not worth listening to, then we can be led to participate in an orgy of feeling. Whether the speaker inspires us to express joy or rage, to celebrate or to conflagrate, to attack others in revenge or to attack the speaker in revenge, all that matters is that the speaker has created an opportunity for an outburst. This perhaps helps to explain why, as a Chapman University survey has shown (and as Jerry Seinfeld liked to joke about), people are more afraid of public speaking than they are of dying.[2]

Public speaking, the very idea of public speaking, creates anxiety for many of us. Perhaps the reason for this anxiety—an anxiety that apparently ranks above that produced by the thought of death—is that we intuitively grasp the threat that public speaking carries with it, the threat of getting the attention of a crowd, of a crowd that could at any moment turn into a mob. Yet a megaphone or a soapbox can lead us not to *overcome* our anxieties about public speaking but to *forget* them. Techno-hypnotically, a megaphone or a soapbox can serve to lead us to not necessarily want to *become* public speakers but to at least *play* at public speaking, to forget the world we belong to and instead belong to the worlds we have seen in TV and movies, worlds where a hero rallied a crowd with a megaphone or gave a stirring speech from a soapbox.

A megaphone or a soapbox can also serve, as an embodiment relation, to amplify our voices and to reduce our awareness of the technologies artificially amplifying our voices. In other words, it is easy to be seduced, while using a megaphone or a soapbox, into not taking seriously the possible ramifications of suddenly being heard by a much larger crowd than that to which one is accustomed. But if a megaphone or a soapbox can lead us to speak before we know *what* to say, and to speak before we even know *that* we are speaking, then how much more pervasive is this phenomenon, how much more dangerous is the crowd that is gathered, when one speaks instead through a digital megaphone like YouTube or a soapbox with instant push notifications like Twitter?

8.3 NEVER READ THE COMMENTS

Whether one is watching puppy videos or reading recipe blogs, it only takes an accidental scroll too far down the page to be confronted with the worst hate-filled non sequiturs humanity has to offer. Consequently, if there is one universally agreed-upon law of the internet, it is: *Never read the comments*. And yet according to a study conducted by the British newspaper the *Guardian*, of the over 70 million comments their site had received between 1999 and 2016, only 1.4 million (or 2 percent of the total number of comments) were considered to be so "abusive" or "off-topic" as to require that the comment be blocked from the site for having "violated the *Guardian*'s community standards."[3] So why do the 2 percent seem to so outweigh the 98 percent that we practically take no notice of them? Why do we advise each other to avoid comments sections? Why do we take it for granted that there is nothing but hate to be found in comments sections?

Indeed the *Guardian* carried out a study of their comments sections precisely due to the impression that the site was becoming over-whelmed by comments that were "crude, bigoted, or just vile." What the *Guardian* found however was that while, *overall*, the comments on the site were largely in keeping with the spirit of the comments sec-tion—allowing readers to "respond to an article instantly, asking ques-tions, pointing out errors, giving new leads"—this spirit was not neces-sarily found in the comments section of articles written by authors who were not white men:

> Although the majority of our regular opinion writers are white men, we found that those who experienced the highest levels of abuse and dismissive trolling were not. The 10 regular writers who got the most abuse were eight women (four white and four non-white) and two black men. Two of the women and one of the men were gay. And of the eight women in the "top 10", one was Muslim and one Jewish.

And the 10 regular writers who got the least abuse? All men.[4]

Comments sections are spaces for democratic discussion and debate. Comments sections are vile cesspools full of bigotry and sexism. These two perceptions of comments sections are not mutually exclusive. It seems—at least based on the evidence from the study performed by the *Guardian*—that the former perception is true for white men, while the latter perception is true for everyone else. But why is this the case? Even if it were true that all commenters are bigots and sexists, this would not explain why bigots and sexists flock to comments sections, nor would it explain why bigots and sexists post their bigotry and sexism in the way that they tend to post it. So the question remains: What is it about comments sections that invites "crude, bigoted, or just vile" com-ments?

Reading the comments section of any internet page can feel like reading a stall in a public bathroom. And indeed the internet and a public bathroom stall do have much in common, in particular *anonym-ity* and a *captive audience*. However a comments section could also be compared to graffiti. While graffiti does, like a bathroom stall, contain vulgarity, it also contains works of art. A wall is for many a canvas, a blank space crying out to be filled, to be turned into a public display of one's creativity, whether that creativity is fueled by joy, by rage, or by something else entirely. The same could be said for a comments section, if not for the internet itself, and yet whereas graffiti appears to often express the sentiment *I exist!* (for example, "[Name] was here"), a comments section appears to instead often express the sentiment *You should not exist!* (for example, "Kill yourself").

The most obvious explanation for why a comments section is frequently more like a bathroom stall than like graffiti is that both a comments section and a bathroom stall are places where people go, not to be creative, but to relieve themselves of a burden. This need for relief, for "blowing off steam," is what Freud referred to as "sublimation," what Nietzsche referred to as our need to "discharge" our instincts, and what today we refer to as "trolling."

> Feeling repressed from living in a politically correct society? Go to a comments section and tell strangers to kill themselves.
> Feeling unloved and alone? Go to a comments section and call someone a slut.
> Feeling overwhelmed by minorities? Go to a comments section and "make America great again."

The need for sublimation, for discharge, for relief, arises, according to Freud and Nietzsche, due to the pressures of living in a society, of being civilized, of being forced to conform to the needs and expectations of others. Yet, as was discussed in the previous chapter, these pressures of conformity can be seen as self-inflicted to the extent that they are the result of our herd instinct. Were it not for our compulsion to be with others, to be seen and heard by others, to be acknowledged by others, there would be no need to conform and, consequently, no need to troll.

And indeed perhaps it is precisely our herd instinct that these so-called trolls are raging against on comments sections, which would help to explain the aforementioned "non sequitur nature" of the trolling comments found in these sections. For the comments in these sections often appear to have little to do with the other comments, little to do with the content of the page, little to do with the author of the page. The comments section is a space for feedback, for constructive criticism, for dialogue, but instead the comments found in these spaces tend to veer off at some point, for the further down a page one goes, the more likely it is to find comments that are willfully ignoring or rejecting the intended purpose of these spaces, with some comments being attempts at jokes, some being ads placed by bots, and many being some version of "Kill yourself."

If these bottom-dwelling comments are related to the content of the page, they are again often negative, and negative to a degree that appears to be completely disproportionate to whatever in the content of the page the commenter has purportedly found to be so objectionable. Hence perhaps what is truly being objected to is the very existence of the content, of the page, of the internet, of people who feel justified in making their views public, of people who promote the making public of those views, of people who would bother to spend their time reading those views and commenting on those views. In other words, what is truly being objected to is *existence*.

It is due to precisely this sort of reappropriation of comments sections as sites of rage, this sort of trolling culture, that more and more internet sites have moved from moderating their comments sections to de-anonymizing them, to finally removing their comments sections altogether.[5] And yet it may be argued that it is precisely this reappropriation, this rage-release function of comments sections, that makes comments sections not only useful but necessary. For if comments sections provide us with a *virtual* space in which to *virtually* explode like *virtual* monsters, then they perhaps help to prevent us from having to *really* explode in *real life* like *real* monsters.

Such an argument can be found for example in the studies of trolling conducted by psychologists at the University of Manitoba, the University of Winnipeg, and the University of British Columbia, entitled "Trolls Just Want to Have Fun." The authors of the study—Erin E. Buckels, Paul D. Trapnell, and Delroy L. Paulhus—conclude:

> In the final analysis of Study 2, we found clear evidence that sadists tend to troll because they enjoy it. When controlling for enjoyment, sadism's impact on trolling was cut nearly in half; and the indirect effect of sadism through enjoyment was substantial, significant, and remained significant when controlling for overlap with the Dark Triad scores. These findings provide a preliminary glimpse into the mechanism by which sadism fosters trolling behavior. Both trolls and

sadists feel sadistic glee at the distress of others. Sadists just want to
have fun . . . and the Internet is their playground![6]

Having found from their studies of college students and Amazon Mechanical Turk users that trolling correlated with three traits of the
"Dark Tetrad" of personality traits (Machiavellianism, psychopathy,
and, in particular, sadism), Buckels, Trapnell, and Paulhus suggest that
the internet serves as a "playground," as a place for sadists to enjoy their
sadism. In much the same way that parents bring their children to the
playground so that they can play, so that they can indulge their urges to
scream and to destroy in an environment designed for screaming and
for destruction, so too does the internet bring sadists to comments
sections, where they can indulge themselves in an environment perfectly suited to their urges.

   After the publication of this study, Buckels further pushed this view
of the comments section as a sadistic playground in an interview with
Slate. In response to the question of whether punishing trolls for their
behavior could stop them, Buckels argued that "the allure of trolling
may be too strong for sadists, who presumably have limited opportunities to express their sadistic interests in a socially desirable manner."[7]
The claim that sadists are able to release their sadistic urges in comments sections because they find no such release offline suggests that
the removal of comments sections would leave sadists with only socially
undesirable options for release. Hence the internet law of *Never read
the comments* could be interpreted as not only a warning but a compromise, as comments sections continue to exist but primarily as places for
sadists to enjoy and for the rest of society to avoid.

   However, the question of whether sadists become trolls or trolls
become sadists is unclear. On the one hand, Buckels, Trapnell, and
Paulhus raise the question, "Do antisocial persons use technology more
than others because it facilitates their nefarious goals/motives?" and
answer, "The findings of this study suggest that this is indeed the case,
but more empirical work is needed."[8] On the other hand, the authors
argue in the very next paragraph, "The troll persona appears to be a
malicious case of a virtual avatar . . . both actual personality . . . and
one's ideal self." Hence, those who troll are viewed as likely to already
have "nefarious goals/motives," but at the same time a troll is a "virtual

avatar," a "persona," or in other words a mask, a costume one puts on in order to play the game of trolling.

The very language of "troll" encapsulates this confusion. For while the euphemism captures the perceived monstrousness of "nefarious" and "malicious" online behavior, it at the same time likens the individual carrying out the behavior to a mythical or "virtual" beast, thus separating and distancing the *action* from the *actor*. The actor is anonymous, identified only through this euphemism and through an invented screen name. This self-created and socially sustained anonymity leads to a virtual/actual dualism, a dualism that allows the actor to experience trolling as an activity that exists solely *online* and that has no *true* bearing on who the actor *is* "in real life." This expression has become so commonplace in the internet age that it has become shortened to "IRL" (which, perhaps not coincidentally, is very reminiscent of "LOL"), suggesting that this virtual/actual dualism enables the internet to simply be a place for fun, *like a playground*, while ignoring both *who* it is that is having so much fun there, and *what* it is that they find so fun to do there.

In the ideology of IRL, one *becomes* a troll when online, but that does not mean that one *is* a troll when offline. Trolling can thus be seen as a form of nihilistic evasion, an evasion both of one's reality (like techno-hypnosis) and of one's accountability (like data-driven activity). In other words, trolling is nihilistic, not because a troll takes pleasure in demeaning others (like pleasure economics) but because a troll is unwilling to admit *who* he or she *is* (like herd networking), unwilling to admit that he or she *is* a troll, that there is no virtual/actual dualism, that there is no "IRL." Indeed one of the most well-known forms of trolling is to antagonize others precisely by responding to each accusation of antagonism by denying that one is trying to be antagonistic (for example, "It's really about the ethics of gaming journalism").

According to at least Aristotle, Marx, and Nietzsche, *we are what we do*. Thus a person who enjoys posting "Kill yourself" on comments sections, a person who enjoys calling others out for their perceived cowardice while hiding behind the anonymity of euphemisms and screen names, is not a mythical beast but is simply a self-denying and reality-evading nihilist.

8.4 FLASH MOB RULE

In 1973, sci-fi author Larry Niven wrote a novella entitled *Flash Crowd*,[9] in which teleportation devices ("displacement booths") and live television news coverage combine to allow crowds of people to appear instantly at the site of any breaking news story. Niven imagined that the people who would take advantage of this technological combination would be not only the media, curious onlookers, and those wanting to participate in an event, but also criminals, for which reason the first such "flash crowd" quickly turns into a riot of chaos, violence, and looting.

On May 27, 2003, an email from themobproject@yahoo.com with the subject line "MOB #1" was sent anonymously to sixty-three people. The email began:

> You are invited to take part in MOB, the project that creates an inexplicable mob of people in New York City for ten minutes or less. Please forward this to other people you know who might like to join.
>
> FAQ
>
> Q. Why would I want to join an inexplicable mob?
>
> A. Tons of other people are doing it.
>
> > INSTRUCTIONS—MOB #1
> > Location: Claire's Accessories (Broadway between 8th and 9th Sts.)
> > Start Time: Tuesday, June 3rd, 7:24 pm
> > Duration: 7 minutes[10]

Further instructions informed the recipients of the email to enter the store, walk to the back, wait seven minutes, and then leave. It is unknown how many people intended to participate in MOB #1 as the police had preemptively closed the store and were waiting out front, prepared to arrest any potential mob participant.

Bill Wasik, author, editor, and creator of "The MOB Project," learned from this failed first attempt not to give out the mob location in advance, for which reason MOBs #2 through #8 were a success, giving rise to copycat mobs and the birth of the "flash mob" phenomenon. In his subsequent *And Then There's This: How Stories Live and Die in Viral Culture*, Wasik explains:

> I realized I needed to make my idea *lazier*. I could use e-mail to gather an audience for a show, yes, but the point of the show should be no show at all: the e-mail would be straightforward about exactly what people would see, namely nothing but *themselves*, coming together for no reason at all. Such a project would work, I reflected, because it was *meta*, i.e., it was a self-conscious idea for a self-conscious culture, a promise to create something out of nothing.[11]

The flash mob phenomenon was born out of the attempt to "create something out of nothing." Niven predicted this phenomenon, he simply got the medium wrong. We clearly do not need the combined powers of teleportation devices and televised news coverage to get us to form a flash mob—all we need are the combined powers of *boredom* and *communication*. An anonymous email suggesting random people participate in a random activity in a random location at a random time is apparently all it takes to get hundreds of people to "join an inexplicable mob" since "tons of other people are doing it" and they need see "nothing but *themselves*."

Wasik created flash mobs as an experiment in performative narcissism, as an opportunity for a "self-conscious culture" to show the world just how self-conscious they could be. In other words, Wasik was not inviting people to participate in an event, in the creation of a new phenomenon, rather Wasik was *trolling* the people he emailed. The people who responded to the email, the people who participated in the flash mob, were not being invited to be part of a large inside joke, they were being invited to be laughed at, *to be the joke*. And perhaps the discovery by participants that they were being *laughed at* rather than *laughed with* explains why the flash mob phenomenon, much like a flash mob itself, seems to have suddenly disappeared.

Having become so popular that it was even appropriated by marketers looking for viral ad campaigns, the flash mob evolved—like many an internet phenomenon—from something fun into a fad, generating a backlash rather than a buzz. Articles eulogizing the flash mob began popping up around 2011, particularly after flash mobs went from viral YouTube sensations to criminal riots. Whereas Wasik's first successful flash mob sent people into a department store to stare at a carpet, later flash mobs sent people into stores in order to rob them, creating the phenomenon dubbed the "flash rob," a phenomenon that the National Retail Federation reported as having occurred "at a full 10 percent of businesses surveyed."[12]

However, just because Wasik created the flash mob phenomenon does not mean he understood it. For while Wasik looked down upon those who would participate in flash mobs, asserting that they were "coming together for no reason at all," there is no need to assume that this view represents the actual motivations of the participants. Flash mobs could certainly appear to simply be *choreographed silliness*, an opportunity for people to participate in a very elaborate performance, a giant pillow fight, or a recreation of a music video, but they could also be an opportunity for people *to make a statement*.

In January of 2011, youth groups in Egypt used the internet to organize protests in opposition to the Mubarak regime following the successful popular uprisings in Tunisia in December 2010. These protests were largely organized through social media (Facebook), gathering people to all appear simultaneously at a specific time (January 25) and in a specific place (Cairo's Tahrir Square) for a specific purpose (anti-Mubarak demonstration).[13] Social media continued to play an important part in the protests as information and reports were disseminated by the protesters through Facebook and Twitter, helping to gain support both by increasing the number of people participating and by increasing news media coverage. The massive, coordinated crowd of hundreds of thousands of people occupied the square, and led to similar occupations in other cities in Egypt, so overwhelming the police and military that Mubarak resigned eighteen days later on February 11.

In July of 2011, an advertisement in the magazine *Adbusters* asked, "Are you ready for a Tahrir moment?"[14] Below a banner reading "#OC-CUPYWALLSTREET," the ad called for people to "flood into lower Manhattan, set up tents, kitchens, peaceful barricades and occupy Wall Street" and to do so "on September 17." As the chosen date approached, Occupy websites, Reddit threads, Tumblr pages, and Twitter trends all continued to spread and expand on the message of trying to replicate the Tahrir Square protests on Wall Street. On September 17, a few hundred people occupied Wall Street's Zuccotti Park, which is where the Occupy movement was based until the NYPD attempted to clear the park two months later, arresting more than 240 protesters.[15]

During the occupation, social media continued to spread the message of the Occupy movement ("We are the 99%"), leading many tourists, celebrities, politicians, and journalists to show up to Zuccotti Park, as well as leading to the creation of hundreds of Occupy organizations and events in cities all over the world.

It is likely not a coincidence that 2011 was not only the year of Tahrir Square and Occupy Wall Street but also the year of the "flash rob" and the year of the proclaimed death of the flash mob phenomenon. Once flash mobs stopped being fun and games, once flash mobs stopped being the mindless entertainment for the bored and narcissistic that Wasik envisioned, once flash mobs attempted to *serve a purpose*, the potential danger of flash mobs became the focus of media coverage rather than their potential entertainment and commercial value. And indeed the "flash rob" phenomenon was both indicative of precisely the political and economic inequalities protested against in Cairo and New York, and provided a perfect way for opponents to criticize flash mobs as the chaotic and criminal riots that Niven had predicted. The Philadelphia Police Commissioner even suggested in 2011 that a better term for flash mobs would be "rampaging thugs."[16]

Yet what is perhaps most important to recognize here is the *multistability* of flash mobs, the ability of flash mobs to appear in ways as varied as MOB #1 or as Occupy Wall Street. As Wasik asserted, a flash mob is a way to "create something out of nothing." The *something* can be as varied as a performance or a protest. But regardless of what the something is, it does not arise from *nothing*. A flash mob, any flash mob, is an expression, an expression of, on the one hand, the desire of people to be part of *something* and, on the other hand, the desire of people to *not* be a part of *nothing*. The *nothing* can be anything from boredom to loneliness to oppression, as what matters is that the flash mob represents a *transformation*, a transformation both of oneself and of the world.

A flash mob is an opportunity for an individual to transform into a performer and for a space to transform into a stage. Whether one is performing in a tribute to Michael Jackson or in a demonstration against a dictator, what is important is that one is transformed through the performance into someone other than oneself, just as the space of the performance is transformed into something other than what it is taken to be. It should perhaps not surprise us that flash mobs did eventually take the explicit form of a protest as, in a sense, all flash mobs are at least an implicit form of protest. Just as a "flash rob" could be seen as a protest against the inequalities produced by Capitalism, so too could any flash mob, even just a synchronized dance performance, be seen as a protest against normalcy, against predictability, against life's lack of spontaneity, against the taken-for-granted assumption that public spaces can only be used as intended. In other words, a flash mob is *a protest against reality*.

A flash mob in and of itself is not nihilistic. Rather, as Nietzsche suggested, what is nihilistic is the *explosiveness* of the flash mob. It appears suddenly, with little to no warning, and then *disappears*. Even in cases such as Tahrir Square or Occupy Wall Street, where the flash mob remains for days or weeks, the flash mob nevertheless disappears. Like the clock striking midnight on Cinderella, the individuals who had been transformed into performers return to being individuals, individuals who are bored, lonely, or oppressed. Likewise the place that had been transformed into a stage is returned to being a place, a place that is normal, predictable, lacking in spontaneity, and to be used as intended.

It is for this reason that Nietzsche warns that while such explosiveness may allow us to escape from reality for a time, the price of this escape must eventually be *paid back*. It can be painful to be bored and to be surrounded by predictable events in predictable spaces, but it is far more painful to be bored and surrounded by predictability after having experienced freedom and spontaneity. Having revealed to oneself what life *could be like*, it is devastating to then return to how life *is*. The desire to remain within the world of the flash mob can help to explain the importance of the role of YouTube in not only spreading the idea of flash mobs virally but in allowing people to experience a flash mob, techno-hypnotically, over and over again as needed, as a medication. But, as Nietzsche warned, such medication does not cure but instead *makes the sick sicker*. The more we are reminded of how reality could be, the more painful reality becomes, and the more painful reality becomes, the more we need to be reminded of how reality could be.

8.5 CYBERWARRIORS AND SHAME CAMPAIGNS

There is an essential affinity between trolling and flash mobs. Trolling is a way to enjoy attacking others while using the ideology of IRL to hide from the responsibility of being someone who would enjoy attacking others. A flash mob is a way to transform oneself into a performer and the world into a stage, a stage filled with performers who are all following a script, a script that allows each performer to deny responsibility for the performance. In other words, if trolls were to form a flash mob, then they could enjoy attacking others without having to worry about being held responsible for the attack since the attack was not done out of personal pleasure but because "tons of other people are doing it." Rather than sadism, trolling in a flash mob could make attacking others appear instead to be a form of *mob justice*.

Of course such trolling flash mobs not only exist but have become so frequent and so far-reaching that we have been led to believe that flash mobs are a fad of the past rather than the zeitgeist of the present. In the past, social media was a tool for organizing flash mobs. In the present, *social media is the flash mob*. However the flash mob that social media has become no longer transforms participants into performers on a stage, carrying out dance routines or pretending to be mannequins, but rather transforms participants into cyberwarriors on a battlefield, carrying out what Jon Ronson calls "shame campaigns."[17]

In his book, *So You've Been Publicly Shamed*, Ronson interviews people who were the victims of shame campaigns, people who became the object of social media ridicule and vitriol to such a degree that their lives were ruined. Ronson analyzes several shame campaigns but focuses primarily on the campaign against Justine Sacco who, in December of 2013, was a publicist at a major media company who tweeted to her 170 followers: "Going to Africa. Hope I don't get AIDS. Just kidding. I'm white!" Sacco then got on an 11-hour flight, during which time hundreds of thousands of people all over the world participated in a shame campaign against her, a campaign which led her to become the top worldwide trend on Twitter, to have her own trending hashtag (#HasJustineLandedYet), to be threatened, fired from her job, shunned by her family, and led her to move temporarily to a rural area of Addis Ababa, Ethiopia, where there was, coincidentally, no internet.[18]

Social media (Sacco's tweet) led strangers to suddenly appear in the same place (Twitter), in order to carry out the same activity (trolling), over the same period of time (the 11-hour flight). In other words, Sacco's tweet created a flash mob, a flash mob of people who were taking pleasure in attacking someone online, a flash mob, therefore, of trolls. This flash mob transformed trolls into vigilantes and transformed Twitter into a platform for a public execution. The flash mob was supposed to have died off as a fad in 2011, and yet we can see that not just a flash mob but one of the world's largest-ever flash mobs took place in 2013. However, participants likely would not have recognized this shame campaign as a flash mob, just as they would not have recognized shaming Sacco as a form of trolling. Rather they might argue, on the one hand, this was not a *performance* but an act of *justice*, and, on the other hand, this was not attacking someone *out of pleasure* but because it was what she *deserved*.

It is precisely this justification, this justification that the flash trolling of a shame campaign is a well-deserved act of justice, that Ronson wants us to reckon with. It is for this reason that Ronson frames Sacco and those who were similarly pilloried online as *victims*, forcing us to question whether the punishment truly fit the crime and, ultimately, to question if there even was a *crime*. Ronson compares these modern-day social media shame campaigns to the public shaming punishments of the past, punishments—such as being put in the stocks or being whipped in the town square—that were outlawed in the United States and in the United Kingdom in the middle of the nineteenth century.

As Ronson explains, he had presumed that such shaming practices ended because industrialization eroded the geographical localization necessary for shame, that moving from small towns to big cities sapped shaming of its power since everyone became just another face in the crowd. However, his research revealed instead that shaming was stopped because it was *too powerful*. Ronson even discovered arguments against public shaming as early as 1787 from doctor and founding father Benjamin Rush who argued that public shaming rituals result in "outsized cruelty" because "well-meaning people, in a crowd, often take it too far."[19]

This connection between what people think they are doing in public shaming, how many people are involved in public shaming, and how far people are willing to go in public shaming raises the question of whether there is anything specific to social media shame campaigns that distinguishes them from the public shaming rituals of the past. This question is particularly important from a Nietzschean perspective for, as was discussed in chapter 5, Nietzsche argues that being cruel to others, and in particular finding pleasure in being cruel, is part of what it means to be human rather than merely being part of what it means to be online.

The shame campaign against Sacco would simply appear to be the latest example of what Nietzsche describes as our "human, all-too-human" desire to take part in a *festival of cruelty*. Indeed Nietzsche goes so far as to argue that it is not the festival that leads to cruelty but rather *cruelty that leads to the festival*.[20] In other words, contrary to the presumption that social media provides the conditions necessary for shame campaigns—conditions such as anonymity and instant notifications—Nietzsche could be seen to be suggesting that it is our desire for shame campaigns, our desire for cruelty, that is one of the conditions necessary for creating festivals like social media.

Nietzsche here can help us to understand one of the central paradoxes of social media, the paradox of our knowing that social media opens us up to becoming the victim of a shame campaign, of possibly ruining our lives, and yet we nevertheless continue to use social media. If our primary motivation for using social media is *to be social*, to communicate with others, to make friends with others, then it would seem that we would have long recognized the toxicity and explosiveness of social media and have sought safer means for achieving this end. However, if our primary motivation for using social media is actually not to be social but *to be cruel*, to shame others, to make a mockery of others, then our continued use of social media makes much more sense.

Further, Nietzsche could be seen as even pointing to the possibility that these two potential end goals motivating our use of social media—to be social or to be cruel—need not be mutually exclusive. For if cruelty is festive, if from out of our shared desire for cruelty festivities are likely to arise, then it is quite possible that it is not sociality that helps create the conditions for cruelty but rather cruelty that helps to create the conditions for sociality. In other words, *trolling can bring people together*. Trolling may not be divisive but cohesive. Trolling can lead to mobs, the modern-day equivalent of angry, pitchfork-wielding mobs, but, for the people in the mobs, trolling could potentially lead to camaraderie, friendship, and perhaps even to a sense of community.

Evidence of this cohesive aspect of trolling has been found by Whitney Phillips in her ethnographic research into trolling subcultures. Though many tend to assume that trolls, as the euphemism suggests, are loners, attacking strangers anonymously from the dark shadows of a parental basement, Phillips has found instead that trolls can, and indeed do, form communities. According to Phillips, trolls can be "organized," having "flagged themselves" through in-joke screen names so they can find each other, in effect "forming an anti-social network of sorts" by "befriending other troll profiles."[21]

As Phillips points out, trolling on social media—unlike trolling in comments sections or on Reddit forums—requires that one have a profile which, even if fake and invented solely for the purpose of trolling, nevertheless gives each troll an online identity stable enough to form relationships. Phillips writes:

> Facebook trolling was, from the very first moment, predicated on the conventions established by Facebook's programmers; it was through the adoption of these protocols—which don't just encourage but engender user enmeshment—that trolling became a fundamentally social activity. This differed greatly from most forum trolling and certainly trolling on /b/, since trolling in these contexts is almost always blindly anonymous. Trolls may work together during a particular raid, but they rarely stand still long enough to establish social ties and certainly don't have a persistent online identity to which particular successes may be affixed. [. . .] Indeed, given the desire to maintain community ties after a profile had been deleted, and in order to contribute to and receive benefits from this emerging lulz economy, trolls on Facebook tended to stick with the same family of trolling names so that respawn accounts would have an easier time finding and being found by trolling friends.[22]

While trolling can bring people together through the discovery of shared interests in cruelty, social media sites like Facebook play an important mediating role in bringing trolls together. Facebook not only helps trolls to find each other through the creation of stable identities but also helps trolls to find targets for their trolling through the creation of pages and of groups whose purported *purity* tend to outrage and inspire trolls.

As Phillips makes clear, trolls think of themselves not as *sadists* but as *satirists*, satirists whose means may be cruelty, but whose ends are perceived by them as righteous, revealing the impurities beneath the claimed pure intentions of their targets. The trolls Phillips focuses on are "RIP trolls," trolls who attack Facebook memorial pages set up as sites of mourning. This trolling subculture not only shares tricks (for example, attracting users to a memorial page and then turning it from a page devoted to mourning into a page devoted to mockery) and tactics (for example, posting memes on memorial pages that ridicule how the mourned individual died) but also shares a code (for example, only attacking public memorial pages created by strangers, not the private memorial pages created by family members of the deceased).

While shared tricks and tactics help trolls to identify each other, a shared code helps to bond trolls to each other. Having a common mission justifies the trolling, allowing the flash mob of shame-campaigning trolls to transform themselves into warriors in a crusade, while transforming social media into a Holy Land that must be *purified* of infidels. Of course sharing tricks, tactics, and a sense of justice is not unique to trolls as, thanks to *herd networking*, this is increasingly becoming a feature of social media users in general. Or to put it another way—and to return to the claim I made earlier that social media has become a flash mob—the line between trolls and non-trolls, between social media abusers and social media users, is increasingly becoming blurred, if not nonexistent. Trolls the likes of which Phillips studies may occupy an extreme end of the spectrum of social media users, but it is a spectrum and thus trolls are a difference in degree rather than a difference in kind from other social media users.

To suggest that everyone on social media is a troll to one degree or another may seem like, on the one hand, a generalization that normalizes trolling and, on the other hand, a generalization that denies genuine activism. Yet, with regard to the first charge, the difference in degree should be taken seriously, both as an indication of how varied trolling can be and as an indication of how easy it is to slide from the seemingly innocent to the righteously indignant. With regard to the second charge, it is precisely the righteous indignation of online activism that illustrates the dangerous blindness to what *we* are doing, as if only *they* could be trolls.

The euphemism of "troll" not only suggests a mythical creature attacking innocent strangers from the shadows but also distinguishes the *doer* from the *deed*, helping to give the false impression that a troll is a particular kind of person, rather than a person performing a particular kind of activity. A troll is not a narcissistic sadist but instead someone who acts in narcissistic ("Look at how pure I am!") and sadistic ("Look at how impure they are!") ways. Once social media is reduced to a world of Good versus Evil, then, as Socrates argued, everyone identifies themselves as Good and their actions must, consequently, also be Good, whether or not they look similar to the actions of those who are Evil.

This is why one of the most common forms of trolling is to mock those on the opposing side for their hypocrisy while we nevertheless ignore or deny the hypocrisy of our own side. Screen shots have become weaponized, as tweets and status updates can be captured, repackaged, and strategically dropped as truth bombs, revealing through juxtaposition the superficiality and context-dependence of the opposing side's claimed convictions. And of course such weapons are becoming increasingly available, since hypocrisy becomes more common when we define ourselves through our intentions rather than through our actions ("You don't know the real me!") while—hypocritically—we define others through their actions rather than their intentions ("I know who you really are!").

We are doers distinct from our deeds, so we need not care about our deeds.

They are deeds behind which there are no doers, so we need not care about who they are.

In both cases there is denial. To say that *we* are Good, regardless of what we do, is to deny that we are what we do, and is thus to deny the nature of our own existence. To say that *they* are Evil, regardless of who they are, is to deny the humanity of those we oppose, and is thus to deny the nature of their existence. And it is precisely this dual denial that is central to trolling as well as to the aforementioned ideology of IRL that helps to enable and perpetuate trolling. I am not a troll, because I am not what I do online, since what I do online is *virtual*, and I am *real*. The other is not a victim, because the other is merely a *virtual* presence, a presence which is the object of *virtual* attacks. In other words, in the shame campaign against Justine Sacco, there was no one trolling Justine Sacco, because the trolling was performed by *no one* against *no one*, as the trolling was merely *virtual* fun on a *virtual* playground at the expense of a *virtual* entity.

The supposed virtuality, and thus irreality, of both the troll and of the trolled, helps to answer the question that must be asked again, and again, *why does anyone use social media?* As I suggested earlier, to use social media is to regularly provide trolls with ammunition, thus seemingly opening ourselves up to finding cruelty rather than to finding a community. One possible answer I have offered is that cruelty and community are not mutually exclusive but rather co-constitutive (we come together to be cruel, and being cruel keeps us together). Another possible answer is that we do not take seriously the threat social media presents to us because, thanks to the ideology of IRL, we deny the reality of the threat to ourselves that the internet represents when we deny the reality of the selves represented in and through the internet. If what is done online is perceived by us as *not really real*, then reactions by others to what we do online must also be *not really real*.

In other words, contrary to the assumption that it is social media that is leading us to participate in trolling, flash mobs, and shame campaigns, we need to take seriously the possibility that it is our desire to participate in such acts—in acts of cruelty, in acts of protest, in acts of vigilantism—that is leading us to use social media, if not to create it in the first place. Social media is indeed an enabler, but what it enables is the *herd networking* aspects of these acts, the ability for us to band together to perpetrate these acts, to bond over our shared interests in these acts, and to form virtual communities of virtual actors who can and will continue to perpetrate these acts. What social media also enables is the *techno-hypnotic* aspects of these acts, the ability for us to distance ourselves from our online actions, to elevate our *real* selves above our *virtual* actions, and to reduce others to their *virtuality* while denying their *reality*.

It is this combination of herd networking and techno-hypnosis, of communities of like-minded disembodied individuals, that sets the stage for the *orgiastic* aspects of these acts, the ability for us to explode, to explode in rage, to explode in joy, to explode in agony, to explode in any emotion so long as it allows us to feel like we are *doing something*. Trolling, flash mobs, and shame campaigns all have in common this orgiastic experience of *doing something*, of doing something important, something unique, something creative, but also of doing something that *does nothing*, that awakens consciences but causes no *real* pain, that mocks institutions but causes no *real* damage, and that destroys enemies but causes no *real* trauma.

What we do in orgies of clicking *matters* and *does not matter*. These acts *matter* because *everyone is doing it*, and if everyone is doing it, it must be *worth doing*. These acts *do not matter* because *everyone is doing it*, and if everyone is doing it, it must not be anything that *I* did, that *I* can be held accountable for, that *I* need to worry about. #HasJustineLandedYet—or whatever happens to be the latest outrage to light up the social media skies like a Bat Signal—is trending on Twitter, so we tweet vitriol, we make jokes, we trade memes, just like everyone else is doing, and we feel like we have taken down someone who *deserved* it, that we have engaged in an act of *justice*, that we have participated in an *event*. At the same time we feel like we have done *nothing* worth thinking about, *nothing* worth taking responsibility for, *nothing* worth worrying about. We move on, not caring about what we did, or who we did it to, but only caring about when we will get to do it *again*.

8.6 THE DANGERS OF ORGIES OF CLICKING

According to Nietzsche, the danger of orgies of feeling is that it *makes the sick sicker*. Actions that we thought would cure us of our sickness, of our nihilism, instead poison us, making us sicker, more nihilistic, more desperate for cures, and more susceptible to being poisoned again. There is thus something self-destructive about orgies of feeling, a self-destructiveness that arises out of our very attempts at self-preservation. The reason that this attempt at self-preservation leads instead to self-destruction is that, rather than cure the sickness, we are only led to alleviate the symptoms. Though all human-nihilism relations offer alleviation from symptoms rather than a cure for suffering, orgies of feeling alone constitute the "guilty" human-nihilism relation. Unlike the "innocent" human-nihilism relations that serve to help us to hide from who we are and from our suffering, orgies of feeling are instead attempts to atone for who we are, to atone for our suffering, for our having *deserved* to suffer.

Finding no meaning in life, we become depressed, sullen, weary. We may try to distract ourselves in order to avoid our suffering (self-hypnosis), busy ourselves in order to avoid our suffering (mechanical activity), help others in order to avoid our suffering (petty pleasure), or join with others in order to avoid our suffering (herd instinct). Or we may seek out the help of an ascetic priest, of one who is supposedly wise in the ways of suffering, one who should know *why we suffer* and *how to cure our suffering*. The ascetic priest tells us, according to Nietzsche, that we suffer because we deserve to suffer, we suffer because we are impure, because we are sinners, because we have not yet atoned for our sinful impurities. The ascetic priest therefore provides us with a reason for our suffering ("Sin!") and a way to cure ourselves of our suffering ("Atone!").

Orgies of feeling are therefore attempts at atonement, attempts at purifying the self. Purification rituals can, as Nietzsche makes clear, be either joyous or monstrous, as all that matters is that the ritual has at its core an *explosion of affect*, an *ecstatic* experience that allows us, momentarily, to feel relieved of suffering by being briefly overcome with an altogether different feeling, a feeling of *ek-stasis*, of being *outside of ourselves*. But precisely because the effect of this ritual is momentary, because it is explosive, the suffering ultimately returns as we ultimately return to ourselves, though with the added element that we now feel guiltier than before since we apparently not only deserve to suffer but are also unworthy of atonement. In other words, orgies of feeling *make the sick sicker*, trapping us in an endless loop of discontent and destruction.

The problem here then is that rather than question why life has no meaning, rather than attempt to find ways to *make life meaningful*, the ascetic priest instead teaches us to feel guilty for being blind to the *fact* that life *is* meaningful, to feel guilty for having lived *impurely* such that life would seem to *us* as meaningless, to feel guilty for not having lived a life of atonement such that we could put ourselves on the righteous path to meaningfulness. The failure of the purity ritual, of the orgies of feeling, to cure us of our suffering is thus not taken to be a failure of the ascetic priest but of the sufferer, for which reason more purity rituals and more orgies of feeling must be attempted again and again. In this way the sufferer discovers that atonement is not a means to an end but is the end itself, that atonement is the meaning of life, and that what the sufferer had hoped to achieve in life will instead be found only after having lived a life of atonement, that the end of suffering will be found not in life but in death, in the life that the ascetic priest tells us awaits us after death.

The question that arises for us today, the question that this chapter has attempted to answer, is that of what happens when technologies, rather than ascetic priests, serve to mediate our attempts to cure ourselves of our suffering. Or, to put it another way, what happens when technologies take up the role of ascetic priests? As we have seen in the previous chapters, technologies serve to distract us (techno-hypnosis), to command us (data-driven activity), to empower us (pleasure economics), and to unite us (herd networking) so that we can evade ourselves and the suffering that we experience when we are forced instead to confront ourselves. But when we do confront ourselves, when our evasions break down and we do again experience our suffering, then too we turn to technologies, just as we once turned to ascetic priests, seeking explanations and cures for our suffering.

Perhaps the most obvious example of technologies mediating our nihilistic suffering is Apple's voice assistant Siri. The introduction of Siri, of a feature that gives users the impression of talking *with* rather than *to* their iPhone, of a calm and soothing female voice that would attempt to answer any and all questions of the user, led many to discover that Siri could even attempt to answer the ultimate question: What is the meaning of life? Indeed, users have discovered that Siri has at least thirteen answers to this question,[23] including:

1. "It's nothing Nietzsche couldn't teach ya."
2. "A movie."
3. "To think about questions like this."
4. "I don't know. But I think there's an app for that."
5. "All evidence to date suggests it's chocolate."
6. "Life: a principle of force that is considered to underlie the distinctive quality of animate beings. I guess that includes me."
7. "Life: the condition that distinguishes animals and plants from inorganic matter, including the capacity for growth, reproduction, functional activity, and continual change preceding death."
8. "I find it odd that you would ask this of an inanimate object."
9. "I can't answer that now, but give me some time to write a very long play in which nothing happens."

10. "Try and be nice to people, avoid eating fat, read a good book every now and then, get some walking in, and try to live together in peace and harmony with all people of all creeds and nations."
11. "That's easy . . . it's a philosophical question concerning the purpose and significance of life or existence in general."
12. "I Kant answer that. Ha ha!"
13. "I give up."

What is perhaps most illuminating about these answers is not their quality—though it is worth noting that the general theme of the answers is that of mocking the user for even asking Siri about the meaning of life in the first place—but their quantity. The team at Apple who programmed Siri clearly expected that users would not only ask Siri about the meaning of life but would ask *so many times* that *so many answers* would be necessary. Indeed the real answer that Siri seems to be suggesting, which is in keeping with the "Easter egg" element of Siri's unknown catalogue of answers, is that the meaning of life is to keep asking questions (see answer 3) or, more specifically, to keep buying Apple products so that you can keep asking Siri questions (see answer 4).

Though beyond the jokes and beyond the Capitalist impulses behind such jokes, one answer stands out from the rest. In the tenth answer listed above, Siri actually does provide what would appear to be a real answer to the question of the meaning of life, an answer that could be boiled down to: Be a better person. Of course the implication of this answer is that iPhone users can be expected to need to be told to be better people; they can be expected to not be nice, to be eating fat, to not be reading good books, to not be walking, and to not be living harmoniously with others. Such expectations appear to be rooted in stereotypes concerning technophiles, concerning people who would be so addicted to their iPhones that they would ask Siri about the meaning of life. Siri has been programmed to tell users to not only be better people but to not be stereotypical iPhone users, users who would presumably need to be told by an iPhone how to be good people (see also answer 8). In other words, Siri has been programmed to make users feel *guilty* and to tell users how to *atone*. Siri has been programmed to be an ascetic priest.

Ascetic priests need not be religious priests in the traditional sense but merely priests in terms of preaching a path of salvation, religious in the sense of preaching that salvation is to be found through asceticism (self-denial) and in a reality different from the one in which we live (world-denial). The ascetic priests of the past preached orgies of feeling. The ascetic priests of the present preach orgies of clicking. As I have attempted to show, trolling can be seen as a form of self-denial, flash mobs can be seen as a form of world-denial, and shame campaigns can be seen as a form of both self-denial and world-denial. Yet, as is evident even in the example of Siri, orgies of feeling and orgies of clicking, priest-mediated suffering and technology-mediated suffering, share not only denial, not only feelings of guilt and ritualistic acts of atonement but also repetition.

In much the same way that Siri could be seen as having grown out of the endless searching for answers through Google and through Wikipedia, so too can shame campaigns be seen as having grown out of our endless searching for purification through trolling and for transformation through flash mobs. Indeed the technologies that enable orgies of clicking could likewise be seen as having grown out of the endless attempts for atonement through orgies of feeling. In other words, both orgies of feeling and orgies of clicking have in common a cyclical nature, a nature that can be seen as an endlessly repetitive form of torture like that found in the myth of Sisyphus, a form of torture that increases suffering with each repetition. Yet whereas orgies of feeling result in increased suffering for the tortured alone, orgies of clicking allow the tortured to *share* their torture, to *spread* their torture, not unlike what may have happened if Sisyphus had had a Facebook account.

Orgies of clicking are not only cyclical in nature but tend to spiral out of control. Nietzsche points out that the ascetic priests' prescription of orgies of feeling resulted in sufferers who "no longer protested *against* pain" but instead "*thirsted* for pain" and cried "*more* pain! *more* pain!"[24] Similarly, we find that the technological prescription of orgies of clicking results in sufferers turning from protesting against clicking to demanding more clicking. However, whereas the increasing demand for more pain leads to an increase in guilt and in cruelty toward *oneself*, the increasing demand for more clicking leads to an increase in shame and in cruelty toward *others*.

As we have already seen, shame campaigns are combinations of trolling and of flash mobs where massive numbers of people come together suddenly and at the same time to use social media to attack another user of social media. In the case of Justine Sacco, we find thousands of people using Twitter to send vile tweets aimed at Sacco for her having dared to use Twitter to send a tweet that they thought to be vile. Of course whereas Sacco mistakenly assumed she was only sending her taken-to-be-vile tweet to her 170 followers, the shame campaigners were riding a wave of outrage. Sending intended-to-be vile tweets to everyone else riding the wave, shame campaigners were trying to out-vile each other, to get attention from others who could be expected to like and retweet their vitriol, which is probably not all that different from the attention from like-minded people that Sacco was hoping to achieve with her initial tweet.

The answer then to the question of why Sacco was targeted by a shame campaign could be that it was not due to a lack of empathy on the part of other Twitter users, but rather due to *too much empathy*. Twitter users reading Sacco's tweet and discovering the reaction it received may have identified with her, recognizing how easily they themselves could have been the targets of a shame campaign, perhaps realizing how little actually separated her tweet from horrible jokes that they themselves had almost tweeted or had tweeted without anyone taking offense. And it may have been precisely because of this identification with Sacco, because of this recognition of the impulses they shared with Sacco, that they joined in the shame campaign against her.

On the one hand, Sacco's tweet revealed to other Twitter users the dangers that they themselves faced on Twitter, revealed to them their own uncivilized impulses and how easily those impulses could get them into trouble. On the other hand, Sacco's tweet revealed to other Twitter users that she was more daring than they were in her willingness to tweet such a joke, that she was not as inhibited in her use of Twitter as they were. In both instances Sacco's tweet revealed to other Twitter users something about themselves, something about themselves that was deserving of guilt, and that was demanding atonement. Yet because Sacco clearly did not feel guilty, did not apologize, did not delete the tweet, did not feel sufficiently inhibited to have never sent the tweet, it was the purpose of the shame campaign *to make her feel guilty*, to make her atone, to make her regret having sent such a tweet, to make her

experience the regret that they had themselves experienced while reading her tweet.

This situation is not unlike what happens when someone cuts in
front of others waiting in a line. To see someone cut the line is to be
made aware, on the one hand, that cutting the line is possible and, on
the other hand, that you are so well-trained to wait in line that you did
not even think to cut the line. As children, we do not wait in line but
rather demand and expect immediate satisfaction. But after years of
training, after years of being taught good manners, of being yelled at for
having bad manners, of being forcibly made to wait in line, eventually
we become people who wait in line on our own, who wait in line as if it
were natural, as if it were something we wanted to do because we are
civilized rather than something we feel compelled to do because we are
inhibited.

And thus the outrage we feel in seeing someone cut in front of us is
not necessarily due to what the line-cutter *did*, as it could instead be
due to who the line-cutter *is*, as we are not necessarily opposed to line-
cutting as much as we are opposed to people being somehow not as
inhibited as we are. This is what we express when we incredulously
blurt out, "Who does that guy think he is?" In other words, we are
asking: "Who must someone be, such that they think they could get
away with breaking society's rules?" Though of course we don't ask this
of the line-cutter, for we are too inhibited about confrontations as well,
and thus we instead ask this of the others waiting dutifully in line,
together speculating about who this line-cutter *must be*.

On the internet however we need not speculate, we need not project
our rule-breaking fantasies onto others, as we can instead investigate.
We can find out exactly *who would do such things*, such things that we
would never do, such things that perhaps we would do except we are
too good to do them. Indeed we are so good that we are often driven to
find out as much as we can about those we deem to be *bad*, so driven in
fact that we have invented a new method of shaming those we deem
bad, those who do what we would not do, a method of shaming that has
come to be known as *doxing*. To "dox" someone, as the slang suggests, is
to publicly release documents in order to reveal the identity behind an
anonymous account.[25] Doxing represents, on the one hand, *how* orgies
of clicking can escalate and, on the other hand, *why* orgies of clicking
can escalate.

As David Douglas makes clear, doxing can take several forms and can do damage in several different ways:

> I propose categorizing doxing into three types: deanonymization, targeting, and delegitimization. Each attempts to remove or damage something different from the subject: anonymity, obscurity, and credibility, respectively. Each type of doxing also creates new possibilities to further interfere with the life of the person involved. Deanonymization makes it easier to obtain other types of identity knowledge about the subject, and so creates greater opportunities for the other types of doxing to occur. Whatever advantages or protection the subject sought to gain by seeking anonymity or adopting a pseudonym will be lost. Targeting doxing creates the possibility that future harassment may take a physical form, with the uncertainty and risks of harm that it brings. The subject may be harassed and inconvenienced by others using her personal information to impersonate her. Finally, delegitimization presents a motivation for carrying out harassment and potentially further doxing by detailing how the subject is somehow unworthy of respect.[26]

Doxing, as Douglas makes clear, is a way to not only troll someone, to be cruel to someone, but also to *enable others* to be cruel to someone. However doxing not only serves to increase the *number* of people who can be cruel to someone, it also serves to increase the *kind* of cruelty that can be inflicted upon someone. Doxing, in its essence, works by turning the benefits of the internet into methods of torture. The freedom afforded by anonymity can become a tool of oppression. The dream of being able to create any online persona can make one's offline reality into a nightmare. The equality promised by digital media can become the impetus for degradation.

We can imagine here though that the doxer might argue that there is nothing inherently wrong with doxing. On the one hand, the investigation into the identity of the doxed rarely requires going deeper than any information that is already publicly available. On the other hand, the doxed only fears doxing if the doxed has done something that they do not want to be publicly associated with. In the first instance, while it is possible to dox someone without having to hack into private accounts, it is still necessary to do quite a bit of digging, quite a bit of dot connecting, which, if not hacking, can still feel a lot like stalking. In the second instance, the argument that only someone who has done something wrong fears having their identity revealed simply elides the fact that this argument works both ways, for which reason the mere event of identity revelation is enough to give the appearance that the doxed has done something wrong, something worth being doxed over.

Yet what is most important here is the argument operating behind these arguments, the argument that the doxed *deserves* the doxing. Whether because the doxed did not cover their tracks well enough, or because the doxed did something the doxer deems wrong, or both, what we find here again is the same argument used to justify shame campaigns: the target is not a victim being attacked, the target is a criminal receiving justice. And yet, as was suggested earlier with the example of the line-cutter, both the judgment of criminality and the justice sought against the criminal are focused not on the *deed* but on the *doer*. The doxer is concerned not with *what* the doxed did but *that* the doxed did it, as the concern is with discovering *who would do such a thing*, with finding out who this person is who can be so uninhibited as to do something criminal. The doxed is a rule-breaker; the doxer is not motivated by the wrongness of rule-breaking—since, of course, doxing is also a breaking of rules—but is instead motivated by the wrongness of someone being able to break rules, of being able to do that which the rest of us are supposed to be too inhibited to do, that which the doxer is too inhibited to do.

Indeed it is important to focus on the fact that the doxer is a rule-breaker too. Breaking rules is a sign of power, of being *more powerful* than those who do not break the rules. Doxing can thus be seen as an act of revenge against someone who is, or who at least claims to be, more powerful than the rest of society, than the rest of society that does not break the rules. The indication of power shown in the rule-breaking serves to justify the doxing of the rule-breaker as an act of speaking truth to power, the truth that the doxed is not as powerful as they thought themselves to be. But, importantly, doxing is itself a breaking of rules and is thus itself an indication of power; in particular, it is an indication of not only being *more powerful* than others but also of having *power over others*—of having the power to dox, to reveal, to destroy, to destroy even those who thought themselves to be more powerful than the rest of society. Doxing is, therefore, simultaneously an act that tears someone down (the doxed) and builds someone up (the doxer). But, of course, to build oneself up by breaking rules is to make oneself a target worthy of doxing. In other words, doxing invites more doxing, which is why orgies of clicking are not only cyclical but tend to quickly spiral out of control.

Again, as was shown with the example of the line-cutter, doxing—or wanting to make public the identity of a rule-breaker—is not new. Rather what is new is our success in being able to find out who rule-breakers are and our success in being able to make the identity of rule-breakers public. It is this success that technology affords us in our investigations of rule-breakers and in our punishments of rule-breakers that highlights what is precisely so dangerous about orgies of clicking. The move from wanting to atone for our own sins to wanting others to atone for their sins is not new either, but again it is the level of success that we are able to achieve in these endeavors that is both new and dangerous.

Trolling leads to more trolling. Shame campaigns lead to more shame campaigns. Doxing leads to more doxing. Orgies of clicking are thus not only ceaseless but also grow in intensity and scope, as trolling leads to shame campaigns, and shame campaigns lead to doxing. And what doxing leads to is President Donald Trump. For in the Trump campaign we witnessed trolling, shame campaigns, and doxing—all of these orgies of clicking—taking place on social media, in traditional media, and of course by candidate Trump himself. If the essence of orgies of clicking is to reveal how powerless those in power can become, and how powerful those thought to be powerless truly are, then perhaps it was only a matter of time before it was no longer enough to merely target individuals, especially when a political party, or even an entire nation, could be made the target of orgies of clicking.

Just as the benefits of the internet can be turned into tools of torture through orgies of clicking so too can the benefits of democracy be turned into weapons of war. An ominous sign that orgies of clicking could spiral out of control in this manner was exposed when doxing escalated into "swatting," which involves revealing identifying information about a chosen target and using it to give phony tips to the police with the expectation that a SWAT team will be sent to kick in the target's door. If doxing can lead to swatting, if revealing identities as a form of trolling can lead to endangering lives as a form of trolling, then certainly swatting can lead to Trumping, Brexiting, or simply *voting* as even more menacing forms of trolling potentially shift from endangering lives to endangering countries.

Orgies of feeling are dangerous because they put us on the path to self-destruction, but orgies of clicking are dangerous because they put us on the path to world-destruction. According to Nietzsche, ascetic priests should be understood to be on the side of life preservation, as their function is to redirect and channel the destructive impulses of the sick and suffering away from the herd so that they only do damage to themselves and not to others. Yet, as we have seen, when technologies attempt to fill the role once occupied by ascetic priests, when technologies attempt to function *as* ascetic priests, such damage control is no longer possible. Instead the very technologies that try to redirect and channel our destructive impulses only end up redirecting and channeling our self-destruction outward rather than inward. Guilt is altered into shame campaigns and purification rituals become ethno-nationalist rallies as technologies used for distracting us from our suffering become technologies used for inflicting our suffering on the world.

NOTES

1. Nietzsche, *Genealogy*, 139–40.

2. Wilkinson College, "America's Top Fears 2016," *Chapman University Blog*, October 11, 2016, https://blogs.chapman.edu/wilkinson/2016/10/11/americas-top-fears-2016/.

3. Becky Gardiner, et al., "The Dark Side of Guardian Comments," *Guardian*, April 12, 2016, https://www.theguardian.com/technology/2016/apr/12/the-dark-side-of-guardian-comments.

4. Gardiner, "The Dark Side."

5. Klint Finley, "A Brief History of the End of the Comments," *Wired*, October 8, 2015, https://www.wired.com/2015/10/brief-history-of-the-demise-of-the-comments-timeline/.

6. Erin E. Buckels, et al., "Trolls Just Want to Have Fun," *Personality and Individual Differences* 67 (September 2014): 101.

7. Chris Mooney, "Internet Trolls Really Are Horrible People," *Slate*, February 14, 2014, http://www.slate.com/articles/health_and_science/climate_desk/2014/02/internet_troll_personality_study_machiavellianism_narcissism_psychopathy.html.

8. Buckels et al., "Trolls," 101.

9. Larry Niven, "Flash Crowd," in *Three Trips in Time and Space: Original Novellas of Science Fiction*, ed. Robert Silverberg (New York: Hawthorn Books, 1973), 1–64.

10. Bill Wasik, "The Experiments," *And Then There's This*, http://www.andthentheresthis.net/mob.html.

11. Bill Wasik, *And Then There's This: How Stories Live and Die in Viral Culture* (New York: Viking Penguin, 2009), 19.

12. Bill Wasik, "'Flash Robs: Trying to Stop a Meme Gone Wrong," *Wired*, November 23, 2011, https://www.wired.com/2011/11/flash-robs/all/1.

13. Zeynep Tufekci and Christopher Wilson, "Social Media and the Decision to Participate in Political Protest: Observations From Tahrir Square," *Journal of Communication* 62 (2012): 363–79.

14. Don Caldwell, "Occupy Wall Street," *Know Your Meme*, September 8, 2011, http://knowyourmeme.com/memes/events/occupy-wall-street.

15. Ray Sanchez, "Occupy Wall Street: 5 Years Later," *CNN*, September 16, 2016, http://edition.cnn.com/2016/09/16/us/occupy-wall-street-protest-movements/index.html.

16. Jason Plautz, "The Changing Definition of 'Flash Mob'," *Mental Floss*, August 22, 2011, http://mentalfloss.com/article/28578/changing-definition-flash-mob.

17. Jon Ronson, *So You've Been Publicly Shamed* (New York: Riverhead Books, 2016), 10.

18. Ronson, *Publicly Shamed*, 70.

19. Ronson, *Publicly Shamed*, 54.

20. Nietzsche, *Genealogy*, 67.

21. Whitney Phillips, "LOLing at Tragedy: Facebook Trolls, Memorial Pages and Resistance to Grief Online," *First Monday* 16, no. 12 (December 5, 2011): 2, available at: http://firstmonday.org/ojs/index.php/fm/article/view/3168/3115.

22. Phillips, "LOLing," 2.

23. Will Wei, "We Asked Siri the Most Existential Question Ever and She Had a Lot to Say," *Business Insider*, July 9, 2015, http://www.businessinsider.com/siri-meaning-of-life-responses-apple-iphone-2015-7.

24. Nietzsche, *Genealogy*, 141.

25. David M. Douglas, "Doxing: A Conceptual Analysis," *Ethics and Information Technology* 18, no. 3 (2016): 199–210.

26. Douglas, "Doxing," 203.

9

GOOGLE IS DEAD

9.1 THE MADMAN

Have you not heard of that madman who turned on his flashlight app one morning, ran to the nearest Starbucks, and cried incessantly, "I seek Google! I seek Google!" As many of the patrons happened to be hipsters who no longer think it cool to use Google, he provoked much laughter. Is Google lost? asked one. Is Google down and it frightened you? asked another. Is Google hiding? Search ran off with Siri? Thus they yelled and laughed. The madman jumped into their midst and briefly caused them to look up from their laptops.

"Whither is Google?" he cried. "I shall tell you. *We have killed it—* you and I. All of us are Google's murderers. But how have we done this? How could we no longer have faith in Google Search? Who made it possible for us to stop looking at Gmail? What were we doing when we broke the chain connecting the Earth to Google Earth? Whither are we going? Away from all Google Maps? Will we not be wandering lost continually? Backward, sideward, forward, in all directions? Do we hear nothing as yet of the noise of the engineers burying the code of Google? Do we smell nothing yet of its decomposition? Algorithms, too, decompose. Google is dead. Google remains dead. And we have killed it.

"How shall we comfort ourselves, the murderers of all murderers? What was wisest and most powerful of all that Silicon Valley has yet produced has bled to death under our smartphones: who will wipe this blood off? What Genius Bar is there to fix it? What YouTube videos of atonement, what apology tweets shall we have to post? Is not the greatness of this deed too great for us? Must we ourselves not become multiplatform internet companies simply to appear worthy of it? There has never been a greater deed; and whoever is born after us—for the sake of this deed he will belong to a better search history than all search histories hitherto."

Here the madman fell silent and looked again at the Starbucks customers; and they, too, were silent and posted photos of him on Instagram in astonishment. At last he threw his iPhone on the ground, cracking the glass and forcing it to restart. "I have come too early," he said then; "my time is not yet. News of this event has not yet begun trending on Twitter. This deed is still more distant from them than a post hidden by Facebook's algorithms—*and yet they have done it themselves.*"

It has been related further that on the same day the madman forced his way into several other coffee shop chains and there struck up his *requiem aeternam Googleo.* Thrown out by baristas, he is said always to have replied nothing but: "What after all are these Wi-Fi hotspots if they are not the memorial GIFs and RIP hashtags of Google?"[1]

9.2 GOD IS DEAD

Nietzsche begins book three of *The Gay Science* with the following aphorism:

> *New struggles.*—After Buddha was dead, his shadow was still shown for centuries in a cave—a tremendous, gruesome shadow. God is dead; but given the way of men, there may still be caves for thousands of years in which this shadow will be shown. —And we—we still have to vanquish his shadow, too.[2]

Here in aphorism 108 we are first introduced to the famous claim, "God is dead." It is stated by Nietzsche almost as if in passing, almost as if it requires no explanation, for, like the death of Buddha, it is referred to as a historical event. Though, importantly, it is referred to as a historical event that we are unwilling to confront. Recalling Plato's myth of the cave, Nietzsche seems to be suggesting that we would rather worship a nonexistent God through false idols than leave the cave that we call home and be forced to face the truth of our situation.

In aphorism 125, Nietzsche explicitly returns to this claim and expands upon it. There Nietzsche tells us the story of a "madman,"[3] of a man who gets laughed at for searching for God, and who responds to the crowd of skeptics by telling them not only that God is dead but that it is we who have killed God. The madman continues by asking how without God we will find a way to orient ourselves, and by asking whether we must become gods in order to be worthy of this murder. Upon realizing that the crowd does not understand him, he declares that he has come too soon, that we have not yet become aware of the death of God, of this deed that we have ourselves committed but have committed without having realized it.

This aphorism has been reduced to a mantra, to a T-shirt, to the three words that even those who have never heard of Nietzsche know, much like how those who have never read *Hamlet* nevertheless know Shakespeare's six words. To say "God is dead" has thus been taken to be straightforward, as equivalent to saying that we are living in an atheistic world, that nothing is sacred, that we have finally discovered that we should look to scientific research rather than pray to supernatural beings for the answers to our questions. "God is dead" has become a shibboleth, a way to signal one's allegiance, either to atheism and science (if one is proudly declaring these three words) or to nihilism and cynicism (if one is resignedly declaring these three words).

The death of God does not refer to a literal deicide, nor to the end of religion, but rather to the death of what God *means*. God no longer fulfills the role of God, not because science won but because nihilism won. Nihilism—the "radical repudiation of value, meaning, and desirability"—has led us to repudiate the value, meaning, and desirability of God. By soothing rather than curing our nihilism, by prescribing self-hypnosis, mechanical activity, petty pleasures, herd instinct, and orgies of feeling, the ascetic priests protected the Christian moral world from exploding. However this world was preserved for so long that it has instead *imploded*. As Nietzsche writes in the second note from *The Will to Power*, "What does nihilism mean? *That the highest values devalue themselves*. The aim is lacking; 'why?' finds no answer."[4]

God is dead because God is no longer an answer that satisfies our questions. We can only be told "God" as an answer to every "Why?" for so long, we can only be told that we exist because of God, that we suffer because of God, that we die because of God for so long before the answer becomes meaningless. For we are not only told that God is the answer but, each time we are told this, the answer is embellished, enlarged, extended to include ideas about what God is like, what we can expect from God, what we will receive from God. In this way God became so desired, so meaningful, so valued that, as Nietzsche described, the value of God devalued itself. God became a contradiction, an all-powerful, all-knowing, all-loving being who yet lacked the power, the knowledge, the love to fulfill our prayers, to respond to our pleas, to even answer our questions. Eventually, the answer of "God" became no more meaningful than the answer of "Flying Spaghetti Monster."[5]

Once the answer became meaningless, the danger arose that the question itself would become meaningless ("'why?' finds no answer"), at which point life would become meaningless ("the aim is lacking"). Yet if, as Nietzsche argues, life is will to power, then for life to become meaningless so too would willing have to become meaningless. But so long as we live we are incapable of *not willing*, for which reason Nietzsche spends the third essay of the *Genealogy* describing how we instead *will nothingness*. Faced with the possibility that life is meaningless, we reject "God" as an answer to our questions, but only by replacing "God" with structurally equivalent answers. In other words, we are willing to keep coming up with new answers to our old questions because we prefer the illusion of meaning to having to face the meaning of our illusions. We prefer shadows "shown for centuries in a cave" to having to "vanquish" our shadows.

Like Schrödinger's cat, God is both dead and not dead. "God" as *the answer* to our questions is dead. "God" as *the way to answer* our questions is not dead. But so long as we only want answers that allow us to stop asking questions, that allow us to get back to living our lives, then our answers will always end up disappointing us, in the same way that "God" ultimately led us from Christianity to Pastafarianism.[6] For the issue is not our answers but our questions, the need to have someone else tell us what to do and how to live, to tell us our purpose, to tell us that our lives are meaningful, rather than decide for ourselves how to live, rather than create our own purpose, rather than make our lives meaningful in our own way. As Nietzsche's madman asks, God is dead, and we have killed him, but do we not still have to "become gods simply to appear worthy of it?"[7]

9.3 GOOGLE HAS RISEN

And yet perhaps we have "become gods," perhaps we have become
"worthy" of the death of God, for we have created technologies that can
now seemingly overcome rather than replace God, technologies like
those produced by Google. Google stands as proof that humans do not
need gods, that humans are capable of fulfilling the role once reserved
for the gods. As Siva Vaidhyanathan writes in *The Googlization of
Everything*:

> Google seems omniscient, omnipotent, and omnipresent. It also
> claims to be benevolent. It's no surprise that we hold the company in
> almost deific awe and respect. [. . .] Overwhelmingly, we now allow
> Google to determine what is important, relevant, and true on the
> Web and in the world. We trust and believe that Google acts in our
> best interest. [8]

Today it is Google that occupies the role of being all-knowing (Google
Search), all-seeing (Google Earth), all-powerful (Google's DeepMind),
and all-loving (Google Assistant). Google founders Larry Page and Ser-
gey Brin have even made the Ten Commandments obsolete, offering
instead the One Commandment: "Don't be evil." [9]

This commandment, or code of conduct, perfectly encapsulates our
relationship to Google. For it is intuitive, it is efficient, and it is seduc-
tive. Thousands of years of religious and philosophical thought suddenly
seem unnecessarily silly when compared to this statement. The bold-
ness of the claim, and the implied mockery of any competing claim,
further entices us to believe it, to trust it, to put our faith in it. What
Google provides us must be honest and objective, since any falsehood,
any bias, any "evil," would so obviously run counter to Google's code
that users would have to immediately feel betrayed and abandon Google.

Google is many things to many people, it is many companies, many
apps, many devices, but more than anything it is one simple and very
powerful thing: *results*. From its beginning as a search engine to its
growth into a multiservice, multi-platform, multinational empire, Google has never represented anything other than results. And it is here
that we can see why Google provides us what God could not. As the
incongruity between the promise of results and the experience of being

told to just keep waiting became harder and harder to suffer through, we lost faith in God, we were led away from looking to the skies and toward looking at our screens. Google offered what we were desperate for, a world of answers rather than questions, a world of results.

In his article "What Is 'Evil' to Google?" Ian Bogost argues that it is Google's definition of "evil" that "might turn out to be one of Google's lasting legacies,"[10] for which reason "understanding what evil means to Google might be central to grasping its role in contemporary culture."[11] According to Bogost, Google defines "evil" not as a moral category but as an engineering category. What is "evil" for Google is what stands in the way, not of *virtue* but of *progress*, in particular what stands in the way of *Google's* progress. The question as Google users that we need to ask then is whether what Google wants is what we want, whether what we define as "evil" is what Google defines as "evil." For Bogost, the answer is no. Bogost writes:

> This is what makes the whole matter seem so insidious: It's not that Google has announced its intention not to be vicious and failed to meet the bar. Nor is Google, Arendt-style, just manning its station, doing what's expected. No, through its motto Google has effectively *redefined* evil as a matter of unserviceability in general, and unserviceability among corporatized information services in particular. As for virtue, it's a nonissue: Google's acts are by their very nature righteous, a consequence of Google having done them. The company doesn't need to exercise any moral judgement other than whatever it will have done. The biggest risk—the greatest evil—lies in failing to engineer an effective implementation of its own vision. *Don't be evil* is the Silicon Valley version of *Be true to yourself.* It is both tautology and narcissism.[12]

For Google, what is "good" is what Google does, and what is "evil" is what Google avoids. Bogost describes this as "narcissism." Nietzsche would describe this as "slave morality." Yet Nietzsche would agree that this value system is indeed "insidious," though not for the reasons that Bogost offers.

The insidiousness of Google for Bogost is that what it presents as a moral worldview is in reality an *amoral* worldview of self-perpetuation. As we have seen, for Nietzsche, self-perpetuation is precisely the aim of the ascetic priests, for which reason "virtue" has come to be increasingly associated with abstinence, with self-denial, self-sacrifice, and self-effacement. Such denial, sacrifice, and effacement are recognized as "moral," as "righteous," because they serve society. But for Nietzsche such service to society has come to be valued because, on the one hand, it allows us to indulge our instincts for cruelty, even if only by being cruel to ourselves, and, on the other hand, because it allows society to be safe from our antisocial instincts, from our *ressentiment*, and from our nihilism. In other words, morality is not opposed to self-perpetuation but is rather an outgrowth of it.

As was discussed in chapter 2, according to Nietzsche, the concept of "evil" originates with slave morality, with the revaluation of the values of the masters such that what had been "good" became "evil" and what had been "bad" became "good." What was valued by the masters (physicality, violence, pleasure) became devalued by the slaves as "evil" and what was devalued by the masters (contemplation, cunning, abstinence) became valued by the slaves as "good." Though the value systems of the masters and of the slaves opposed each other, they had in common that what one valued was one's own characteristics, and what one devalued were the characteristics that defined those opposed to oneself. But whereas the masters looked down upon those not like themselves, for which reason the masters merely saw the slaves as "bad," the slaves despised and sought to destroy those not like themselves, for which reason the slaves saw the masters as "evil." Those who were "bad" were those who were beneath oneself, but those who were "evil" were those who should not exist. In other words, the value system of the slaves, the value system that gave birth to the Christian moral world and to nihilism, could be summarized: "Don't be evil."

The insidiousness of Google for Nietzsche therefore would be that what it presents as an amoral worldview is in reality a *moral* worldview of self-perpetuation. Google is not evidence that we have become worthy of the death of God, nor is it evidence that we have overcome God. Google is *God 2.0*. But as Bogost points out, "Google's logic is no different from that of other technology companies," as they all share "the belief that its principles should apply to everyone."[13] This logic, though, is not new, as it is shared not only by tech companies but also by ascetic priests.

We put our faith in the ascetic priests because we thought the ascetic priests would cure us of our suffering, of our nihilism. But because our suffering was rooted in the very world that the ascetic priests were trying to preserve, they sought to soothe rather than cure our suffering, prescribing to us ways to avoid ourselves, ways to rechannel our instincts, ways such as self-hypnosis, mechanical activity, petty pleasures, herd instinct, and orgies of feeling. The result of soothing rather than curing our suffering was that it strengthened rather than weakened our nihilism, so much so that our nihilism became strong enough to destroy our faith in the ascetic priests, in God, and in the Christian moral world.

This does not mean that we have lost faith completely however, as we have today put our faith in tech companies, in companies like Google, in companies that produce what we expect will provide us the cure to our suffering, the cure that we could no longer wait for the ascetic priests and God to provide. It is for this reason that these tech companies are so insidious, for in place of the amoral, atheistic, posthuman, post-Christian world that we believe these tech companies are ushering in, we are instead presented only with the illusion of change, of evolution, of *disruption*. For in reality, as Bogost pointed out, these tech companies are interested in self-perpetuation, not self-overcoming, particularly as genuine disruption of the status quo could result in a genuine disruption of their exalted place in the status quo. Hence, like the ascetic priests they replaced, tech companies too only soothe rather than cure our suffering, providing us not disruption but *distraction*, thereby preserving the Christian moral world that they present themselves as having overcome.

9.4 GOOGLING OURSELVES TO DEATH

As we have seen in previous chapters, the ways of soothing our suffering may have changed—as we now have techno-hypnosis, data-driven activity, pleasure economics, herd networking, and orgies of clicking—but the result of such "priestly medications" has not changed. Our nihilism is still being strengthened rather than weakened. Thanks to tech companies, we can zone out, we can be more efficient, we can help strangers, we can make friends, and we can attack enemies. And while we may indeed find these activities meaningful, and may even find they make us happy, that does not mean that these activities are not nihilistic. For nihilism does not mean that life is meaningless but rather that our search for a transcendent source of meaning, for a source of meaning external to us, external to our lives, results in our lives *not being lived*. It is for this reason that what should concern us is not what we find to be meaningless but rather what we find to be meaningful.

Nietzsche wanted us to question the value of our values, not in order to show that our values were meaningless but in order to show that our values do not necessarily provide us what we assume they provide. The high value we attribute to being good does not necessarily result in our being benefited by such goodness, particularly if "being good" requires that we deny our instincts, deny our individuality, and deny what Nietzsche refers to as our "indeterminacy." In *Beyond Good and Evil*, Nietzsche argues that "humans are *the still undetermined animals*," for which reason religions like Christianity and Buddhism are "uncanny dangers" because "they give rights to all those who suffer life like a disease, and try to make every other feeling for life seem wrong and become impossible."[14] Rather than viewing life as challenges to be overcome, as challenges that force us to adapt and to grow, the attitude of ascetic religions instills in us a view of life as suffering, thereby exploiting and perpetuating our weaknesses and worst tendencies by teaching us to view life as a burden we must suffer through in order to prove our worthiness for the afterlife.

Nietzsche does not challenge the belief that ascetic religions have helped to make the world a better place, a safer place, a place where the weak need not fear the strong. Rather Nietzsche tries to show why the better, safer, moral world is a nihilistic world, a world where we can stagnate, where we can remain suffering, where we can remain determined, determined as the beings who suffer. For Nietzsche, we are the beings who suffer, but we suffer not because life *is* suffering but because *we suffer from life*, because we have accepted—and because we continue to accept—the gospel that a *better* world than this is waiting for us. Ascetic religions manifest and multiply our nihilism because they turn us against life, against the world, and against ourselves, and turn us instead toward lifelessness, toward worldlessness, and toward the supernatural. Human-nihilism relations therefore soothe our suffering because they provide us a taste of the afterlife we have been promised, allowing us to experience death while alive. This is achieved by allowing us to experience freedom from the burdens of living, from the burdens of introspection, of decision-making, of weakness, of loneliness, and of responsibility.

Here again we can see how tech companies operate like ascetic priests, and how technology has become our new ascetic religion. As was seen in the discussion of transhumanism in chapter 2, technologies can point us away from life and point us toward an afterlife, a *posthuman* life, a life free of suffering, free of the suffering of the *merely human* life. For transhumanism, just as for Christianity and Buddhism, to be human means to be suffering. Yet, according to transhumanism, while suffering is who we are, who we are can be overcome, though not by embracing human freedom but by embracing technological freedom. Nihilism-technology relations therefore soothe our suffering because they provide us a taste of the posthuman life we have been promised, allowing us to experience *being technology* while being human. This is achieved by allowing us to experience freedom from the burdens of being human, from the burdens of limited imagination, of limited information, of limited influence, of limited interaction, and of limited impact.

In other words, tech companies are trying to make the world a better place, a safer place, a place where there are no weak, there are no strong, there are only the more or less limited. The dream of tech companies is the dream of smart devices, smart cities, and smart people, a world where everything and everyone is connected, integrated, always on, always up-to-date, and always overcoming limitations. But what must be recognized is that this is not a dream *imposed on us* by tech companies. This dream is our dream too. And indeed tech companies are not wrong to justify their practices by arguing that they are only providing us with *what we want*. Wanting, though, as was discussed in chapter 3, is not immune to the influences of technologies, as technologies mediate our experience of the world and of ourselves.

If today we experience life as suffering because we experience life as limited, that is because our technologies reveal life to us as limited, and reveal such limitations by presenting them as *unnecessary* sources of suffering. Technologies enable us to do things we never thought possible, things like using a headset to enter virtual worlds, using algorithms to predict behavior, using a website to rent out our bedrooms, using a hashtag to connect with strangers, and using a handheld box to participate in protests from our couch. Yet because we never thought such activities were possible, we did not feel limited by the impossibility of doing these activities. We did not feel that human abilities were lacking in these ways until these new technologically enabled abilities appeared. Once these abilities did appear—or even when they were simply advertised to us as possibilities on the horizon—then we began to see ourselves differently, to see ourselves dualistically, dividing *who we are* from *what we can do*, for which reason enhancement could be seen as providing us "freedom" rather than as producing unforeseeable, and possibly undesirable, changes to our identity. This "neo-Cartesian"[15] attitude elevated our minds while lowering our bodies, seeing our bodies only in terms of our abilities, our abilities only in terms of their limitations, and seeing these limitations only as unnecessary, unwanted, and unfair.

For example, tech companies have shown us that traditional face-to-face communication is inefficient. As talking can be broken down into listening and speaking, and listening to someone does not require looking at someone, we could be looking at something else while talking, we could be doing something else, we could be *multitasking*. With a phone, we could be talking to someone while still having our hands and eyes free to work. With a laptop, we could be talking to someone while still trying to work in one window and checking Facebook in another window. With a video conferencing app, we could be talking to multiple people while still trying to work and still checking Facebook, all while we are still in our pajamas. These innovations have enabled us to expand our communicative abilities, but they have achieved this not by making communication a richer, more meaningful experience but by reducing communication to mental tasks achieved by bodily abilities, abilities that could be isolated and enhanced to allow us to accomplish more and more tasks, as if communication was a goal-driven activity and accomplishing tasks was the only goal driving communication.

Tech companies therefore do give us what we want, but they also play a vital role in shaping what we think it is even possible to want. Thanks to tech companies we not only want these technologically enabled abilities, we crave them. In their article "The 'Myth' of Media Multitasking," Zheng Wang and John Tchernev write that their research revealed that "although cognitive needs are not gratified by media multitasking, emotional needs are, such as feeling entertained or relaxed," the result of which is that we become less productive and yet more motivated "to engage . . . in media multitasking again and again."[16] Technologies that isolate and enhance our abilities do not satisfy the cravings—whether cognitive or emotional—they create in us, they only exacerbate them. This is the danger of reducing humanity to abilities and abilities to limits, as the pleasure of exceeding limits eventually wears off, leaving any new ability to be seen as a new limit that must itself be overcome. Having been led by technologies to see abilities as to-be-upgraded rather than as to-be-appreciated, we quickly lose our excitement over whatever new limit-breaking ability a new upgrade has brought us and begin to focus instead on what the *next* new upgrade will bring.

The more we use these technology-enabled abilities, the more these abilities become, as Aristotle put it, *second nature* to us. But as we have learned from tech companies to look down upon what is natural, to see what is natural as merely a limit to be overcome, we end up not only incorporating these new technology-enabled abilities into our sense of what is natural but also looking down upon these new abilities as a *new natural* to be overcome. It is for this reason that nihilism-technology relations can only soothe our suffering rather than cure it, as any technology that overcomes a limit must itself be reduced to a limit to be overcome. The cyclical nature of our relationship with technologies—a cycle that repeats more rapidly as our habituation to technologies is achieved more rapidly—must ultimately result in technologies no longer being able to even soothe our suffering. Instead our technologies will themselves become sources of suffering, of the very suffering that they were meant to overcome, of the very suffering that they provoked in us in the first place. In other words, our highest values are devaluing themselves.

So long as we continue to expect new technologies to cure our suffering, to cure even the suffering created by the technologies previously expected to cure our suffering, these cycles of excitement and disappointment will not only increase our suffering but also our nihilism. For we are increasingly asking technologies to grow and to adapt to the challenges of life so that we do not have to. Technologies protect us from the chaotic and the unexpected as well as from the boring and the mundane, allowing us to stagnate in insulated, media-rich environments, enticing us to accept the gospel of tech companies and of transhumanism that life lived through technologies is the *only* life worth living. If we are to break free of these cycles, to break free of this nihilistic death spiral, then we must begin by learning to recognize the dangerous as well as the desirable effects of our relationships with technologies, and to recognize the pervasiveness of these dangerous effects. We need not reject technologies, nor reject attempts to better ourselves, rather we must develop a more critical perspective toward our single-minded devotion to technologies, toward our ideological faith that *better* can only mean *more technological*.

Tech companies cannot justify their actions on the basis of what we want unless we are first able to determine *for ourselves* what it is that we want. Yet because technologies mediate our experience of ourselves and of the world, there is no way to discover what we want without technologies playing an active role in such discovery. For this reason we must not attempt to escape from technology, as if taking a phone-free walk in the woods would allow us to find unmediated experience rather than finding that even without our devices we are still nevertheless experiencing the world through our devices. The mediating influences of our technologies operate on us whether they are in our hands or just in our minds as, for example, when we see an animal as not merely cute but as Instagram-worthy, or experience an event as not merely memorable but as Twitter-worthy. Or to put it another way, the influence of technologies like Instagram and Twitter on us is such that Instagram-worthiness can determine what is cute and Twitter-worthiness can determine what is memorable, as if we saw the world not through our eyes but through the eyes of Instagram and Twitter.

We may log out of our apps and our devices, but our apps and our devices do not log out of us. This is why we must not try to flee from our technologies or try to somehow get outside of technological mediation, as the belief that such escape is possible merely reinforces the illusion that technologies only influence us so long as we are using them. Technologies are invasive not only in terms of our privacy but also in terms of our perceptivity. Debates over how to improve our technologies — about how to make them safer, more secure, more resilient, more available—are so consuming our attention that we forget to first question how to improve ourselves, to question whether improving technologies helps or hinders our attempts to improve ourselves, to question where our idea of what "improvement" means comes from. From a Nietzschean perspective, this is a feature, not a bug. Time spent thinking about technologies is time spent not thinking about ourselves. And our need to not think about ourselves, to not question ourselves, to not reckon with ourselves, is precisely what draws our nihilism to embrace technologies and draws tech companies to embrace our nihilism.

9.5 BEYOND GOOGLE AND EVIL

Let us conclude by returning to Nietzsche's distinction between *passive nihilism* and *active nihilism*. In chapter 2 I suggested that passive nihilism can give rise to active nihilism, that the devaluation of values can open up the space necessary for the creation of new values, and I also left open the question of whether we should think of technological nihilism as passive or as active. Having now seen how we are becoming more and more disappointed, disillusioned, and destructive in our attempts to use technologies to improve ourselves, we can also see that we are becoming more and more ready to ask the question that passive nihilism provokes: What is our *aim* with regard to technologies? What is the *why?* of our technological pursuits?

The answer to these questions would appear to be that our aim is human progress, and that we believe that human progress can and must arise solely through technological progress. This is the answer provided not only by Kevin Warwick, Ray Kurzweil, and Nick Bostrom (see chapter 2) but by contemporary philosophers of technology as varied as Luciano Floridi, Peter-Paul Verbeek, and Shannon Vallor. As Floridi writes:

> any apocalyptic vision of AI can be disregarded. We are and shall remain, for any foreseeable future, the problem, not our technology . . . [W]e should make AI make us more human. The serious risk is that we might misuse our smart technologies, to the detriment of most of humanity and the whole planet. Winston Churchill said that 'we shape our buildings and afterwards our buildings shape us'. This applies to the infosphere and its smart technologies as well. [17]

As Verbeek writes:

> If technology fundamentally mediates what kind of humans we are, this does not imply that "humanity" is mastered by "technology," as

those advocating some Heideggerian positions want us to believe. [. . .] Ethics, then, should not aim at protecting "humanity" from "technology" but should consist in carefully assessing and experimenting with technological mediations, in order to explicitly fashion the ways they help to shape subjects in our technological culture.[18]

As Vallor writes:

> The choice is not between surrendering to technology or liberating ourselves from it. We are *technomoral creatures* to the core; that is, we allow and have always allowed the things we make to reshape us. The only question is whether this process is deliberate and wise or unreflective and reckless.[19]

For Floridi, Verbeek, and Vallor, human progress is shaped by technologies, for which reason we must learn how to best shape technologies if we are to learn how to best shape ourselves.

For Nietzsche, human progress is shaped by nihilism, for which reason human progress did not begin until the slaves defeated the masters, until ascetic values replaced warrior values, until using self-denial to shape ourselves supplanted using self-expression to shape the world. In other words, technological progress and human progress are indeed intertwined, but if our definition of "progress" is fundamentally nihilistic, then it should not surprise us that technological progress has resulted in techno-hypnosis, data-driven activity, pleasure economics, herd networking, and orgies of clicking.

Nietzsche would therefore agree with Floridi, Verbeek, and Vallor that technological progress has furthered human progress, or at least what we take for granted to be human progress. We are indeed using technologies to shape ourselves into the beings we want to be. But from a Nietzschean perspective we can see that this *aim* is nihilistic, that the answer to the *why?* of our technological progress is that we do not want the reality in which we find ourselves. As we saw in chapter 3, Ihde describes our desire for technologies as a "desire for a change in situation," a desire to "inhabit the earth, or even to go beyond the earth." Our relationship to technologies is thus not only nihilistic, it is *passively* nihilistic. Though we are destroying traditions with creative aims, what we seek to create are not new values but new humans, *posthumans*. Yet these posthumans would nevertheless be shaped in accordance with human aims, with the human, *all-too-human* aims that formerly led to the creation of the Christian moral world and that are presently leading to the creation of a "technomoral" world.

Rather than try to overcome our nihilism, we must try to turn our passive nihilism into active nihilism. Our willingness to destroy any and all traditional ways of life, traditional relations with others, and traditional forms of engagement with the world in the pursuit of the posthuman is simultaneously our greatest danger and our greatest opportunity. Our dissatisfaction with reality, our disappointment with all new realities that technologies have brought into being, can either lead us to destroy ourselves or it can lead us to destroy the values that have put us on this path to self-destruction. If passive nihilism has so far led us to question every value that is seen as contrary to technological progress, then passive nihilism may soon lead us to question the value of technological progress itself, and with it the value of human progress.

As I suggested earlier, such a stage would herald the death of Google but, like the death of God, the loss of perspective, of certainty, of orientation that such a death would bring could lead us to simply seek out new Googles rather than new perspectives. It is for this reason that we must seek out new perspectives now in anticipation of our reaching such a nihilistic stage. We must attempt to take advantage of where passive nihilism has already led us so that, as Nietzsche did, we can motivate in advance a critique of our values, a critique of what values lurk beneath such seemingly benign ideas as those concerning the relationship between "human progress" and "technological progress."

To see why such a critique is necessary and what such a critique may look like, let us focus on a rather mundane example of technological progress, such as the development of productivity-enhancing lighting systems in office buildings. Rather than have workers be desperate to leave the office, buildings are now being designed to bring the outdoors into the office, as can be achieved for example by replacing fluorescent lighting with daylight-replicating lighting, with lighting that not only seems more natural but can even be regulated to conform with circadian rhythms.[20] Based on studies of employee performance and employee attitudes, such lighting interventions have a quantifiable impact on employee well-being. In other words, these new lighting systems are a proven technological solution to the problem of employee productivity.

However, from a Nietzschean perspective, rather than ask whether such lighting systems increase productivity and well-being, we must ask what it means to think of productivity and well-being as problems to be solved by technologies. Lighting systems that are designed to make employees feel better carry with them the normative weight that employees working in such an environment *should* feel better. Consequently, to not feel well at work, to not be happy, to not be more productive, is no longer a sign that there is something wrong with the work, it is instead a sign that there is something wrong with *the worker*, with the *individual* worker who somehow does not feel happy in an environment *designed* to increase happiness. Rather than being motivated by our unhappiness to question the world around us, to question the structures of the world that produce unhappiness, technological interventions such as these lighting systems motivate us to question only ourselves. These technological interventions motivate us to feel that there must be something wrong with us if we are not as happy as we are *supposed to be*, if we are not as happy as studies have shown *humans would be* in the technological environment we have been provided.

Yet even the studies that show these technological interventions produce the benefits they were designed to produce may only have such positive results because the people who were surveyed knew how humans were supposed to respond to these interventions. When asked if we are made happier by technologies designed to make humans happier, we are likely to respond positively, if only because we know—whether consciously or unconsciously—that to be seen as *unhappy* is to risk being seen as *inhuman*. Hence if we only evaluate technological innovations by metrics like productivity and well-being, we will not only be ignoring how such technological innovations can influence our understanding of our identity and of our humanity, we will also be ignoring how technological innovations can even influence the trustworthiness of our evaluations.

A critical, Nietzschean perspective on technologies can help us to recognize how we use technologies nihilistically, such as when we use technologies to try to *make* people be happier in particular environments rather than questioning *why* people are not happy in those environments. A critical, Nietzschean perspective on technologies can also help us to recognize how we evaluate technologies nihilistically, such as when we take for granted what it means to be human, and when we take for granted that we need not question the relationship between human progress and technological progress.

Passive nihilism has led us to see in technologies a way to become better humans, humans who are more productive and who are—or at least *should be*—happier while being productive. But passive nihilism is also leading us to see in technologies a way to become sicker humans, humans who are trapped in an endless cycle of never being satisfied with how much "better" we have become. In other words, passive nihilism is leading us toward active nihilism, toward being able to question if we know what "better" means; to question if we know what purpose such betterment is meant to serve; to question whether we are trying to become better only for the sake of being better, for the sake of being different, for the sake of not being who we are; to question whether our pursuit of the posthuman is leading us to risk becoming inhuman because of our nihilistic desire to be anything other than *merely human*. It is through exploring such questions that we can destroy in order to create, in order to create new values, new goals, and new perspectives on the relationship between human progress and technological progress.

NOTES

1. For the original version of this prophecy, see Nietzsche, *The Gay Science*, 181–82.

2. Nietzsche, *The Gay Science*, 167.

3. Nietzsche, *The Gay Science*, 181–82.

4. Nietzsche, *The Will to Power*, 9.

5. Kathy Gilsinan, "Big in Europe: The Church of the Flying Spaghetti Monster," *The Atlantic*, November 2016, https://www.theatlantic.com/magazine/archive/2016/11/big-in-europe/501131/.

6. See Bobby Henderson, "About," *Church of the Flying Spaghetti Monster*, https://www.venganza.org/about/.

7. Nietzsche, *The Will to Power*, 181.

8. Siva Vaidhyanathan, *The Googlization of Everything: (And Why We Should Worry)* (Berkeley and Los Angeles, University of California Press, 2011), *xi*.

9. Alphabet, "Google Code of Conduct," *Alphabet Investor Relations*, https://abc.xyz/investor/other/google-code-of-conduct.html.

10. Ian Bogost, "What Is 'Evil' to Google?," *The Atlantic*, October 15, 2013, https://www.theatlantic.com/technology/archive/2013/10/what-is-evil-to-google/280573/, 6.

11. Bogost, "Evil," 3.

12. Bogost, "Evil," 6.

13. Bogost, "Evil," 7.

14. Friedrich Nietzsche, *Beyond Good and Evil*, ed. Rolf-Peter Horstmann, trans. Judith Norman (Cambridge: Cambridge University Press, 2002), 55–56.

15. Ian Hacking, "Our Neo-Cartesian Bodies in Parts," *Critical Inquiry* 34 (August 2007): 78–105.

16. Zheng Wang and John Tchernev, "The 'Myth' of Media Multitasking: Reciprocal Dynamics of Media Multitasking, Personal Needs, and Gratifications," *Journal of Communication* 62, no. 3 (2012): 509.

17. Luciano Floridi, "Should We Be Afraid of AI?," *Aeon*, May 9, 2016, https://aeon.co/essays/true-ai-is-both-logically-possible-and-utterly-implausible.

18. Peter-Paul Verbeek, *Moralizing Technology: Understanding and Designing the Morality of Things* (Chicago and London: University of Chicago Press, 2011), 82.

19. Shannon Vallor, "Moral Deskilling and Upskilling in a New Machine Age: Reflections on the Ambiguous Future of Character," *Philosophy of Technology* 28 (2015): 118.

20. Molly Greenberg, "Flick of a Switch: How Lighting Affects Productivity and Mood," *Business*, February 22, 2017, https://www.business.com/articles/flick-of-a-switch-how-lighting-affects-productivity-and-mood/.

BIBLIOGRAPHY

Adorno, Theodor. "How to Look at Television." In *The Culture Industry*, edited by J. M. Bernstein, 158–77. London and New York: Routledge Classics, 2001.

Alleyne, Richard. "YouTube: Overnight Success Has Sparked a Backlash." *Telegraph*, July 31, 2008. Accessed August 13, 2017. http://www.telegraph.co.uk/news/uknews/2480280/YouTube-Overnight-success-has-sparked-a-backlash.html.

Alphabet. "Google Code of Conduct." *Alphabet Investor Relations*. Accessed October 24, 2017. https://abc.xyz/investor/other/google-code-of-conduct.html.

Anders, Günther. "The World as Phantom and as Matrix." *Dissent* 3, no. 1 (Winter 1956): 14–24.

Aristotle. *Nicomachean Ethics*. Edited by Roger Crisp. Cambridge: Cambridge University Press, 2000.

Aydin, Ciano. "The Posthuman as Hollow Idol: A Nietzschean Critique of Human Enhancement." *Journal of Medicine and Philosophy* 42, iss. 3 (June 1, 2017): 304–27.

Ayers J. W., E. C. Leas, M. Dredze, J. Allem, J. G. Grabowski, and L. Hill. "Pokémon GO—A New Distraction for Drivers and Pedestrians." *JAMA Internal Medicine* 176, no. 12 (December 1, 2016): 1865–66.

Babich, Babette. *"Ex aliquo nihil*: Nietzsche on Science, Anarchy, and Democratic Nihilism." *American Catholic Philosophical Quarterly* 84, no. 2 (2010): 231–56.

———. *The Hallelujah Effect: Philosophical Reflections on Music, Performance Practice, and Technology*. Farnham: Ashgate, 2013.

———. "Nietzsche's Post-Human Imperative: On the 'All-too-Human' Dream of Transhumanism." In *Nietzsche and Transhumanism: Precursor or Enemy?*, edited by Yunus Tuncel, 101–32. Cambridge: Cambridge Scholars Publishing, 2017.

———. "On Schrödinger and Nietzsche: Eternal Return and the Moment." In *Antonio T. de Nicolas: Poet of Eternal Return*, edited by Christopher Key Chapple, 157–206. Ahmedabad, India: Sriyogi Publications & Nalanda International, 2014.

Bauman, Zygmunt. *Liquid Modernity*. Cambridge: Polity Press, 2000.

BBC News. "Google Buys YouTube for $1.65bn." *BBC News*, October 10, 2006. Accessed August 13, 2017. http://news.bbc.co.uk/1/hi/business/6034577.stm.

Biegler, Paul. "Tech Support: How Our Phones Could Save Our Lives by Detecting Mood Shifts." *Sunday Morning Herald*, November 12, 2017. Accessed November 13, 2017. http://www.smh.com.au/technology/innovation/tech-support-how-our-phones-could-save-our-lives-by-detecting-mood-shifts-20171106-gzfrg5.html.

bigkif. "Ivan Sutherland : Sketchpad Demo (1/2)." *YouTube*. Published on November 17, 2007. Accessed August 20, 2017. https://www.youtube.com/watch?v=USyoT_Ha_bA.

Bignell, Paul. "Happy 30th Birthday Emoticon! :-)" *Independent*, September 8, 2012. Accessed April 4, 2017. http://www.independent.co.uk/life-style/gadgets-and-tech/news/happy-30th-birthday-emoticon-8120158.html.

Blagdon, Jeff. "How Emoji Conquered the World." *The Verge*, March 4, 2013. Accessed April 4, 2017. http://www.theverge.com/2013/3/4/3966140/how-emoji-conquered-the-world.

Bogost, Ian. "What Is 'Evil' to Google?" *The Atlantic*, October 15, 2013. Accessed October 20, 2017. https://www.theatlantic.com/technology/archive/2013/10/what-is-evil-to-google/280573/.

Bostrom, Nick. "In Defense of Posthuman Dignity." *Bioethics* 19, no. 3 (2005): 202–214.

Bowerman, Mary. "Driver Slams into Baltimore Cop Car While Playing Pokemon Go." *USA Today*, July 20, 2016. Accessed February 8, 2017. http://www.usatoday.com/story/news/nation-now/2016/07/20/driver-slams-into-baltimore-cop-car-while-playing-pokemon-go-accident/87333892/.

Buckels, Erin E., Paul D. Trapnell, and Delroy L. Paulhus. "Trolls Just Want to Have Fun." *Personality and Individual Differences* 67 (September 2014): 97–102.

Burnham, Douglas. *The Nietzsche Dictionary*. London and New York: Bloomsbury, 2015.

Burrell, Jenna. "How the Machine 'Thinks': Understanding Opacity in Machine Learning Algorithms." *Big Data & Society* 3, iss. 1 (January–June 2016): 1–12.

Caldwell, Don. "Occupy Wall Street." *Know Your Meme*, September 8, 2011. Accessed June 3, 2017. http://knowyourmeme.com/memes/events/occupy-wall-street.

Cicero. *On the Good Life*. Translated by Michael Grant. London: Penguin Books, 1971.

Clarke, Kristen. "Does Airbnb Enable Racism?" *New York Times*, August 23, 2016. Accessed February 24, 2017. https://www.nytimes.com/2016/08/23/opinion/how-airbnb-can-fight-racial-discrimination.html.

Crystal, Bonnie, and Jeffrey Keating. *The World of CB Radio*. Summertown, NY: Book Publishing Company, 1987.

Deloitte. "70 Percent of US Consumers Binge Watch TV, Bingers Average Five Episodes per Sitting." *Deloitte Press Releases*, March 23, 2016. Accessed August 20, 2017. https://www2.deloitte.com/us/en/pages/about-deloitte/articles/press-releases/digital-democracy-survey-tenth-edition.html.

Dent, Steve. "The Roomba 960 Is iRobot's Cheaper App-Driven Robot Vacuum." *engadget*, August 4, 2016. Accessed November 1, 2016. https://www.engadget.com/2016/08/04/irobots-roomba-960-is-its-cheaper-app-driven-robot-vacuum/.

Douglas, David M. "Doxing: A Conceptual Analysis." *Ethics and Information Technology* 18, no. 3 (2016): 199–210.

Dvorak, John C. "Chat Rooms Are Dead! Long Live the Chat Room!" *PCMag*, December 11, 2007. Accessed March 28, 2017. http://www.pcmag.com/article2/0,2817,2231493,00.asp.

Economist, The. "The Rise of the Sharing Economy." *The Economist*, March 9, 2013. Accessed February 22, 2017. http://www.economist.com/news/leaders/21573104-internet-everything-hire-rise-sharing-economy.

Edelman, Benjamin, Michael Luca, and Dan Svirsky. "Racial Discrimination in the Sharing Economy: Evidence from a Field Experiment." *American Economic Journal: Applied Economics* (forthcoming). Available online: http://www.benedelman.org/publications/airbnb-guest-discrimination-2016-09-16.pdf.

Edgar, James. "'Captain Cyborg': The Man Behind the Controversial Turing Test Claims," *Telegraph*. June 10, 2014. Accessed February 17, 2018. http://www.telegraph.co.uk/news/science/science-news/10888828/Captain-Cyborg-the-man-behind-the-controversial-Turing-Test-claims.html.

Eldrick, Ted. "I Love Lucy." *Director's Guild of America Quarterly*, July 2003. Accessed August 13, 2017. https://www.dga.org/Craft/DGAQ/All-Articles/0307-July-2003/I-Love-Lucy.aspx.

Ellul, Jacques. *The Technological Society*. Translated by John Wilkinson. New York: Vintage Books, 1963.

Evans, Vyvyan. "Beyond Words: How Language-like Is Emoji?" *OUPblog*, April 16, 2016. Accessed April 8, 2017. https://blog.oup.com/2016/04/how-language-like-is-emoji/.

Federal Trade Commission. "Data Brokers: A Call for Transparency and Accountability." *Federal Trade Commission*, May 2014. Accessed February 9, 2017. https://www.ftc.gov/system/files/documents/reports/data-brokers-call-transparency-accountability-report-federal-trade-commission-may-2014/140527databrokerreport.pdf.

Feron, James. "Problems Plague Citizens Band Radio." *New York Times*, April 2, 1974. Accessed March 28, 2017. http://www.nytimes.com/1974/04/02/archives/problems-plague-citizens-band-radio-violations-abound.html.

Finley, Klint. "A Brief History of the End of the Comments." *Wired*, October 8, 2015. Accessed May 9, 2017. https://www.wired.com/2015/10/brief-history-of-the-demise-of-the-comments-timeline/.

Fitbit. "How Does My Fitbit Device Count Steps?" *Fitbit Help*. Accessed February 6, 2017. https://help.fitbit.com/articles/en_US/Help_article/1143.

Floridi, Luciano. "Should We Be Afraid of AI?" *Aeon*, May 9, 2016. Accessed September 22, 2017. https://aeon.co/essays/true-ai-is-both-logically-possible-and-utterly-implausible.

Fuller, Steve. "We May Look Crazy to Them, But They Look Like Zombies to Us: Transhumanism as a Political Challenge." *Institute for Ethics and Emerging Technologies*, September 8, 2015. Accessed October 3, 2016. https://ieet.org/index.php/IEET2/more/fuller20150909.

Gardiner, Becky, Mahana Mansfield, Ian Anderson, Josh Holder, Daan Louter, and Monica Ulmanu. "The Dark Side of Guardian Comments." *Guardian*, April 12, 2016. Accessed May 12, 2017. https://www.theguardian.com/technology/2016/apr/12/the-dark-side-of-guardian-comments.

Gertz, Nolen. "Autonomy Online: Jacques Ellul and the Facebook Emotional Manipulation Study." *Research Ethics* 12, no. 1 (2016): 55–61.

———. *The Philosophy of War and Exile*. Basingstoke: Palgrave Macmillan, 2014.

Gilsinan, Kathy. "Big in Europe: The Church of the Flying Spaghetti Monster." *The Atlantic*, November 2016. Accessed October 22, 2017. https://www.theatlantic.com/magazine/archive/2016/11/big-in-europe/501131/.

Goodrow, Cristos. "You Know What's Cool? A Billion Hours." *YouTube Official Blog*, February 27, 2017. Accessed August 14, 2017. https://youtube.googleblog.com/2017/02/you-know-whats-cool-billion-hours.html.

Graham, Jefferson. "YouTube Keeps Video Makers Rolling in Dough." *USA Today*, December 16, 2009. Accessed August 12, 2017. https://usatoday30.usatoday.com/tech/news/2009-12-16-youtube16_CV_N.htm.

Greenberg, Molly. "Flick of a Switch: How Lighting Affects Productivity and Mood." *Business*, February 22, 2017. Accessed December 19, 2017. https://www.business.com/articles/flick-of-a-switch-how-lighting-affects-productivity-and-mood/.

Grossman, Lev. "2045: The Year Man Becomes Immortal." *TIME*, February 10, 2011. Accessed February 17, 2018. http://content.time.com/time/magazine/article/0,9171,2048299,00.html.

Hacking, Ian. "Our Neo-Cartesian Bodies in Parts." *Critical Inquiry* 34 (August 2007): 78–105.

Hall, Melinda. *The Bioethics of Enhancement: Transhumanism, Disability, and Biopolitics*. Lanham, MD: Lexington Books, 2017.

Harwell, Drew. "Online Dating's Age Wars: Inside Tinder and eHarmony's Fight for Our Love Lives." *Washington Post*, April 6, 2015. Accessed March 3, 2017. https://www.washingtonpost.com/news/business/wp/2015/04/06/online-datings-age-wars-inside-tinder-and-eharmonys-fight-for-our-love-lives/.

Heidegger, Martin. *Being and Time*. Translated by John Macquarrie and Edward Robinson. New York: Harper & Row, 1962.

———. *The Essence of Human Freedom: An Introduction to Philosophy*. Translated by Ted Sadler. London and New York: Continuum, 2002.

———. "Letter on 'Humanism'." In *Pathmarks*, edited by William McNeill, translated by Frank A. Capuzzi, 239–76. Cambridge: Cambridge University Press, 1998.

————. "The Question Concerning Technology." In *The Question Concerning Technology and Other Essays*, translated by William Lovitt, 3–35. New York: Harper & Row, 1977.

————. "The Word of Nietzsche: 'God is Dead'." In *The Question Concerning Technology and Other Essays*, translated by William Lovitt, 53–112. New York: Harper & Row, 1977.

Henderson, Bobby. "About." *Church of the Flying Spaghetti Monster*. Accessed October 22, 2017. https://www.venganza.org/about/.

Hill, Kashmir. "Facebook Manipulated 689,003 Users' Emotions for Science." *Forbes*, June 28, 2014. Accessed April 11, 2017. https://www.forbes.com/sites/kashmirhill/2014/06/28/facebook-manipulated-689003-users-emotions-for-science/.

Holsendolph, Ernest. "Fading CB Craze Signals End to Licensing." *New York Times*, April 28, 1983. Accessed March 26, 2017. http://www.nytimes.com/1983/04/28/us/fading-cb-craze-signals-end-to-licensing.html.

Ihde, Don. *Technics and Praxis*. Dordrecht: D. Reidel, 1979.

————. *Technology and the Lifeworld*. Bloomington and Indianapolis: Indiana University Press, 1990.

IMDb. "Schizopolis (1996) Quotes." *IMDb*. Accessed February 14, 2017. http://www.imdb.com/title/tt0117561/quotes?ref_=tt_ql_trv_4.

Kelly, Heather. "Apple Replaces the Pistol Emoji with a Water Gun." *CNN*, August 2, 2016. Accessed April 8, 2017. http://money.cnn.com/2016/08/01/technology/apple-pistol-emoji/.

Koblin, John. "Netflix Studied Your Binge-Watching Habit. That Didn't Take Long." *New York Times*, June 8, 2016. Accessed August 20, 2017. https://www.nytimes.com/2016/06/09/business/media/netflix-studied-your-binge-watching-habit-it-didnt-take-long.html.

Kooragayala, Shiva, and Tanaya Srini. "Pokémon GO Is Changing How Cities Use Public Space, But Could It Be More Inclusive?" *Urban Wire*, August 1, 2016. Accessed August 26, 2017. http://www.urban.org/urban-wire/pokemon-go-changing-how-cities-use-public-space-could-it-be-more-inclusive.

Kramer, Adam D. I., Jamie E. Guillory, and Jeffrey T. Hancock. "Experimental Evidence of Massive-Scale Emotional Contagion through Social Networks." *PNAS* 111, no. 24 (2014): 8788–90.

Kriss, Sam. "Emojis Are the Most Advanced Form of Literature Known to Man." *Vice*, November 18, 2015. Accessed April 6, 2017. https://www.vice.com/en_dk/article/sam-kriss-laughing-and-crying.

LaFrance, Adrienne. "Not Even the People Who Write Algorithms Really Know How They Work." *The Atlantic*, September 18, 2015. Accessed February 15, 2017. https://www.theatlantic.com/technology/archive/2015/09/not-even-the-people-who-write-algorithms-really-know-how-they-work/406099/.

————. "Why Can't Americans Find Out What Big Data Knows About Them?" *The Atlantic*, May 28, 2014. Accessed February 9, 2017. https://www.theatlantic.com/technology/archive/2014/05/why-americans-cant-find-out-what-big-data-knows-about-them/371758/.

Lee, Stephanie M. "How Many People Actually Use Their Fitbits?" *BuzzFeed News*, May 9, 2015. Accessed February 7, 2017. https://www.buzzfeed.com/stephaniemlee/how-many-people-actually-use-their-fitbits.

Luckerson, Victor. "Here's How Facebook's News Feed Actually Works." *TIME*, July 9, 2015. Accessed February 9, 2017. http://time.com/collection-post/3950525/facebook-news-feed-algorithm/.

Luminoso. "Emoji Are More Common than Hyphens. Is Your Software Ready?" *Luminoso Blog*, September 4, 2013. Accessed April 8, 2017. https://blog.luminoso.com/2013/09/04/emoji-are-more-common-than-hyphens/.

Marx, Karl. "Alienated Labor." In *Karl Marx: Selected Writings*, edited by Lawrence H. Simon, 58–67. Indianapolis: Hackett, 1994.

————. "The Communist Manifesto." In *Karl Marx: Selected Writings*, edited by Lawrence H. Simon, 157–86. Indianapolis: Hackett, 1994.

Matofska, Benita. "The Secret of the Sharing Economy." *TEDxFrankfurt*, November 29, 2016. Accessed February 26, 2017. Available at: https://www.youtube.com/watch?v=-uv3JwpHjrw.

McDowell, Edwin. "C.B. Radio Industry Is More in Tune After 2 Years of Static." *New York Times*, April 17, 1978. Accessed March 27, 2017. http://www.nytimes.com/1978/04/17/archives/cb-radio-industry-is-more-in-tune-after-2-years-of-static-added.html.

Miller, Ryan W. "Teens Used Pokémon Go App to Lure Robbery Victims, Police Say." *USA Today*, July 11, 2016. Accessed February 8, 2017. http://www.usatoday.com/story/tech/2016/07/10/four-suspects-arrested-string-pokemon-go-related-armed-robberies/86922474/.

Mooney, Chris. "Internet Trolls Really Are Horrible People." *Slate*, February 14, 2014. Accessed May 16, 2017. http://www.slate.com/articles/health_and_science/climate_desk/2014/02/internet_troll_personality_study_machiavellianism_narcissism_psychopathy.html.

Mufson, Beckett. "Author Translates All of 'Alice in Wonderland' into Emojis." *Vice*, January 2, 2015. Accessed April 8, 2017. https://creators.vice.com/en_uk/article/author-translates-all-of-alice-in-wonderland-into-emojis.

Netflix. "How Does Netflix Work?" *Netflix Help Center*. Accessed February 9, 2017. https://help.netflix.com/en/node/412.

Nietzsche, Friedrich. *Beyond Good and Evil*. Edited by Rolf-Peter Horstmann. Translated by Judith Norman. Cambridge: Cambridge University Press, 2002.

———. *The Gay Science*. Translated by Walter Kaufmann. New York: Random House, 1974.

———. *On the Genealogy of Morality*. Translated by Carol Diethe. Cambridge: Cambridge University Press, 1994.

———. *On the Genealogy of Morals and Ecce Homo*. Translated by Walter Kaufmann. New York: Vintage Books, 1989.

———. *Twilight of the Idols*. Translated by Duncan Large. Oxford: Oxford University Press, 1998.

———. *The Will to Power*. Translated by Walter Kaufmann and R. J. Hollingdale. New York: Vintage Books, 1967.

Niven, Larry. "Flash Crowd." In *Three Trips in Time and Space: Original Novellas of Science Fiction*, edited by Robert Silverberg, 1–64. New York: Hawthorn Books, 1973.

Olson, Dan. "Vlogs and the Hyperreal." *Folding Ideas*, July 6, 2016. Accessed August 19, 2017. https://www.youtube.com/watch?v=GSnktB2N2sQ.

Oxford Dictionaries. "Word of the Year 2015." *Oxford Dictionaries Blog*. Accessed April 7, 2017. http://blog.oxforddictionaries.com/2015/11/word-of-the-year-2015-emoji/.

Pasquale, Frank. *The Black Box Society: The Secret Algorithms that Control Money and Information*. Cambridge, MA: Harvard University Press, 2015.

———. "Digital Star Chamber." *Aeon*, August 18, 2015. Accessed February 10, 2017. https://aeon.co/essays/judge-jury-and-executioner-the-unaccountable-algorithm.

Pew Research Center. "The Future of World Religions: Population Growth Projections, 2010–2050." *Pew Research Center*, April 2, 2015. Accessed April 10, 2017. http://www.pewforum.org/2015/04/02/religious-projections-2010-2050/.

Phillips, Whitney. "LOLing at Tragedy: Facebook Trolls, Memorial Pages and Resistance to Grief Online." *First Monday* 16, no. 12 (December 5, 2011). Accessed August 1, 2017. Available at: http://firstmonday.org/ojs/index.php/fm/article/view/3168/3115.

Pinsker, Joe. "How to Succeed in Crowdfunding: Be Thin, White, and Attractive." *The Atlantic*, August 3, 2015. Accessed February 26, 2017. https://www.theatlantic.com/business/archive/2015/08/crowdfunding-success-kickstarter-kiva-succeed/400232/.

Plato. *Republic*. Translated by G. M. A. Grube. Indianapolis: Hackett, 1992.

Plautz, Jason. "The Changing Definition of 'Flash Mob'." *Mental Floss*, August 22, 2011. Accessed June 1, 2017. http://mentalfloss.com/article/28578/changing-definition-flash-mob.

Plotz, David. "My Fake Facebook Birthdays." *Slate*, August 2, 2011. Accessed April 19, 2017. http://www.slate.com/articles/technology/technology/2011/08/my_fake_facebook_birthdays.html.

Pokémon Company, The. "Pokémon GO Safety Tips." *Pokémon GO*. Accessed February 7, 2017. http://www.pokemongo.com/en-us/news/pokemon-go-safety-tips.

Purvis, Jeanette. "Finding Love in a Hopeless Place: Why Tinder Is So 'Evilly Satisfying'." *Salon*, February 12, 2017. Accessed February 20, 2017. http://www.salon.com/2017/02/12/finding-love-in-a-hopeless-place-why-tinder-is-so-evilly-satisfying/.

Raffoul, François. *The Origins of Responsibility*. Bloomington and Indianapolis: Indiana University Press, 2010.

Richter, Felix. "The Fastest-Growing App Categories in 2015." *Statista*, January 22, 2016. Accessed April 1, 2017. https://www.statista.com/chart/4267/fastest-growing-app-categories-in-2015/.

Ronson, Jon. *So You've Been Publicly Shamed*. New York: Riverhead Books, 2016.

Roose, Kevin. "'Netflix and Chill': The Complete History of a Viral Sex Catchphrase." *Splinter*, August 27, 2015. Accessed August 19, 2017. http://splinternews.com/netflix-and-chill-the-complete-history-of-a-viral-sex-1793850444.

Rosenberger, Robert, and Peter-Paul Verbeek. "A Field Guide to Postphenomenology." In *Postphenomenological Investigations: Essays on Human-Technology Relations*, edited by Robert Rosenberger and Peter-Paul Verbeek, 9–41. London: Lexington Books, 2015.

Ryckaert, Vic. "Sex Offender Caught Playing Pokémon Go with Teen." *USA Today*, July 14, 2016. Accessed February 8, 2017. http://www.usatoday.com/story/news/nation-now/2016/07/14/indiana-sex-offender-caught-playing-pokemon-go-teen/87083504/.

Sanchez, Ray. "Occupy Wall Street: 5 Years Later." *CNN*, September 16, 2016. Accessed June 4, 2017. http://edition.cnn.com/2016/09/16/us/occupy-wall-street-protest-movements/index.html.

Sartre, Jean-Paul. *Being and Nothingness*. Translated by Hazel Barnes. New York: Washington Square Press, 1992.

———. "The Humanism of Existentialism." In *Essays in Existentialism*, edited by Wade Baskin, 31–62. New York: Citadel Press, 1965.

Schneier, Matthew. "The Post-Binge-Watching Blues: A Malady of Our Times." *New York Times*, December 6, 2015. Accessed August 20, 2017. https://www.nytimes.com/2015/12/06/fashion/post-binge-watching-blues.html.

Small, Alonzo. "Pokémon Go Player Assaulted, Robbed in Dover." *USA Today*, July 20, 2016. Accessed February 8, 2017. http://www.usatoday.com/story/news/crime/2016/07/19/pokemon-go-player-assaulted-robbed-dover/87304022/.

Sommer, Andreas Urs. "Nihilism and Skepticism in Nietzsche." In *A Companion to Nietzsche*, edited by Keith Ansell-Pearson, 250–69. Oxford: Blackwell, 2006.

Spinello, Richard A. "Privacy and Social Networking Technology." *International Review of Information Ethics* 16 (12/2011): 41–46.

Statista. "Fitbit—Statistics & Facts." *Statista*. Accessed February 7, 2017. https://www.statista.com/topics/2595/fitbit/.

———. "Leading Reasons for Using Emojis According to U.S. Internet Users as of August 2015." *Statista*. Accessed April 1, 2017. https://www.statista.com/statistics/476354/reasons-usage-emojis-internet-users-us/.

———. "Most Famous Social Network Sites Worldwide as of September 2017, Ranked by Number of Active Users (in Millions)." *Statista*. Accessed August 13, 2017. https://www.statista.com/statistics/272014/global-social-networks-ranked-by-number-of-users/.

———. "Negative Effects of Binge Viewing TV Shows According to TiVo Subscribers in the United States as of March 2015." *Statista*. Accessed August 20, 2017. https://www.statista.com/statistics/448177/tv-show-binging-negative-effects-usa/.

———. "Number of Monthly Active Facebook Users Worldwide as of 3rd Quarter 2017 (in Millions)." *Statista*. Accessed April 9, 2017. https://www.statista.com/statistics/264810/number-of-monthly-active-facebook-users-worldwide/.

———. "Reasons for Binge Viewing TV Shows among TV Viewers in the United States as of September 2017." *Statista*. Accessed 20 August 2017. https://www.statista.com/statistics/620114/tv-show-binging-reactions-usa/.

Steinicke, Frank. *Being Really Virtual: Immersive Natives and the Future of Virtual Reality*. Cham, Switzerland: Springer International, 2016.

Sterling, Bruce. "Augmented Reality: 'The Ultimate Display' by Ivan Sutherland, 1965." *Wired*, citing the *Proceedings of IFIP Congress*, 1965: 506–8, available online at: https://

www.wired.com/2009/09/augmented-reality-the-ultimate-display-by-ivan-sutherland-1965/.

Sternbergh, Adam. "Smile, You're Speaking Emoji." *New York Magazine*, November 16, 2014. Accessed April 4, 2017. http://nymag.com/daily/intelligencer/2014/11/emojis-rapid-evolution.html.

Sunstein, Cass. *Republic.com 2.0*. Princeton, NJ: Princeton University Press, 2007.

Sydell, Laura. "How Twitter's Trending Topics Algorithm Picks Its Topics." *NPR*, December 7, 2011. Accessed April 25, 2017. http://www.npr.org/2011/12/07/143013503/how-twitters-trending-algorithm-picks-its-topics.

Symonds, John Addington. "Twenty-three Sonnets from Michael Angelo." *Contemporary Review* 20 (1872): 505–15.

Trend Watching. "5 Consumer Trends for 2017." *Trend Watching*. Accessed January 15, 2017. http://trendwatching.com/trends/5-trends-for-2017/.

Tufekci, Zeynep, and Christopher Wilson. "Social Media and the Decision to Participate in Political Protest: Observations from Tahrir Square." *Journal of Communication* 62 (2012): 363–79.

Tuncel, Yunus, editor. *Nietzsche and Transhumanism: Precursor or Enemy?* Cambridge: Cambridge Scholars Publishing, 2017.

TV Tropes. "Red Shirt." *TV Tropes*. Accessed August 14, 2017. http://tvtropes.org/pmwiki/pmwiki.php/Main/RedShirt.

Tyson, Gareth, Vasile C. Perta, Hamed Haddadi, and Michael C. Seto. "A First Look at User Activity on Tinder." *arXiv*, July 7, 2016. https://arxiv.org/pdf/1607.01952v1.pdf.

Vaidhyanathan, Siva. *The Googlization of Everything: (And Why We Should Worry)*. Berkeley and Los Angeles, University of California Press, 2011.

Vallor, Shannon. "Moral Deskilling and Upskilling in a New Machine Age: Reflections on the Ambiguous Future of Character." *Philosophy of Technology* 28, no. 1 (2015): 107–24.

Verbeek, Peter-Paul. *Moralizing Technology: Understanding and Designing the Morality of Things*. Chicago and London: University of Chicago Press, 2011.

———. *What Things Do*. Translated by Robert P. Crease. University Park: Pennsylvania State University Press, 2005.

Wang, Zheng, and John Tchernev. "The 'Myth' of Media Multitasking: Reciprocal Dynamics of Media Multitasking, Personal Needs, and Gratifications." *Journal of Communication* 62, no. 3 (2012): 493–513.

Warzel, Charlie. "How Ferguson Exposed Facebook's Breaking News Problem." *BuzzFeed*, August 19, 2014. Accessed April 19, 2017. https://www.buzzfeed.com/charliewarzel/in-ferguson-facebook-cant-deliver-on-its-promise-to-deliver.

Wasik, Bill. *And Then There's This: How Stories Live and Die in Viral Culture*. New York: Viking Penguin, 2009.

———. "The Experiments." *And Then There's This*. Accessed May 24, 2017. http://www.andthentheresthis.net/mob.html.

———. "'Flash Robs': Trying to Stop a Meme Gone Wrong." *Wired*, November 23, 2011. Accessed June 1, 2017. https://www.wired.com/2011/11/flash-robs/all/1.

Wei, Will. "We Asked Siri the Most Existential Question Ever and She Had a Lot to Say." *Business Insider*, July 9, 2015. Accessed August 1, 2017. http://www.businessinsider.com/siri-meaning-of-life-responses-apple-iphone-2015-7.

White, Gillian B. "Uber and Lyft Are Failing Black Riders." *The Atlantic*, October 31, 2016. Accessed February 26, 2017. https://www.theatlantic.com/business/archive/2016/10/uber-lyft-and-the-false-promise-of-fair-rides/506000/.

Wilkinson College. "America's Top Fears 2016." *Chapman University Blog*, October 11, 2016. Accessed May 5, 2017. https://blogs.chapman.edu/wilkinson/2016/10/11/americas-top-fears-2016/.

YouTube. "Advertiser-Friendly Content Guidelines." *YouTube Help*. Accessed August 18, 2017. https://support.google.com/youtube/answer/6162278?hl=en&ref_topic=1121317.

———. "History of Monetization at YouTube." *YouTube 5 Year Anniversary Press Site*. Accessed August 14, 2017. https://sites.google.com/a/pressatgoogle.com/youtube5year/home/history-of-monetization-at-youtube.

Zoia, Christopher. "This Guy Makes Millions Playing Video Games on YouTube." *The Atlantic*, March 14, 2014. Accessed August 15, 2017. https://www.theatlantic.com/business/archive/2014/03/this-guy-makes-millions-playing-video-games-on-youtube/284402/.

Zuckerberg, Mark. "We Just Passed an Important Milestone." *Facebook*, August 27, 2015. Accessed April 9, 2017. https://www.facebook.com/zuck/posts/10102329188394581.

INDEX

ABOUT THE AUTHOR

Nolen Gertz is assistant professor of applied philosophy at the University of Twente, and a senior researcher at the 4TU.Centre for Ethics and Technology. He is the author of *The Philosophy of War and Exile* (2014). His work has appeared in the *Atlantic*, the *Washington Post*, and on ABC Australia. He can be found continuing his research into the relationship between nihilism and technology at @ethicistforhire.